More
Natural "Cures"
Revealed

More
Natural "Cures"
Revealed

---

*Previously Censored
Brand Name Products
That Cure Disease*

KEVIN TRUDEAU

Alliance Publishing Group, Inc.

More Natural "Cures" Revealed
Copyright © 2006 by Kevin Trudeau
All rights reserved.

Alliance Publishing Group, Inc.
P.O. Box 207
Elk Grove Village, IL 60009

A CIP catalog record for this book is available from the Library of
Congress.
ISBN-10: 0-97878-513-4
ISBN-13: 978-0-97878-513-0

Manufactured in the United States of America.
10 9 8 7 6 5 4 3 2 1

Contents

Disclaimer

This book is considered by some a work of fiction, yet inspired by a true story. Some truth is sprinkled in to spice things up. On occasion, names, dates, and events have been changed or made up for fun. It contains the opinions, theories, and conclusions of what some people call a raving lunatic, conspiracy theorist, snake oil salesman, political activist, consumer advocate, believer in immortality, and delusional fraudster. Believe what you will. It is for entertainment purposes only. Remember, the author is not a doctor and has no medical training. He is a two-time convicted felon. Yet . . . then again, did he say it's all 100 percent true?

Acknowledgments

This book is dedicated to the hundreds of thousands of people that have read my first book, *Natural Cures "They" Don't Want You to Know About*, and have sent me their stories, appreciation, and letters of gratitude relating to me how the information I exposed has positively influenced their lives. Without your prayers and letters I could have never survived the ongoing and continued onslaught and attacks from the government, the media, and the worldwide pharmaceutical medical cartels. I acknowledge you all. I thank you all. Please continue your steadfast support.

CHAPTER 1

How to Use This Book

One of the first duties of the physician is to educate the masses not to take medicine.

—Sir William Osler

You could have bought this book for several reasons. Maybe you are sick and you want to know a natural alternative to drugs and surgery that has no negative side effects. Maybe you are concerned about becoming sick or developing a serious condition such as cancer, diabetes, heart disease, etc. Maybe you are just curious as to what all the controversy is regarding me, my books, and my constant battles with government regulators.

No matter what the reason you are reading this book, the best way to read it is from start to finish. Ideally, read the book as it was written. Start with page 1 and read the book through until the end. Ideally, do not jump around. If you jump to the end of the book, what you read or see will be incomplete. You may think you understand what I wrote and why, but I can assure you without reading the book in its entirety you will have missed the whole point. Imagine walking into a movie and seeing the last ten minutes. Could you give an honest evaluation of the true meaning of the entire movie? Of course not. Imagine looking at a small corner of a masterpiece painting. Could you really understand why the painting is classified as a masterpiece without seeing the entire work as it was meant to be viewed? Of course not.

This book is designed to give you knowledge about natural non-drug and non-surgical ways to prevent and cure disease. These products, remedies, therapies, and treatments are inexpensive, have no negative side effects, and absolutely 100 percent work. There is documentation and substantiation verifying these facts. The evidence is overwhelmingly clear. However, the pharmaceutical companies whose profits are adversely affected by people having access to this information do not want you to know the truth. Governments, bought and paid by the pharmaceutical medical cartels around the world, do not want you to know the truth about these inexpensive, safe, and effective non-drug and non-surgical ways to prevent, treat, and cure disease.

This book is designed as a sequel to my first book *Natural Cures "They" Don't Want You to Know About*. It is designed to fill in the gaps and answer questions from the first book, and pick up where the first book left off. Therefore, the very best way to get the most benefit out of this book is to do the following.

1. Read my first book *Natural Cures "They" Don't Want You to Know About* cover to cover. Doing so gives you the foundation for which this book has been based.

2. Read this book cover to cover. Don't jump around.

3. This book can never replace personalized medical care by a licensed healthcare practitioner. You must always seek advice and treatments from a licensed healthcare practitioner.

4. Do all the things in Chapter Six of my first book. The "natural cures" for every disease is doing the things listed in Chapter Six.

Cures do not come in the form of a pill, a shot, or some magical medical surgical procedure or treatment. The drug companies want you to believe that "cures" must be bought in the form of some expensive drug or treatment that they sell. They've even lobbied governments around the world to pass laws which state that only a drug or approved medical device can prevent, treat, and cure disease. It doesn't matter that even medical scientists around the world concur that most disease is caused by nutritional deficiencies. Have we forgotten that the horrible disease of scurvy is simply a Vitamin C deficiency, or the disease of osteoporosis is a calcium deficiency?

Are the products listed in this book and the protocol outlined in Chapter Six of my first book "cures"? Although it may be a simple matter of semantics, it could be said that only the body heals and cures itself. Pills, potions, and all medical and health treatments either suppress the symptoms by making the body do something unnatural, or help the body heal itself by eliminating nutritional deficiencies and/or toxins and putting the body in a state of balance so that healing can occur.

To use this book properly is to understand that drug companies and the entire pharmaceutical and medical industry only have an interest in selling you drugs and getting you to use their expensive medical tests and treatments. They are all profit-based businesses. Most are publicly traded corporations whose only objective is to increase profits. To use this book effectively you must at least consider that all the advertising we see for drugs is misleading. Drug companies are no longer selling drugs to save lives. They are manufacturing and selling drugs that are used to treat the simplest and mildest of conditions. This trend is more than just worrisome. It is scandalous and the most reprehensible of all actions. Drug companies are taking advantage of people's vulnerabilities and selling you ineffective drugs that all have negative side effects. These drugs and medical treatments do not work as advertised. They are ineffective. At best, they suppress the symptom for a short time. However, because they work by making the body do something unnatural, and because they are highly poisonous chemicals, they all cause the body to break down in other areas, causing more illness and disease. If you are under sixty years old and taking nonprescription, over-the-counter, or prescription drugs on a regular basis, researchers and scientists can assure you that these drugs will cause you serious medical conditions later on in life. That's the fact.

I am routinely attacked for suggesting that people not take drugs. My policy of "just say no to drugs" is said to be irresponsible and outrageous. The governments around the world and the drug companies want people to believe the myth that every person on planet earth will be healthier and happier in direct proportion to the amount of nonprescription and prescription drugs they take on a regular basis! I am, therefore, an insane lunatic. I must be a moron, an idiot, and a very unhealthy person ... hmmm ... let me think. I have not taken a nonprescription or prescription drug in over twenty years. I rarely, if ever, get sick. If I do get a sniffle, or a cough, the severity and duration is a fraction of what other people experience. I do take herbs, homeopathics, nutritional supplements, and eat organic fruits, vegetables, nuts, seeds, and other nutritious food. I exercise. I get massage, chiropractic care, live cell therapy, energetic rebalancing, etc. I virtually do all the things listed in Chapter Six of my first book. I am not a good customer for the drug companies.

Is there a place for drugs, surgery, and western medical treatment? Absolutely yes! The way I see it, drugs and surgery are incredibly effective in crisis situations when the patient is dying, and when a person is so far engulfed in illness and disease that only these aggressive treatments can stop the patient from dying, relieve symptoms, and make the patient more comfortable. I've always said if I'm in a horrible car crash please rush me to the closest emergency room and use drugs and surgery to save my life.

Today, however, things are out of control in relation to how drugs are marketed and sold. Years ago certain people were known to be shy or slightly introverted. Today there are ads on television stating that if you are shy you have a new disease called "social anxiety disorder." The ads tell us that this "disease" can be cured by taking a new drug every day for the rest of your life! How insane is that? The ad quickly goes on to state all the negative side effects, including heart disease, stroke, blood in the urine, seizure, and death. The drug ads are so ridiculous they would be laughable. The bad news is the only people laughing are the drug company executives, all the way to the bank. These ads have been produced using brainwashing techniques developed by the CIA and KGB. These ads work; they get people to buy more drugs. It's sad, but true. I should know, I helped develop some of them! (More on how I did this later.)

So, to get the most out of this book make sure you read my first book *Natural Cures "They" Don't Want You to Know About*, do all the things in Chapter Six of that book, read this book cover to cover without skipping around, then do the following:

- Go to several licensed healthcare practitioners to get specialized, customized, and personalized product and treatment choices for your condition.
- Go to www.naturalcures.com and talk to one of our health specialists who can help you with options regarding natural cures for your specific condition.
- Use the websites and phone numbers listed in this book, and use the products recommended under the supervision of a licensed healthcare practitioner.

Remember, the "natural cure" for your condition must be personalized and customized based on a variety of factors. The first thing that must be addressed is finding the cause of your symptoms, illness, and disease. This is why doing all the things in Chapter Six of my first book cures virtually every disease. The items in Chapter Six address virtually all the potential causes for virtually all diseases.

How do I know this to be true? How do I, with no formalized medical schooling, a convicted felon, learn these insider secrets to health? Let me tell you a story ...

CHAPTER 2

An Offer I Couldn't Refuse

A life spent making mistakes is not only more honorable, but more useful than a life spent doing nothing.

—George Bernard Shaw

Saint Mary's High School. Lynn, Massachusetts. I went into my guidance counselor's office to take the required aptitude and IQ tests. I liked tests. They were a game to me. I liked figuring out things. First came the IQ test. I always thought I was relatively quick and bright. I never considered having a high IQ. Those were reserved for the well-to-do of society, whose parents were alumni of the Ivy League colleges with friends in powerful government positions and captains of industry. That was not me. Dad was a regular guy. A blue-collar welder and member of the union. He liked hunting, fishing, and doing work with his hands. He was a real man. I don't think he graduated from high school. I remember, however, that when he built something out of brick, or wood, or steel, his math skills were excellent. Mom ran the house. Being Italian, we ate the best food. She was full-time cook, maid, gardener, and taxi driver for us kids in the neighborhood. She had perfect penmanship. I don't think she graduated high school either. It didn't matter. Heads up, both my mom and dad could beat any high school graduate today in a math, spelling, or English grammar test. Plus, and most importantly, they knew how to solve problems and figure out solutions when needed. They unknowingly adhered to Mark Twain's axiom about never letting schooling interfere with one's education.

When I received the IQ test from the guidance counselor I didn't expect to do very well. Having parents who never went to college and living in a blue-collar community meant my friends and I were not very well read. This equated to not having a good vocabulary. IQ tests at the time were impossible if your English vocabulary was not very strong. Both the IQ test and aptitude test were required of all students. I figured I would rush through them, finish early, and take off for the afternoon. I actually enjoyed school, but enjoyed figuring out a way to miss a class without being punished even more. I received the IQ test and answered the questions as quickly as I could without much thought. I really didn't care what the results were. I had already decided I wasn't going to college. Not because my parents couldn't afford it; I knew they would do whatever they had to do to send me if I wanted to go, but rather out of a combination of not wanting to burden my parents with undue stress and, mostly, an almost compulsive desire and need for me to make money and prove my self worth as soon and as quickly as possible.

I finished the three-hour IQ test in a little over an hour. Next, the aptitude test. It was multiple choice. After the fourth question I found the test to be utterly ridiculous, useless, and a waste of time. I proceeded to then quickly mark every answer "d" on the multiple choice answer sheet. I was done in twenty minutes. The guidance counselor was not pleased. I left school early as planned and hopped in my 1967 Firebird convertible to enjoy my freedom from the classroom.

Three days later I was called into the guidance counselor's office to discuss my test results and receive "guidance" from the "counselor." I was anticipating some long drawn-out lecture about what kind of job or career would be best suited for me. My counseling session was quite different than I had anticipated. When I arrived at the "guidance office" there were approximately thirty other students waiting their turn. These students were serious about their test results and had serious questions and concerns about college and career options. It was obvious to the guidance counselor that I viewed the whole process as a joke. Seeing me into the room elicited a very public and personally embarrassing and humiliating comment from this very powerful person in authority: "Trudeau, you don't need to waste my time. Your test scores were terrible. You should consider being a forester. This way you can work for long periods of time by yourself. You're a loser and you'll always be a loser." Snickers and whispers filled the room. I turned beet red with embarrassment. I tried to put on a cocky "I could care less" smile. I don't think I fooled anyone. I turned around and walked out of the room. I distinctly remember mumbling to myself, "You're going to eat those words, baby. You're going to eat those words."

I heard a phrase "success is the best revenge." Ironically, just a few short years later, I was going to dinner at one of the most expensive restaurants in the Boston area, The Baytower Room. I was driving a brand-new Lincoln Continental. I was wearing a $1,000 Armani suit and a $25,000 solid gold Rolex watch. When I pulled up to have my car valeted, can you imagine my surprise to see that one of the valets was my old guidance counselor. He was working this second job parking cars to help pay his bills. I had a great dinner that night!

Let's go back to Saint Mary's High School again. I had just been humiliated and embarrassed by my guidance counselor in front of many other students. By the end of the day it seemed the entire school knew what had happened. I knew the aptitude test scores meant nothing because I put the same answer for every question, but I was curious what the IQ results were. I found out it was well above 140. Allegedly, this was very high. I wondered if maybe I was one of these "gifted kids" that were talked about at the time. When I actually spent some time doing homework, or studying for an exam, everything came easy and I would get 100 percent correct answers. It also occurred to me that my verbal and written communication skills were said to be very good. I got my points across concisely and with clarity. I also knew that if I indeed wanted to make large amounts of money, I had to use the talents I had.

Remember, my family had no money. We had no connections. I had no relatives that were alumni of prestigious universities. We knew no one in high places of business or government. Plus, I wasn't going to college. The only way I imagined that I could overcome my low self-esteem, self-doubts, and feelings of unworthiness was to achieve huge financial success. In those days, having a poor self-image, or low self-esteem, was thought to be caused by a number of different issues. Maybe the fact that I was adopted as an infant, or maybe because I was a fat kid, or maybe because I wore glasses and was "four eyes," or maybe because we lived at the outskirts of town, all could have played a part in my personality development.

Realizing that maybe I actually could be considered super intelligent, I decided to find out if there was a way to accurately determine whether this was true or not. Along came MENSA, a society restricted to only those who have a super IQ. I decided to take the MENSA test. I sat in the room, nervous yet confident that I would do well. I looked around at the others taking the exam and figured that I was much smarter than all of them. Then came the shock. I opened the exam booklet and found a very different kind of IQ test. First was a series of problem-solving questions. The problem I faced was there were certain words I was expected to know the definitions of. There were certain mathematical formulas that I was expected to have committed to memory. I remember one specific question on the test. "A building is 20 stories high, built at sea level. Using a barometer, how do you determine the height of a building?" I don't know how to use barometric pressure to figure the height of a building. I did, however, give two solutions that would work. First, I suggested you simply go to the top of the building, tie a string around the barometer, lower it down the outside of the building to the ground, then haul it up and simply measure the string with a ruler. This would give you the height of the building. Next, I said the simplest way would be to walk into the superintendent's office of the building and say, "I will gladly give you this beautiful barometer as a gift if you simply tell me the exact height of the building." Both are correct answers to the question.

I quickly realized, however, that I was going too slowly, and that there was an excellent probability that they would not accept my creative, although correct, answers. I became panicky and afraid that my score would not be high enough and I would be denied membership into MENSA. For some unknown reason, this horrified me and depressed me beyond comprehension. I could not face failure and rejection. I took my unfinished test and presented it to the supervisor. I informed the test administrator that I had suddenly fallen ill and would like to reschedule the test. Although unusual, the administrator assured me that they would destroy my unfinished exam, and make a notation that I did not take the test at all. I left the building and threw up.

Three months later I took the test again. I was told that there was a three-hour time limit. I was told not to worry if I did not get to all the questions on the test. It seems that no one can finish the exam in just three hours. I sat down with full confidence and began putting answers to all the questions. In forty-five minutes I had completed and answered every question. With a big smile on my face, I walked to the front of the room and handed the administrator my fully completed MENSA IQ exam. I proudly and confidently said, "I scored a 100 percent on this test. Every question is correct. The reason I know this is because I cheated. Now, you are a member of MENSA. If you can't figure out how I cheated then that means that I'm smarter than you and I deserve to be admitted."

No one has ever figured out how I cheated on that test. I have never yet been admitted to MENSA.

Because of these and many other factors, I fit a certain "profile." Being adopted, needing to prove myself, obsessive desire to make money, no real family attachments, high IQ, willing to bend or even break the rules, all put me in a category of being an excellent candidate to be approached and made an offer that I couldn't refuse. Big Brother is bigger than you could ever imagine. Today, it is worse than ever before. I can assure you that throughout history Big Brother has been watching us. The letters and e-mails you write, the books you read, the conversations you have, the websites you visit, where and when you spend your money, all are being reviewed and scrutinized. When two men approached me in a very public bowling alley it seemed a little surreal. They had obviously been watching me for quite some time. The conversation was straightforward, serious, and to the point. They knew about me in great detail. They knew my most powerful motivation was making money. They knew I had an obsessive need to feel "wanted." They told me they were members of a secret society, and that I had the attributes that qualified me for potential entry into this secret society. They wanted me. Being a member of this secret society would give me access to the secrets of lifelong incredible health, and allow me to make tens of millions of dollars. I would have access to some of the richest and most powerful people on planet earth. It was a simple exchange. They wanted to use my talents and abilities for their purposes of increasing their own billions and their own power, control, and influence over the masses, and in exchange, I would receive health secrets, access to the inner circles of the rich and powerful, and the ability to live a life of luxury.

This book is specifically about the secret non-drug and non-surgical ways to cure and prevent disease. Therefore, I will not go into great detail about my history, this secret society, and my exploits as a member of this society. Those details will be revealed and exposed in a future book unless I have some "unfortunate accident." The threats are real and are already coming in. I mention this secret society and my involvement here so that you have a general idea of how I have come to know what I know. As a member of this secret society I have sat in private meetings with the heads of state from countries around the world. I have attended secret international business meetings where business leaders, politicians, and media moguls coerce together to create the new world order with global control over individual people everywhere. I have been shown and have seen with my own eyes secret government and corporate documents. I have heard with my own ears how Big Pharma, the food industry, and the oil industry are working together with governments and media outlets around the world. I have been in over sixty countries, yet there are no stamps of evidence in any of my passports. I have been to Area 51 in Nevada. (This top secret military installation is still denied to exist by the U.S. government.) This is where much of our technology has been developed. Area 51 houses most extraterrestrial artifacts, including a working spacecraft and dead alien bodies. I've seen these things with my own two eyes.

As a member of this secret society I was used in covert operations around the world. You need to know that multinational corporations, the wealthiest families on earth, and governments all work together to increase their own power, influence, control, and profits. They all are using each other for their own purposes of creating ultimate global monopolies. Since the fall of the Soviet Union the truth about covert operatives has been exposed in the mainstream media. Even in America the *New York Times* and other journalistic media sources are exposing the true facts about how "normal people" working in "normal jobs" were in fact agents for the CIA, KGB, and other underground secret agencies.

In my role I was used at the behest of whichever society member needed my unique talents and abilities. I was virtually on call twenty-four hours a day, seven days a week. Throughout my almost twenty-year involvement, I became privy to startling insider secrets. I was shown the real cause of disease and exactly how this information is kept secret from the public. I was exposed to the hidden research and data about how non-prescription and prescription drugs all are being purposely used to cause disease. I have been in the factories and laboratories where food additives are being produced, and secretly and illegally being added to food, for the specific purpose of increasing people's appetites, getting people physically addicted to the food, and specifically designed to cause illness and disease. I have been in factories where food is being genetically modified and manufactured with the sole purpose of making people fatter. I was taught secret brainwashing techniques developed by the CIA that are being used in the news media and in advertisements for certain products.

During my involvement I made hundreds of millions of dollars. I drove Porsches, Ferraris, Rolls-Royces, and Mercedes. I lived in homes worth millions of dollars. I dined in the finest restaurants, eating the most expensive caviar and drinking wine that cost over $1,000 a bottle. I flew in private jets and stayed in the most expensive hotel suites in the world. I had custom-made jewelry valued in the millions of dollars. I lived an opulent and luxurious lifestyle that most people could never imagine. Even when I was in prison the secret society guaranteed that I receive benefits and perks that would outrage the public. While in prison I actually spent much of my time in the officers club at Edwards Air Force Base! That's right, while I was doing my time, I and other inmates would actually spend our days eating the best food and enjoying ourselves at a U.S. military base officer's club. Can you imagine convicts having complete access to a U.S. military installation? Can you imagine that convicts would be eating the finest food in a club generally restricted to U.S. military officers? (The society needed me to go to prison for a very specific mission.)

The government denies all of this. The government denies Area 51 exists. Yet everyone can see it with their own two eyes. The government denied the mafia existed, yet it flourished throughout New York in virtually every aspect of business, government, and law enforcement. Most recently, President Bush denied knowing or even meeting the corrupt lobbyist Jack Abramoff. Despite his denials, dozens of pictures emerged proving that not only did the president know and meet Mr. Abramoff, but seemed to be very close and friendly with him. Did the president lie or is his memory that bad? I wonder if he remembers what he ate for breakfast.

When I was offered membership into this secret society they made me an offer I couldn't refuse. If I accepted, health, money, and a lifestyle of the rich and famous would be mine. Not accepting would mean a life of meritocracy, financial struggles, and unfulfillment. It was simply an offer I couldn't refuse.

Once I was in, I began to find out that this secret society was actually broken down into two groups. The first group used the society, its insider secrets, and power to add value to society and make society a better place. The other faction used the same insider secrets and power for personal gain at the expense of society. One group worked for people and society. The other group lived off the people and society. One group added value to the world, the other group were parasites living off the production of others. It fascinates me now, looking back, that the world's most powerful people fall into one of these two categories.

Never in history has someone left the society and exposed its members, and exposed its insider secrets. Think about, for a moment, that no one in history has exposed the secret rituals of the Masons. No one has exposed the secret writings kept at the Vatican, or Mormon Church headquarters. I am the first member of this society that is coming forward. Members of this society include politicians, captains of industry, news journalists, celebrities, musicians, writers, scientists, law enforcement officials, movie stars, and more.

This is one of the reasons why the government and media attacks are so vicious. I swore a vow of secrecy and silence. But I have seen the light. I was on the dark side doing evil; now I have repented, changed my ways, and turned my life around. I regret and am very sorry for all of the bad things I have done in my life. Now, I am going against the masters that I once served. I am telling people the truth about Big Pharma, the food industry, the oil industry, governments, and the media. For those who listen, and have experienced positive changes in your lives for the better, your letters of appreciation give me the strength to carry on with this mission. I am not the devil, a con man, charlatan, or snake oil salesman. I am not the messiah, superman, or some radical conspiracy theory extremist. I am a real guy who has turned his life around. I am simply sharing with you what I know. Some suggest my thoughts and opinions are dangerous. I would propose that any suppression of the free expression of thoughts and opinions is the real danger.

Live free or die!

CHAPTER 3

Read This or They'll Kill Me

The First Amendment is often inconvenient. But that is beside the point. Inconvenience does not absolve the government from its obligation to tolerate speech.

—Justice Anthony Kennedy

The United States Government and governments around the world have colluded together with international drug and pharmaceutical companies to create a "medical cartel," a virtual monopoly on what is the "truth" regarding health, and the treatment of illness and disease. Individuals around the world have been charged criminally for stating their opinions regarding the best ways to prevent and cure disease. This occurs when these "opinions" go against what the "medical cartel" has already established as "truth." Therefore, I must write a disclaimer. There is no freedom of speech or freedom of expression in the world when it comes to health. Like it was in Nazi Germany and Stalinist Russia, if a person says something that the government, in its supreme infinite wisdom, deems detrimental to society, that person will be severely ridiculed, debunked, discredited, attacked, and in many cases persecuted and prosecuted beyond the wildest imaginations of even the most ardent conspiracy theorists. Therefore, this disclaimer must be put forth. It is irrelevant if I believe these words. If I do not say them it is almost guaranteed that I will be sued for expressing my opinions. If I do not submit to the government's requirement of writing this disclaimer, I am convinced that agents from some renegade governmental agency, such as the United States Food and Drug Administration, Federal Trade Commission, or some other world regulatory body, will simply arrest me for writing a book where I simply express my personal beliefs, opinions, and observations in my capacity as a journalist.

Therefore, do not believe anything you read in this book. It is a combination of a work of fiction, memoir, "inspired by a true story," opinion, individual conclusions, and reporting on subjects and information that has not been documented or verified, or even fact checked, to the satisfaction of anyone in a position of authority.

Although I personally believe that everything in this book is 100 percent true, please be aware that I could be totally delusional in my thoughts, opinions, and beliefs and a complete insane lunatic conspiracy theorist. Read this book for entertainment purposes only. It is not meant to educate, as I am not an educator. (The government says I am not anything and no one should listen to anything I say!)

Although I believe I am a journalist, consumer advocate, investigative reporter, and exposer of government and corporate corruption, news agencies and government organizations around the world will repeatedly tell you I am nothing more than a convicted felon, liar, and a con man, who should not be allowed to express his opinions to anyone. I warn you, therefore, that before you read this book you should consider that the government, news organizations, and the multinational corporations all agree that the information presented here is nothing more than a fraud and a pack of lies.

You should consider burning this book. Be careful, however, when burning it, because in some countries the governments have established that this is not a book at all, but rather an unlicensed and ineffective medical device that can cause great harm to people who "use it."

Remember too that the government requires you to seek "proper" medical treatment from only "proper" licensed medical professionals. If you have a serious medical condition you must obey the law and follow blindly the advice of the licensed medical doctor that the government has determined knows the only treatment options that work. Never question the government. Never question what the drug companies say. Never question what the government-approved medical doctor tells you to do! Yes, following these steps may lead to more illness, disease, or death, but rest assured you'll not be sued or arrested!

No matter what I say in this book, remember that the only cures for disease come from patented drugs, surgical procedures, or medical treatments that publicly traded international pharmaceutical companies sell and politicians and governments have approved. NOTHING

ELSE ON PLANET EARTH CAN PREVENT, TREAT, OR CURE DIS-EASE! That's the law!

By the way, although I look like I am in my early forties, I am really seventy years old ... but that means nothing. The stuff in this book really doesn't work!

CHAPTER 4

Trust Me, I'm Not a Doctor

The reasonable man adapts himself to the world; the unreasonable one persists in trying to adapt the world to himself. Therefore, all progress depends on the unreasonable man.

—George Bernard Shaw

My first book on health, *Natural Cures "They" Don't Want You to Know About*, sold over five million copies in a little over a year. I wrote the book because I was fed up with the United States Federal Trade Commission repeatedly suppressing the dissemination of truthful information regarding inexpensive non-drug and non-surgical ways to prevent and cure illness and disease. I watched government agencies around the world, including the ITC in Great Britian, the Department of Fair Trading in Australia, and the Federal Trade Commission and Food and Drug Administration in America, as well as hundreds of other local government agencies, routinely attack and persecute individual citizens and companies for doing nothing more than exposing people to truthful information and opinions about natural inexpensive ways to treat, prevent, and cure disease.

When I wrote the book I simply reported, as a journalist, information, observations, and studies from around the world that show the various ways to prevent, treat, and cure disease without drugs and surgery. I exposed the obvious fact that there is a major conflict of interest with the way healthcare is provided to people around the world. For the first time in history a writer put in a book, that had major distribution, the fact that pharmaceutical drug companies are virtually all publicly traded corporations. This means that all drug companies have a legal responsibility to increase shareholder value above everything else. This means that all drug, pharmaceutical, and healthcare companies have only one goal ... to sell more drugs and their expensive treatments! This is the major conflict of interest that I exposed. I was like the kid in the fable of the Emperor's New Clothes. I pointed out what everyone knew, but were all afraid to acknowledge.

Immediately, everyone that I exposed in my first book went on a major attack to discredit me, debunk what I had to say, and stop people from buying and reading the book. The onslaught of attacks was unlike anything the publishing industry or an author has ever been subject to. If you have not read *Natural Cures "They" Don't Want You to Know About,* you need to read it. In it I expose and blow the lid off some of the most well-kept secrets in healthcare and government. As a longtime covert operative for both the U.S. Government and pharmaceutical industry, I know information that few people have been privy to. The reason I have been so violently attacked is because the "powers that be" know that I in fact know the truth. Powerful people of governments around the world and some of the richest people on the planet are fully aware that I can "name names."

The first book was viciously attacked in the media. I appeared on CNN's Paula Zahn, NBC's *Today Show with Matt Lauer,* the CBS *Early Show,* ABC's *20/20* and *Dateline,* and numerous other television and radio shows. Stories about me and my book were run on Fox, *The O'Reilly Factor, Inside Edition,* the *Wall Street Journal,* the *Washington Post, USA Today,* the *New York Times,* and hundreds of other newspapers and magazines around the world. My staff has reviewed virtually every one of these interviews, articles, and reports. It is absolutely astounding that in virtually every case there are facts that are 100 percent inaccurate and have not been fact checked, statements are made that are categorically untrue, false, and flat-out lies, and most importantly, virtually every one of these "news reporting organizations" produced a piece that in my opinion was blatantly and flagrantly misleading and dishonest!

Why would these reputable journalists and news organizations so willfully deceive the public about me and my book? Simple, read my first book! When you do you will see that I expose the truth about how virtually every news organization, television station, radio station, newspaper, and magazine is controlled by, and has financial interests in, drug companies, fast food companies, and the oil industry! The good news is that the axiom "there is no such thing as bad publicity" holds true. All the exposure for the book caused massive numbers of people to read the book.

I exposed the corruption at the various fraudulent governmental agencies that allegedly are in place to protect consumers. Remember, I have met secretly with the heads of many of these agencies around the world in my role as a covert operative. I was physically at meetings when deals were made between the heads of these agencies and major corporations. I know how the bribes, payoffs, and illegal coercion work between politicians, government regulators, and corporations. In this respect I have been compared to Joe Valachi. Joe Valachi came forward and said he was a member of La Cosa Nostra, the mafia. At the time the mafia consisted of five families in New York. It also consisted of other families throughout America, Italy, and Sicily. This criminal underground empire was reportedly bigger than U.S. Steel. At the time, the mafia was at its height in size and power. Amazingly, however, there was no proof that the mafia existed. It was called a myth by law enforcement officials and politicians. The head of the FBI stated emphatically that the mafia did not exist and was nothing more than a fantasy and urban legend. When Joe Valachi came forward it was the first time in history that an insider acknowledged that this huge underground criminal organization did not only exist, but flourished. He exposed how law enforcement officials, politicians, and officers and directors of major corporations all belonged to, knew about, and worked with the mafia! Looking back it is obvious now why law enforcement officials, politicians, and government regulators all violently denied the existence of the mafia. They denied its existence because they were a part of it! The same is happening now. I am exposing that politicians, government regulators, and the heads of pharmaceutical companies, food manufacturers, news organizations, and the oil industry are working together to hide from you the truth about inexpensive home remedies and natural non-drug and non-surgical ways to cure, prevent, and treat disease.

This is not a conspiracy theory. This is simple economics. It is in the economic best interest of the drug companies to hide any information about inexpensive non-patentable ways to prevent and cure disease. It is in the economic best interest of virtually every television station and network, radio station and network, newspapers, and almost all magazines to keep hidden from you any information that would have an adverse effect on the drug companies, food companies, or oil companies. It is in the best interests of every politician and government regulator to protect the financial interests of the drug industry, food industry, and oil industry. I and the hundreds of authors, consumer advocates, scientists, researchers, and alternative healthcare practitioners are a major threat to the profits of the medical cartel, food industry, and oil industry that are being exploited from the unknowing citizenry around the globe.

You may question whether this is true. First, I highly recommend you read my first book. It gives hundreds of specific examples and facts showing the obvious collusion that is keeping you sick. Also consider a few other interesting tidbits:

- In many countries around the world my first book, and I believe this book, is being called a medical device! How absurd.
- The New York Consumer Protection Board violated my First Amendment rights by trying to stop people from buying and reading my first book. It is my opinion and belief that members of this government agency knowingly lied in press releases and purposely misled the public, and deceived the public, about the true facts regarding me and my book. They even tried to get people in the media, including Oprah, to run negative stories about me and my book. The head of this agency was recently arrested for possession of crack cocaine. How ironic.
- Several drugstore chains stopped selling my book even though it was the best-selling title they ever had. This was done because the book exposes the truth about the dangers of non-prescription and prescription drugs. Since the drugstore chain sells drugs, it is in their financial best interests to have people NOT read my book. When people read the book they get healthier and therefore buy fewer drugs! Drugstore chains and drug companies do not want people to be healthy. Healthy people do not buy drugs.
- Several newspapers, magazines, and television networks will not allow me to advertise my book! These companies have major financial ties to the drug industry and food industry. They have no problem running ads for drugs like Vioxx even though it killed over 100,000 people. These vehicles of free speech do not promote the free flow of opinions and ideas at all! TV, radio, newspapers, and magazines are propaganda machines controlled by the drug industry, the food industry, and the oil industry.
- My first book was, I believe, the first book in U.S. history to be censored by the United States Government! I was told in so many words that if I put certain things in my first book my books would be confiscated and burned. The regulators at the FTC, FDA, and

other government agencies threatened me in such a way that I believed if I exercised my First Amendment right by saying certain things that I wanted to say, that I would in fact have been persecuted, arrested, and prosecuted.

- Since the writing of my first book I have been repeatedly harassed by government agents all around the world!

Most of the attacks revolve around the same few areas:

I am not a medical doctor.
In every interview one of the first things that comes up is how can I write a book on health and natural cures when I am not a "medical doctor"? I am viciously attacked for having the audacity to write a book about health when I have not gone to a western medical school, have no medical training, and am not a licensed healthcare expert. The arrogance of politicians, federal regulators, and the media is that only a person who is an "M.D." is qualified to write a book or talk about health or ways to treat, prevent, and cure disease. This is the great lie. This is the brainwashing that the American Medical Association has purposely perpetuated throughout America. The American Medical Association, a union owned and controlled by the drug industry, wants to have a monopoly on what is true relating to health. They want you to believe that only an M.D. should be listened to regarding your health. They want you to believe that anyone else other than an M.D. is a "quack." This thinking protects their monopoly. I am not a medical doctor! I have no formal medical or health training. I am simply a reporter. I am a journalist. I am an advocate for consumers around the world. I am an exposer of corporate and government corruption.

The AMA does not want people to know the truth. There are millions of people around the world that are not M.D.s who routinely treat patients without drugs and surgery. These millions of "doctors" prevent, cure, and treat illness and disease with natural non-patentable remedies. In many cases their success rates are much better than drugs and surgery. The American Medical Association, the U.S. Food and Drug Administration, and medical associations around the world, because they are controlled by the drug industry, want you to believe that these results do not exist and anyone other than an M.D. is a quack. The facts are "doctors" in China use natural non-patentable methods such as herbs, acupuncture, and chi gong, with spectacular results. "They" don't want you to know about these treatment options.

"Doctors" in India use the inexpensive all-natural ayurvedic methods of curing disease with amazing results. "They" don't want you to know about these healing methods. "Doctors" throughout the Amazon use herbs and plants to cure and prevent disease and have miraculous results. "They" don't want you to have information about these inexpensive non-patentable treatments. Chiropractors have been proven in court to reduce and eliminate back pain better than any drug or surgical procedure. "They" don't want you to know these facts. Researchers in Canada were curing breast cancer with linseed oil better than chemotherapy. Why wasn't this discovery front page headline news? Women around the world should be outraged that the truth and effectiveness about linseed oil treating breast cancer is being hidden from them. Drug company executives years ago told me directly that anything that would cut into the profits of chemotherapy has to be debunked, discredited, and hidden from the public!

Remember, according to the news media and government officials, nobody is a legitimate "doctor" unless they have gone to a western medical school and are a licensed M.D. This is the great lie. When you watch television, an M.D. is brought on and asked a health question. The M.D. answers factually as if the answer is without dispute. Never once does the M.D. say, "This is my opinion." Never once does the M.D. state, "Other doctors may have a different viewpoint." Never once does the M.D. state, "Based on the information we currently have it appears that this is the case, however, other health experts have different opinions and as more information becomes available this conclusion may change." Never once does the M.D. state, "This information comes directly from the drug companies that actually pay me."

I am not a doctor. I do not treat patients. I have, however, traveled over five million miles interviewing doctors, patients, researchers, and scientists. I have read thousands of books on preventing, treating, and curing disease. I have interviewed and talked to hundreds of authors, health editors, and medical industry insiders. I, myself, was a former secret insider. The facts are indisputable. There absolutely is a need for drugs and surgery. In crisis situations drugs and surgery can and do save lives. The facts are also indisputable that there are inexpensive non-drug and non-surgical ways to prevent and cure disease. These treatments and discoveries are being hidden from the population because it will adversely affect the profits of the drug companies. The facts are also indisputable that the food industry, in a desire to increase profits, is producing food that is causing illness and disease. The food industry knows this to be true. Remember the tobacco industry, fifty years ago, knew that cigarette smoking caused disease, and lied about it over and over again. The food industry today is doing the same thing. They know they are producing food that causes disease. I have personally seen the evidence in secret meetings. They are lying about it.

The facts are indisputable. Non-prescription and prescription drugs all have negative side effects. The drug industry today, as a business model, is based on getting as many people around the world, as young as possible, to take drugs every day for the rest of their lives. I know it sounds like a cocaine or heroin dealer. The facts are indisputable. The drug industry can only increase profits by getting more people to take more drugs on a regular basis. The pharmaceutical industry has no financial interest in healthy people. I am their worst nightmare. I haven't taken an over-the-counter or prescription drug in over twenty years. If everyone was as healthy as me every drug company would be out of business!

Remember, no one has a monopoly on the truth. The media, the government, the American Medical Association, and every special interest group want you to believe that no one on planet earth can intelligently talk about health issues unless they went to a western medical school and have an "M.D." after their name. This is arrogant, ludicrous, and nonsensical. Remember, too, that western medical schools virtually only teach how to prescribe drugs and how to cut out parts of a person's anatomy! If you believe that only an M.D. knows anything about treating or preventing disease, consider this: M.D.s virtually know absolutely nothing about chiropractic, acupuncture, herbology, homeopathy, nutritional therapy, enzyme therapy, traditional Chinese medicine, the use of chi gong, cranial-sacral therapy, high-dose nutritional therapy, chelation, ozone therapy, oxygen therapy, energetic rebalancing, radionics, thought field therapy, ayurvedic medicine, rainforest medicine, and the hundreds if not thousands of other technologies and therapies used by doctors around the world with miraculous results!

M.D.s have the arrogance to believe that the two things they are trained in, drugs and surgery, are the only things on planet earth that are successful in the prevention, treatment, and curing of disease. How wrong they are.

No scientific research?

One of the completely false misrepresentations about my first book and this book is that there is no "scientific evidence" to back up any of the claims that natural remedies can prevent, cure, and treat disease. This is categorically false. There are thousands of studies around the world that conclusively prove that natural remedies are in fact effective. This is discussed in great detail in my first book. Let me summarize. Consider the definition of "scientific study." All studies are funded by someone. When a study is commissioned there is a specific reason why the study is being ordered. Studies are commissioned and paid for to prove that something works, or to prove that something doesn't work. Studies are never commissioned to find the truth. They are always paid for to give a specific preplanned result. Drug companies have a very specific way that they organize studies. They first produce secret studies to get preliminary information on how to produce a final study that will give them the required result. These secret preliminary studies are never released to the public. They are produced to figure out the best way to organize a final study that will give the drug company the desired end result. Drug companies fund 99 percent of all studies, directly or indirectly. Sometimes the funding is ten times removed! It is almost comical in the way that the drug companies distance themselves from the true fact that they are the vested interest behind the result of the study. These studies that produce results that "prove" that a particular drug is safe and effective are completely false and misleading!

Consider also that these same drug companies will directly or indirectly fund and produce studies that prove that their competing products are ineffective and unsafe. This happens routinely. Drug companies, directly or indirectly, engage in hundreds of secret preliminary studies on natural remedies. These secret preliminary studies are conducted to figure out a way to organize a "final study" that will prove the natural remedy is ineffective and unsafe. The public never hears about these preliminary studies. The public also does not know that the final study was indirectly paid for by the drug company. It is then reported in the news that the natural remedy has been proven in a scientific study to be unsafe and ineffective. This is a flagrant and blatant lie, deception, and falsehood. The few true independent real studies, real observations and experiences from doctors and patients around the world, are ignored.

The fact is there are huge amounts of evidence and proof that natural remedies are effective and safe.

No real doctors agree with you.

First, let's define "real doctor." The fact is that hundreds of thousands of doctors around the world agree with many of the things I report on regarding natural remedies because I am simply reporting to the public what these doctors are saying themselves! Doctor Andrew Weil, M.D., has written several books. In those books he suggests that reducing stress can prevent and treat disease. Those are not my words, those are his. I report that information. James Balch, M.D., co-author of *Prescription for Nutritional Healing* and *Prescription for Natural Cures,* says that homeopathic remedies, flower essences, vitamins, aromatherapy, and even food can prevent and treat disease. I report to you his findings. There are thousands of M.D.s, naturopaths, Ph.D.s, scientists, authors, and researchers that have concluded that the natural remedies that I expound upon do in fact work. Remember, these are not my natural cures. In my first book, and in this book, I am simply reporting on the natural non-drug and non-surgical ways to prevent and cure disease that M.D.s and other doctors have found to be safe and effective. In the book *The World's Greatest Treasury of Health Secrets* published by Bottom Line Publications, over 300 M.D.s are quoted, many with inexpensive all-natural ways to cure and prevent disease.

The bottom line is that these natural cures come from licensed healthcare practitioners, healers, doctors, and M.D.s from around the world. It is impossible to suggest that a person will agree with everything in this book. I am simply reporting on what the doctors and researchers have discovered.

The FTC says you are a habitual false advertiser.

This is standard operating procedure used by the government and media. When a whistleblower like me comes forward and exposes the corruption in government and big business, the procedure used is to debunk, discredit, and file false accusations. Smear campaigns and political dirty tricks are not new. Filing false charges and publishing false and misleading press releases to discredit those individuals whom the government deems as having undesirable opinions is the modus operandi used by the powers that be. Debunking campaigns are even part of official government documents when outlining the procedures to be used against individuals who blow the whistle on corruption or reveal and expose information government and corporations want to remain hidden.

The entire FTC and attorney general story will be available at www.kevinfightsback.com. Every bit of correspondence, secret government documents, e-mails, and court transcripts, with commentary, will be available in chronological order. See for yourself with your own eyes. To summarize my public fights with both the FTC and various attorneys general in America, as well as government regulatory agencies around the world, I present these interesting facts.

Over fifteen years ago I uncovered a secret government program that was designed to systematically stop teaching children how to read and simultaneously get children numbed up on psychiatric prescribed drugs such as Ritalin, as well as other drugs. This secret program involved removing the teaching of phonics from the classroom. If children were not taught phonics and instead were taught the "look see method" they would effectively be dumbed down and be incapable of reading and true education. At the same time, the amount of mercury-laced vaccines, which have been proven to produce autism and other learning disabilities, was dramatically increased. Schools were given $500 per month per child that was on Ritalin®, Prozac, or some other psychiatric prescribed drug. The combination of taking phonics out of the schools together with increasing the amount of drugs being forced on our children created a dumbing down and demotivating of our youth. This produces a less intelligent, less motivated populace much more susceptible to advertising campaigns produced by drug companies and fast food companies.

Sean Shanahan produced an educational program called "Hooked on Phonics." He advertised this home study informational publication primarily on the radio. Some of you may remember the clever telephone number 1-800-ABCDEFG! Sean Shanahan committed a heinous crime. He was helping to teach children how to read. Hundreds of thousands of satisfied customers were incredibly grateful for the "Hooked on Phonics" program. The government, however, was not happy at all. With virtually zero customer complaints, the Federal Trade Commission was ordered to put Shanahan out of business. They then used their unlimited resources to conduct a secret investigation into Shanahan. They coordinated these secret investigations with the news media. Shanahan was never contacted, interviewed, or questioned. If he was, the government would have found him to be cooperative in every way, as his only mission was to help children read. Without warning, in one massive attack, the FTC sued Shanahan, attempted to freeze all of his personal and business assets, and demanded over $100 million. The FTC sent out false and misleading press releases stating that he had misled the public and ripped off consumers. Simultaneously, the news media, working in conjunction with the government, put out a massive negative smear campaign against Hooked on Phonics. Hooked on Phonics was crushed and nearly bankrupted.

Shanahan did nothing wrong. He did not rip off consumers: he did not mislead anyone. He had happy customers. He was teaching kids how to read. The FTC is the wrongdoer. The FTC is the deceiver. The FTC is the group that is hurting consumers.

Around this same time I was beginning my breakaway from my activities within the secret society. I published *Mega Memory*. Like Shanahan, I knew what was going on in the educational system. I knew firsthand. One of my required missions was to discuss with high members of the Department of Education how specifically we could turn children into zombies, making them lifelong users of products the pharmaceutical industry and food industry were selling. I was secretly involved in many of these meetings. Many of my suggestions are still in use today within the school lunch program and the vending machine systems used to get children hooked on the new crack, diet sodas. My covert activities made certain corporations billions of dollars in profits.

With the publishing of *Mega Memory* I had turned the corner and now was trying to help the children instead of the corporations. When I went on television and exposed the drugging of children in schools and the lack of teaching children how to learn, I had crossed the line with the government. I exposed the fact that attention deficit disorder or attention deficit hyperactivity disorder was simply a "made up syndrome" caused primarily from growth hormones in meat and dairy, food dyes, chemical additives and preservatives, artificial sweeteners, and specifically manufactured sugars such as high fructose corn syrup. I was fully aware that these learning disabilities were labels put on children who had symptoms that were being specifically manufactured so that the kids could be drugged and kept stupid. Exposing this secret outraged those in government. Their former boy wonder genius who they've paid millions of dollars to was now blowing the whistle on the secrets he knew. I had to be stopped. Like Hooked on Phonics, *Mega Memory*, and all the products I sold, including the Callahan Addiction Breaking System, Hair Farming for thinning and balding hair, Action Reading, Nature's Pure Body Program, Mega Math, Mega Speed Reading, Dr. Duarte's Health Alternatives, Jaws For Life, the story of shark cartilage, Dr. Morter's Dynamic Health, Biotape, Snore Away, Coral Calcium, and several other products—all are incredibly effective, excellent products. They all work. They all do what we say they do. People who bought them loved them. There were virtually no consumer complaints. Everything we said about the products was documented and substantiated.

The truth does not stop the government. Like with Hooked on Phonics and virtually hundreds of other honest people and companies I became a target for the FTC and various state attorneys general. Remember, there were virtually no consumer complaints. There were only happy, satisfied customers. This doesn't matter. The government always acts as the ruthless tyrants that they are. They are not interested in protecting consumers. They are only interested in protecting the corporations that in effect pay them, and protecting their own power and influence.

Without warning I was sued by the FTC. Later, I was sued by eighteen state attorney general offices. I have been sued in various countries around the world by government regulators. The actions that these agencies take are always the same. These agencies always make up the most outrageous lies and false accusations. They attempt to seize all assets and do everything in their power to bankrupt you and shut you up forever. They send out false and misleading press releases and get the media to make you appear like you are an evil con man rip-off artist.

I, like most of the other hundreds of marketers wrongly attacked and accused by the FTC, wind up signing consent decrees. What is never published is that in every single case after complete and full investigations the government always dropped every charge and allegation. The agencies were required to sign a document stating after the complete investigation there was no finding of any wrongdoing on Mr. Trudeau's part or any of his companies. If I am such a bad guy, if I am a habitual false advertiser who has ripped off millions of people around the world, why would the government sign a document stating, "After a complete investigation there is no finding of any wrongdoing on the part of Mr. Trudeau or any of his companies." If I am in fact a false advertiser who has ripped off millions, why is it that I have never been found guilty in a court of law of this fact? Why is it that I have never been ordered to pay a single penny in fines? If I have ripped off millions, where are they? I have virtually hundreds of thousands of completely satisfied and happy customer comments in my files. Certainly you can't please all the people all the time. No matter who you are or what you sell, or what kind of business you have, you can find an unhappy customer. The fact remains that the overwhelming majority of people who have purchased any product from me over the years are completely satisfied with that product.

All these allegations and trumped-up charges are nothing more than politically motivated smear campaigns designed to stop me from blowing the whistle on the insider secrets that I have been exposed to over the last twenty years.

You're a convicted felon.

Old news. Virtually every interview I do starts off with the fact that I pled guilty to two felonies that I committed over twenty years ago. I explain this in great detail in my first book. In my youth I bounced several checks, and applied for several credit cards and put false information on the applications. I took full responsibility for my actions, paid full restitution, and spent two years in prison. I learned a very important lesson and turned my life around. When I traveled through New Zealand and Australia with past president Gorbachev of the Soviet Union and General Norman Schwarzkopf, as part of the WORLD MASTERS OF BUSINESS, it was because I am regarded as a great American turnaround story. The experience was very humbling. Many people in life do bad things. Many people make errors in judgment. Many people get consumed with greed, money, and power. I learned that when you make a mistake, do a bad thing, and do something very wrong, that you must take full responsibility for your actions, blame no one but yourself, and most importantly, learn so that you can become and be a better person. The reason why I wrote my first book and I am writing this one is that I have "seen the light." I was the bad guy. I was on the dark side. And now, truth, justice, and honesty are the pillars of my life.

The government and the media use the fact that I am a convicted felon as a perfect platform to attack my credibility. This is the reason why, they say, you should not buy my book or listen to what I have to say. I would say that because I am an ex-felon is exactly the reason why you should read these words. I am the insider coming forward revealing the secrets that I know.

The bottom line is who should you believe? Who should you listen to when it comes to truthful and honest unbiased information about your health, the safety and effectiveness of medical treatment, and the use of natural remedies? You cannot believe the media. You cannot believe anything you hear on TV and radio, or read in newspapers and magazines. These media outlets are controlled by the drug industry, the food industry, and the oil companies. It has been proven repeatedly that the information coming from the media is biased and slanted because of the financial conflicts of interests that exist.

You cannot believe doctors, medical clinics, or hospitals. Doctors are only trained in drugs and surgery. They are trained by the drug companies and pharmaceutical industry itself. They are legal drug pushers. They only tell you what they know. Most importantly, they only tell you what they sell! Even the *Journal of the American Medical Association* published an article that suggested that doctors should stop accepting bribes from drug companies. Most people don't know that Big Pharma spends almost $19 billion a year enticing and influencing doctors on how they treat patients. How can you believe a doctor when he has so little health information other than drugs and surgery? How can you believe a doctor when he has major financial incentives and simply makes more money by getting you to use the expensive drugs, testing procedures, and treatments that he is paid to sell for the pharmaceutical industry?

People forget that medical clinics, hospitals, and doctors' offices are businesses set up to make a profit! People forget that when these doctors purchase an expensive machine, they have to use it or lose all that money. How do you know that when the doctor says you need an expensive treatment that he happens to sell, that in fact you really need it? How could that doctor tell you about a better, more effective, and less expensive treatment option even if he knew about it? The doctor is stuck, he has to pay his bills, he has to get a return on the money he invested in his equipment. This is the major conflict of interest no one wants to talk about. You simply cannot believe and trust doctors. It is imperative that you always get multiple opinions.

A perfect example of this is the story I heard of the man who was diagnosed with prostate cancer. He went to a doctor and was told he needed surgery. The doctor he went to was a surgeon. This is how the doctor makes his money. The more surgeries he performs, the more money he makes. The surgeon said that nothing else would cure his prostate cancer. The patient sought a second opinion. He went to a medical clinic that specialized in men's health. The medical doctors at this clinic said that surgery was absolutely not needed. There was a new form of chemotherapy, which they happened to offer, that would cure his prostate cancer. These doctors make ninety percent of their profits from selling this chemotherapy treatment. The patient was told there was no other treatment available in the world that could cure his prostate cancer. The patient sought yet another opinion. He went to Europe and met with a group of medical doctors at a prestigious hospital. These doctors told the patient that there was only one treatment that could cure his prostate cancer. This treatment was a revolutionary freezing of the prostate. It required no surgery and no chemotherapy. Interestingly enough, these doctors did not perform surgery in their clinic, nor did they offer chemotherapy. They did, however, offer this freezing medical treatment. The profits on this treatment were enormous. The patient was very confused. While in Europe he heard about an anti-aging medical facility run by a medical doctor. He decided to get yet another opinion. This M.D. examined the patient and concluded that neither surgery, chemotherapy, nor freezing of the prostate was needed. He suggested some herbs, nutrients, and live cell therapy. Of course, this is what the doctor sold. The patient was confused and went home. He went on a thirty-day juice fast with herbs to contemplate which treatment option he should choose. The patient realized that if he visited doctors around the world, that he would probably continue to receive different opinions as to what the best treatment options were. He realized that these doctors may in fact truly believe that their treatment suggestion was in his best interest. However, he also realized that none of these doctors could possibly be knowledgeable about all the potential treatment options, their success rates, and potential negative side effects. While fasting and meditating, the patient came to grips with the fact that he had to choose a treatment soon or he could die. He decided to just cut the prostate out and take the surgery route.

The story ends on an amazing note. When the patient went to the surgeon to schedule prostate removal surgery the surgeon conducted a basic pre-surgical evaluation. Lo and behold, the prostate was no longer cancerous. The surgeon could not understand this. He suggested that perhaps there was never any prostate cancer to begin with. Maybe there was a misdiagnosis. Maybe there was some miraculous spontaneous healing. The patient obviously was elated at this good news and informed the doctor that he had just concluded a thirty-day fast with herbs and colonics. The doctor said that doing fasts, taking herbs, and doing colonics is very dangerous and never do them again. The patient left wondering how his prostate cancer was cured.

Can you really trust and believe everything doctors say?

So who can you believe? Remember, if they are selling you something, how can you believe and trust what they have to say? If they are telling you to take something that they sell and not take something that they don't sell, how do you know they are being truthful and honest instead of just trying to make money? Think about authors and health experts that manufacture and sell products. Doctor Andrew Weil, Deepak Chopra, and Dr. Gary Null are regarded as legitimate, credible authorities on health, nutrition, and alternatives to drugs and surgery. Did you know, however, that they all sell and have financial interests in various nutritional products? If Dr. Weil said do not take coral calcium, but rather buy this calcium that I sell, it's much, much better, how do you know that what he says is something he actually believes to be true or rather is he just trying to sell you something and make a profit?

How can you believe what is written in medical journals and magazines when the authors of the articles are being paid by drug or supplement manufacturers to say either positive things or negative things about a particular subject or product? How can you believe any scientific study when we know they are virtually all bought and paid for, directly or indirectly, from a company that has a financial interest in what the study says? How can we believe what the government says when it has now been proven that corporations give millions of dollars to lobbyists who in turn pay off the politicians who then direct the various government regulators to say what is in the best interests of the corporations that put up the money to start with!?

That leaves little old me. If you read the papers, I am either the messiah or the antichrist when it comes to informing people about health. Why listen to me? First, I actually believe everything I write in my books, publish in my newsletters and website, and say in speaking forums around the world. I believe it so strongly to be true that I actually live my life this way. Most importantly, I have no financial interests with any of the recommendations that I make. If I tell you that a certain supplement is the best, you can be assured that I take it myself and I have no financial interest whether you buy it or not. This is a huge difference. Lastly, unlike any medical doctor, I have not been trained in any one discipline. I am not biased based on my schooling that any one form of medical or health protocol is the best. I have traveled the world, observed firsthand, experienced in my own life, and seen with my own eyes what I am reporting to you regarding health. I believe that I am truly one of the only unbiased sources of health journalism and reporting in the world.

You can trust me ... I am NOT a doctor!

CHAPTER 5

The Health Basics

A hospital is no place to be sick.

—Samuel Goldwyn

Everything you need to know about the cause of disease, as well as the best way to prevent and cure disease without any drugs or surgery, can be found in my first book, *Natural Cures "They" Don't Want You to Know About*. If you have not read this book I strongly suggest that you read it cover to cover. I receive astronomical amounts of correspondence from people that share with me their stories of how they used the information in that book to cure themselves of all kinds of terrible illnesses and diseases. People have told me that the information in the book cured asthma, allergies, acid reflux, arthritis, back pain, migraines, frequent colds and flus, herpes, addictions, depression, sleep disorders, prostate problems, breast cancer, high blood pressure, high cholesterol, and the list goes on. Since I wrote that first book I have published dozens of articles in my monthly newsletter and on my website www.naturalcures.com. No one has all the answers regarding health. Every day, all around the world, millions of doctors, scientists, researchers, and everyday people are making discoveries regarding ways to prevent and cure illness and disease without drugs and surgery.

This is why I have a monthly newsletter and the website www.naturalcures.com. My goal is to scour the world and report to you on the newest discoveries and breakthroughs regarding anti-aging, and preventing and curing disease. Remember, as I am on my quest to find and report this life-changing information to you, the drug companies are at the same time trying to hide these discoveries from you, or turn them into patented drugs so that they can make billions more in profits. While I and others like me are on a quest for uncovering inexpensive natural health remedies, the medical cartel is on a well-funded mission to debunk, discredit, and destroy me and those like me.

Which brings us to this book. When I wrote my first book, the United States Government said in effect if I mentioned any product by brand name or wrote where you could obtain any product that I recommended, the books would be confiscated and burned, and I believe I would have most assuredly been arrested and prosecuted under some trumped-up charge of "practicing medicine without a license" or deceiving the public. I have been in court with the U.S. Federal Trade Commission as well as other government regulators regarding these issues. I have decided to put myself in grave danger by writing this book. In this book I am going to do what the U.S. Government does not want me to do. I am going to tell you the names of specific products that after years of investigation and research I have concluded may prevent and cure various diseases. These are products that I have no financial interest in. Other people looking at the same data may come to different conclusions. The government repeatedly says that there is no evidence that these products prevent and cure disease. The government claims that only a drug can prevent, treat, or cure disease. I think the government is wrong. So I am going to report to you my findings.

First, you must understand where I am coming from.

MY MISSION

What I'm all about.

It is important that you all realize what my mission in life is, what the mission of my newsletters, books, and website is, and what the mission of my entire business enterprise is. I believe in positively impacting individual people and society. My mission statement, both personal and corporate, is: "We positively impact the whole person." What this means is I do things that I believe have a positive impact on individuals and society. I believe in doing things that have a positive impact on the "whole person." That includes doing things that I believe are beneficial to a person's physical health, emotional well being, financial status, intellectual endeavors, spiritual development, and personal fulfillment. My whole career has been primarily about selling information. I have in the past, on occasion, sold products that I believe so strongly in that I personally use them and encourage all of my friends and family to use as well. However, in the last few years I came to realize that my opinions were actually costing millions of dollars in profits to major multinational corporations. These multinational corporations, as well as other special interest groups, do not want me to actively, in any wide-scale way, disseminate my personal beliefs and opinions.

Most people do not know how the system works in America. We think there is a constitution; we think there is a bill of rights. We think that each individual person has the right under the law to life, liberty, and the pursuit of happiness. We think that the First Amendment of the United States Constitution guarantees that every person has the right of free speech, which means that every person has the right, in any format, to express his opinions and beliefs even though the government or the majority may disagree with and dislike those opinions and beliefs. We believe as Americans that no one has a monopoly on the truth, that scientific facts are generally not facts at all, but merely theories and opinions that history has shown to change as new information becomes available. The way our system works is when a large publicly traded company has their profits affected by the voice and opinions of an individual like me, those companies and special interest groups take certain measures to suppress and stifle that individual's expression of his First Amendment free speech right.

Here is how it works as I see it. This, in my opinion, is exactly what has happened to me. I went on television and interviewed a man by the name of Bob Barefoot, who is an author of several books. Bob Barefoot, in his books, offers his opinions about how calcium is one of the most important nutrients needed for a person's health and the prevention of disease. Mr. Barefoot quotes Nobel Prize–winning authors and makes his case based on his opinions, observations, and conclusions. Bob Barefoot's conclusion is that virtually everyone is deficient in calcium, which leads to acidosis, which makes a person susceptible to cancer. Thus, if a person supplements his diet with calcium, his body pH has a chance to go back to alkaline and any and all cancers that may be there cannot live in an alkaline state, thus go into remission and the person is healed.

Those opinions, according to the scientific community and medical community at large, are heresy. Although a rather large, yet minority percentage of scientists and doctors around the world believe in Mr. Barefoot's conclusions, the majority does not. Since the cancer industry is one of the most profitable industries in the world, anything that would adversely affect the profits of the cancer industry must be suppressed. On our TV infomercial, we sold Bob Barefoot's books, but I made a huge error. I also sold Bob Barefoot's recommended source of calcium, which is coral calcium of Okinawa, Japan. In doing so I became subject to the attacks of both the Federal Trade Commission and the Food and Drug Administration.

So, here is how our beautiful system works. The corporations whose profits are affected by my speech give millions of dollars to their lobbyists in Washington. These lobbyists in turn talk to senators and congressmen, as well as cabinet members and other Washington insiders. They take these millions of dollars and funnel them into the politicians' and Washington insiders' pockets through various means, all of which have been made legal by the politicians themselves. These "payoffs," although legal, are by any logical normal person's account, what they are—100 percent bribes and payoffs. I state this as my opinion and I state this exercising my First Amendment right. These politicians then use the agencies, which they control, including the FDA and FTC, to do their dirty work. The FTC and FDA, in my opinion, are like the Gestapo and the SS of Nazi Germany, or the KGB under Stalinist Russia. They do the dirty work of the politicians. They do not do what they are designed and commissioned to do, which is to protect consumers. They do the exact opposite. They in fact protect the profits and monopolies of the major corporations.

My Washington insiders tell me that this is exactly what has happened in relation to my dealings with both the FDA and the FTC. The most senior people in these organizations have gotten direct orders from very powerful people in Washington who need to protect the profits of the multinational pharmaceutical companies. These direct orders are to squash Kevin Trudeau, and suppress Kevin Trudeau at any cost. The orders are to make sure that Kevin Trudeau is not on TV and is not disseminating his views and opinions. My insiders tell me that the FTC is on a mission to find any technicality, any loophole, and do all it can to drive me into the ground and strip me of my First Amendment right of free speech. Their harassing tactics over the last few months should be viewed as civil rights violations, personal attacks, and retaliation against my very public negative comments against these government renegade agencies.

When I saw this happen, I re-evaluated my business enterprise around the world, my personal mission statement, and my life's priorities. This is the conclusion that I have come to. My life is not about making money. My life is not about accumulation of wealth. My life is about my mission, which is to positively impact individual people and society. I have decided that the best way to achieve this objective is to virtually give away everything that I own so that I have no wealth, I have no net worth, and that people can know that my intentions are pure. I have decided to set up a series of foundations and charities around the world that virtually anything and everything I own will be donated to. This way people will know that my intention is pure, true, and honest. This is in the process of happening now, and it is my intention to achieve this in a very short period of time.

My second conclusion was that I cannot, in any way, shape, or form, sell any products anywhere in the world any longer. The FTC's position is that I misled the public into buying useless products. Their assertions are totally insane and outrageous. The FTC's press releases that they have published since the signing of my consent decree should be viewed as false and misleading, but who will sue the FTC for producing a false and misleading press release? Their press releases are filled with defamatory statements, yet they are immune from prosecution because they are the government. The FTC's press releases state that they have shut down Kevin Trudeau's empire and stopped me from doing what I have done for years, which is mislead the public by producing false, unsubstantiated and misleading advertisements. They claim I have ripped off consumers and they have finally come to the rescue of these poor individuals who were taken advantage of by me.

The FTC is full of bravado in their assertions. Their statements are misleading, false, untrue, and fraudulent. Their statements are totally unsubstantiated themselves. If, as they claim, I have produced such false and misleading advertising and have ripped off so many American consumers, why wouldn't they actively pursue these things instead of signing consent decrees where there is no finding or admission of wrongdoing? If I am such an evildoer, where are the thousands of angry consumers? Where are all the consumer complaints? Where are the massive requests for refunds? They do not exist. The reason they do not exist is there are no angry customers, there are no massive refund requests, there are no consumer complaints on file in virtually any organization in the world from people who have purchased products that I sell. The fact is the people who have purchased my products overwhelmingly love my products. They do not feel misled in my advertising; they feel blessed that they have seen my ads and purchased the products that I endorse and recommend.

Here is the conclusion that I have come to: I will not sell any products anywhere in the world. This way I am no longer under potential attack from the Food and Drug Administration, and I am no longer under potential attack from the Federal Trade Commission. I will not sell any products anywhere in the world. Not only that, but I will not accept any conflicting advertising for my newsletter or my websites, www.naturalcures.com, www.thewhistleblower.com, and www.kevinfightsback.com. This way you can be assured and guaranteed that the information I am giving is unbiased and there are no conflicts of interest. As far as I know, mine is the only health newsletter and website that does not sell supplements or take advertising. I am going one step beyond. In addition to all of the above, I am not going to receive any compensation in any form, directly or indirectly, from any of the products that I endorse or recommend. This way my newsletter, the books that I write, and all the informational publications I publish, on DVD, VHS tape, and internet websites, can be produced and sold without the FTC being able to do anything about it. Why? Because I am not selling (promoting) products, because I do not take advertising, and because I am not compensated on any products that I talk about or recommend. All of these informational publications are in fact informational publications. They are what they are. They are me in various forms giving my opinions, which not only is my right to do under the First Amendment, but also has been specifically carved out in my consent decree with the Federal Trade Commission.

Even with all of this being true, I believe the Federal Trade Commission, because they are under direct orders from their superiors, will try everything they can to find some loophole, some technicality to stop me from expressing my opinions in my newsletter, books, and websites. I believe they will try to stop me from publishing my newsletter. I believe they will try to stop me from publishing my website. I believe they will try to stop me from publishing and selling my books, videocassettes, DVDs, and CDs. I believe they will try to stop me from lecturing around the world. I believe they will try to stop me from doing all of the things I intend to do, including producing radio and television networks and programs. The FTC is not trying to protect consumers, the FTC is under direct orders from their superiors to stop and suppress Kevin Trudeau from disseminating his views and opinions. The reason is these views and opinions are going to cost the publicly traded drug industry and food industry profits. They are afraid of me being and exercising my right as a journalist. They are afraid of me exercising my right as a whistleblower. They are afraid of me exercising my right as an investigative reporter. They are afraid of me because tens of millions of people all around the world believe what I say and love the fact that I am standing up to the suppressive tyrants in government and in the corporate boardrooms around the world. They are afraid of me because they know like Gandhi, Cesar Chavez, Martin Luther King, Ralph Nader, and David Horowitz, I will have a major political following around the world. They know that like these great men, millions of people will follow me and listen to what I have to say. They know that unless they stop me now, my voice is going to make a change. Their power, profits, and influence are at risk. They are afraid that I will run for political office, which I have every intention of doing. They are afraid that I will name names and expose these individuals for the cowards and frauds that they are.

Let me be perfectly clear, and to summarize my mission and what I intend to do. My mission is to positively impact the whole person, as well as society. I intend on doing this by:

a. I will not, directly or indirectly, sell any products.

b. I will not take any conflicting advertising in my newsletter or website.

c. I intend on selling off or giving away most of my assets to charities and foundations.

d. I will not receive any compensation in any form, directly or indirectly, for any products that I endorse or recommend.

With that said, I intend on:

1. *Continuing to publish my newsletter called the "Natural Cures Newsletter,"* and selling subscriptions to this newsletter to people all around the world.

2. *Continuing to produce NaturalCures.com.* NaturalCures.com is a website where people can go to and must join to become a member. As a private member, they will be a member of my political association and a member of this website community. As a member on the website community, they will have access to all my views and opinions, as well as be able to share views and opinions specifically relating to natural ways to cure and prevent all disease.

3. *"Natural Cures Radio Network."* I intend on producing a radio network, which will be broadcast 24 hours a day, 7 days a week, called the "Natural Cures Radio Network." Initially, this will be broadcast on the web and I intend on negotiating with broadcasting this through other channels as well, including satellite radio. This radio network may in fact take some advertising, but not for any of the products that

we talk about on the network. It will take advertising for only informational publications or other generic, mundane products and services.

4. *Books.* My intention is to write very specific books on very specific subjects. The current books I am working on are *The Diabetes Cure They Don't Want You to Know About, The Cancer Cure They Don't Want You to Know About, The Heart Disease Cure They Don't Want You to Know About, The Attention Deficit Disorder Cure They Don't Want You to Know About, The Herpes Cure They Don't Want You to Know About, The Fibromyalgia Cure They Don't Want You to Know About, The Muscular Dystrophy Cure They Don't Want You to Know About, The Multiple Sclerosis Cure They Don't Want You to Know About,* etc., etc., etc.

Additionally, I am writing books on finances. My first book that I am writing now is entitled *How Anyone Can Make Millions: The Money Making Secrets They Don't Want You to Know About.*

I will also author a book which explains in great detail my firsthand eyewitness accounts of what I have seen at Area 51 relating to extraterrestrial artifacts, spacecraft, alien technology, and actual alien beings.

I am writing books on weight loss and exercise. My first book will be entitled *Lose 30 Pounds in 30 Days: The Weight Loss Secrets They Don't Want You to Know About.*

I am also in the process of writing a complete detailed manuscript about my twenty-year activities in the secret society. It will name names and I will reveal the insider secrets that up until now have been reserved for the privileged few in the world that the society has deemed worthy enough to benefit from these powerful methods of achieving financial freedom and vibrant health.

I will also be writing books on prayer, spirituality, government corruption, corporate corruption, etc.

It is interesting to note that the Federal Trade Commission, in one of their letters to me, had the arrogance to state that I could not title my books the way I want to. The FTC has stated in their letters to me that the title of the book claims that the book will do something; therefore, I could not title my books the way I want. They claim that any book with the words "how to" in the title would be making an efficacy claim. Therefore, I could not sell a book entitled how to do anything. For example, the FTC's position is that if I wrote a book on "How to Play the Piano in 30 Days," that book title would, in fact, be making a claim; therefore, I could not sell that book on television. The FTC is out of control. The FTC is certainly trying to overstep the bounds of the order that they signed with me, and are taking retaliatory action because I am talking about them in a negative way. It is obvious to everyone. For the FTC to say that I can't title a book the way I want is nothing but 100 percent pure suppression of my First Amendment right. I can write a book entitled *How to See God*. I can write a book that is entitled *How to Travel to Mars*. I can write a book entitled *How to Re-grow Limbs That Have Been Amputated*. I can write a book and entitle it anything I want. This is America, we have the First Amendment.

5. *Public appearances*. I intend on making speeches all around the country, be a guest on radio shows, and be a guest on TV shows. I also intend on writing articles that will be published in newspapers and magazines. In all of these forms I totally intend on expressing my opinions, and totally 100 percent will be exercising my First Amendment rights.

I believe the FTC is going to try to find any loophole or technicality to stop me from doing this. Why? Because, simply, they don't like me and they don't like my opinions. I am a person who has been targeted by the Federal Trade Commission. How do I know this to be true? Well, let's look specifically at the facts again. There are virtually no customer complaints, there are no massive refunds, and there are virtually no angry customers anywhere. In my industry, I have the highest customer satisfaction rate of virtually anyone. I have the highest repeat buy rate of virtually anyone. Customers love me and love my products. Virtually no one feels ripped off, virtually no one feels misled, and anyone who ever wanted a refund got a refund at any time. With virtually no unhappy customers, how can the FTC say I am ripping off consumers?

The other thing that points out the fact that the FTC is targeting me is very simply this—what they allege I am doing, they consistently let other people do exactly the same thing. Additionally, they use me as their poster child at every conference they can around the country. At the Electronic Retailing Association convention, as well as other conventions, on stage they publicly humiliate me, defame me, and make false and misleading statements about their case against me. They hold me up as an evildoer and someone who is ripping off the public yet, again, there are virtually no customers complaining. When I pointed out to the FTC that the vice president of the United States had purchased one of my products and wrote me a letter saying how much he loved it, as well as a federal judge who did the same thing, they pointed out that the people who buy my products, including the vice president and this federal judge, were too stupid to know that they were ripped off.

The Federal Trade Commission also coordinates with the news media to produce negative stories about me. There is obviously a campaign in Washington that is politically motivated. Washington insiders know that I am going to be running for political office and are trying everything they can to stop me and discredit me. They know that my following is a major political force and, quite frankly, they are afraid of me.

Now, in all of the above informational publications and venues where I will be expressing my right of free speech, including my newsletter, I intend to do exactly what I told the FTC I was going to do and that they agreed to. I intend to be a journalist, an investigative reporter, a consumer advocate, an author, an activist, and politician. In all of these venues, I am going to talk freely about anything I want and express my opinions about any subject I choose.

6. *Buyers guides.* These are going to be guides published in book form and on my website where I personally review products and as a consumer advocate, investigative reporter, and journalist, I will tell you what I think these products are good for and what they are not good for. I intend on reviewing individual brand name products and giving my opinions and thoughts about those products. I intend on telling you which products I think are good and which products I think are bad, and I specifically intend on highly recommending and endorsing certain products, keeping in mind that I am not compensated in any way, shape or form, directly or indirectly, on any products that I talk about, endorse, or recommend. This is an important point because all around the world individual people are paid huge sums of money by companies to talk glowingly about products. This happens in the magazine industry, the radio industry, the newspaper industry, the news media, and virtually any venue. These large payments are usually never disclosed. A good example is when a doctor appears on a news program and seems to be giving his unbiased professional opinion about a certain drug or treatment. Everyone believes that this "expert," whether it is a doctor, professor, researcher, or an author, is giving an unbiased opinion with no conflicts of interest. Well, guess what? It was reported in the *Wall Street Journal*, and I have been saying this for years, that these people are actually paid huge sums of money by the respective companies to talk glowingly about the particular products. This happens in every venue. I personally know publishers who write glowing

reports on cars or products in exchange for huge advertising contracts by those same respective manufacturers.

The free flow of information in journalism is not unbiased, but in many cases, it is bought and paid for. In the news media, for example, when you see a segment on a certain news channel where a doctor comes on to give a health update, you think it is news. It certainly appears to be news. You are being led to believe it is news. You are being led to believe that it is unbiased, impartial, and the information is "objective." You are being misled and lied to. Where is the FTC in relation to this? Hmm, hmm—they seem to be silent. They are turning their heads. This is flagrant and obvious. It is misleading and fraudulent information. These "experts" are paid spokespersons for the companies whose products they talk about. This is never disclosed and the FTC takes no action. The FTC should be ashamed of themselves, but they are what they are—puppets for the multinational corporations and politicians. They are the thugs, henchmen, and act like the Gestapo doing the dirty work to protect the profits of special interests.

7. *I intend to sell videotapes, DVDs, audiotapes, CDs, and a host of informational publications where I say specific things about any subject I want.* This is totally protected free speech because, again, I sell no products, I promote no products, and I am not getting compensated on any products I talk about or recommend. I am simply a journalist, a consumer advocate, an author, an activist, a future politician, and an investigative reporter exercising my rights of free speech. The interesting thing is that the Federal Trade Commission is taking an insane position. They claim that certain books are not books. The FTC claims that certain videotapes are no longer videotapes, that certain CDs are no longer CDs, that a certain tape of a lecture is not a lecture. They claim, at their discretion, that these things are "programs." Therefore, I am forbidden to market and sell them. I went to the dictionary. I tried to find the definition of "book." I tried to find the definition of "informational publication." I tried to find the definition of "program." For the life of me I can't understand how the FTC is coming to the conclusion that a book is not a book, that a lecture is not a lecture, but rather, program. Do you see what I mean? They are looking for any technicality they can find to stop me from expressing my opinions. The fact is this, so long as I am not selling products or getting compensated on products I can write a book about anything; I can title it anything I want. That is exercising my First Amendment right of free speech.

The FTC cannot stop me from doing that and they cannot stop me from selling it. No court in the land can. The only caveat is when I produce an ad selling that book, videotape, CD, website, newsletter, or any informational publication. As long as the ad accurately describes the contents of that informational publication it is protected by the First Amendment. For example, my book coming out is entitled *Lose 30 Pounds in 30 Days: The Weight Loss Secrets They Don't Want You to Know About*. That's the title of the book. If I tell you, "Buy this book and you will read my opinions on how to lose 30 pounds in 30 days, and what I believe are the weight loss secrets they don't want to you to know about," then that is an accurate description of the contents of the book and that ad should be fine. However, if I were to say, "Buy this book and you will lose 30 pounds in 30 days, guaranteed," then that is an efficacy claim which would need substantiation. My intention is to be very specific. My intention is to run all advertising through my attorneys to make sure that all of my ads accurately describe the contents of the book, which cannot be censored by the Federal Trade Commission or anyone else. As long as my ads accurately describe the contents of the books and not the efficacy or results a person will achieve by reading the book or other informational publication, I have a free hand under the Constitution of the United States and the spirit of the agreement I entered into with the Federal Trade Commission. The FTC agreed to this in open court and it is on the record!

But as I mentioned, the Federal Trade Commission is trying to find any loophole or any technicality they can to stop me from expressing my opinions. The FTC is out of control. They have lost the plot. They are not doing what they are supposed to be doing. They are supposed to be protecting consumers from rip-offs. Instead, they are on a vendetta mission to stop Kevin Trudeau from expressing his opinions strictly because they don't like my opinions and these opinions are costing multinational corporations profits. Maybe the General Accounting Office should do a complete investigation and review all internal documents to find out exactly why, and who is ordering this vicious personal vendetta attack against me.

With these things in mind, all of my informational publications will have the following disclaimer:

Everything in this informational publication is my opinion, or the opinions of the writers. Many people disagree with these opinions. Nothing in this published work is intended to diag-

nose, prevent, cure, or treat any disease. It is presented as informational material only, and for educational purposes only. If you do anything in this published work, you do so at your own risk. It is highly advisable that before you do anything in relation to your health you consult with a licensed healthcare practitioner, and do so under the supervision of a licensed healthcare practitioner of your choice. If you do anything contained in this published work there may be serious medical consequences. I am not a doctor, am not a scientist, and I am not offering any medical advice. I am not practicing medicine; I am simply a consumer advocate, a future politician, an activist, a journalist, and an investigative reporter. I am presenting information that I believe to be accurate at the time of printing. These are my opinions and views only.

As an example, in this book, in my future books, in my newsletter, websites, and other informational publications I am going to specifically tell you about specific branded products. I will absolutely tell you what my opinions are regarding whether or not I believe that these products can prevent, treat, or cure disease. This is very important for you to understand. If I sold a product or had any financial interest in the product for which I claimed could prevent, treat, or cure a disease I would be breaking the law. I could be charged criminally and imprisoned! For example, there is a company called "The Amazon Herb Company." Their website is www.amazonherb.net. Their phone number is (800) 835-0850. They sell a whole line of all-natural herbs from the Amazon. They cannot say, suggest, or imply that any of their products are effective in the prevention, treatment, or curing of any disease. Doing so would be in violation of various laws around the world. These laws, bought and paid for by the pharmaceutical cartels, protect the drug company monopoly; therefore, this company and thousands like it can only produce and sell their products and say nothing about them other than what is actually the ingredients. They sell, for example, a product called "100% Pure Camu." The label says, "Contains hand picked chemical free camu camu (Myrciaria dubia) fruit, which has never been irradiated or fumigated." That is all the company can say about it. Because I do not sell this product, am not compensated in any way on the sale of this product, directly or indirectly, and have no financial interest in the product or company, directly or indirectly, or even ten times removed, I am free to give you my opinion based on reviewing the research about this product. My opinion is this product can absolutely prevent and cure disease! It can be used as an effective non-drug treatment for herpes, immune disorders, colds and flus, and is even a potential cure for SARS and the Asian Bird Flu! I challenge the FTC, the FDA, or any other local, state, or federal regulator or law enforcement agency to come and arrest me for speaking such heresy. It is interesting to note and remember that people were put to death for saying such outrageous things such as the earth is round and not flat, bloodletting does not cure disease, or the sun does not revolve around the earth!

This feels good and is liberating! Let me do it again.

Dr. Lorraine Day Videotapes

Dr. Lorraine Day had cancer. She was told by the medical doctors that she was going to die. She told the medical doctors that they were not God and that by using natural means she believed she could cure her cancer. Without drugs or surgery and using only all-natural alternative therapies Dr. Day cured herself of what was thought to be terminal cancer. If you have cancer, in my opinion, you need to watch these videos. These videos are not a "program," they are in fact videotapes. They are a videotape of Dr. Lorraine Day giving a lecture. They are informational only. But, if you have cancer, you need to watch these videotapes. In my opinion, you will learn information about how to cure all cancer without drugs, surgery, or chemotherapy. Buy these videotapes now. I do sell these videotapes because they are informational publications, and I do make money when you buy them from me. Dr. Lorraine Day has also written a book about how to cure cancer without drugs and surgery, and I will encourage you to buy the book as well. The book is not a program; it is in fact a book. It is pages with words written on them. It is not an advertisement for any products, as Lorraine Day does not sell any products. It is a book in which Lorraine Day gives her opinions. You can buy her videotapes and books at www.naturalcures.com.

Lose 30 Pounds in 30 Days:
The Weight Loss Secrets They Don't Want
You to Know About

I have a book coming out by the above title. If you are overweight, in my opinion you need to read this book. When you read this book you will learn how I believe anyone can lose 30 pounds in 30 days. You will also learn about what I believe to be the weight loss secrets that they don't want you to know about. If you don't want to read the book, I have narrated the book in an abridged version on a single CD. The CD is not a program; it is in fact a CD. When you listen to the CD it is me reading the book, but giving you the abridged version of it. The book is not available now, but will be available sometime next year. The CD is available now. You can purchase the weight loss CD at www.natural-cures.com.

The Supplement Shopper Book

I sent a letter to the Federal Trade Commission with a copy of this great book called *The Supplement Shopper*. In *The Supplement Shopper* book, the authors list a very large number of diseases and tell you specifically the products that they recommend that prevent, treat, and cure that disease. All the products recommended in this book are all-natural vitamins, minerals, herbs, homeopathics, and the like. In addition to giving the specific product by brand name, the book also tells you exactly where to buy that product. It gives you an 800 number, a website address, and ordering information. I actually sent this book to the Federal Trade Commission and asked them if I could sell it. They told me I could. It was amusing to me the reasons why. In the letter I received from the Federal Trade Commission they said that I could sell this book and market this book because, "Trudeau's proposed dissemination of advertising for 'The Supplement Shopper' provided that the advertising for the book accurately conveyed the contents of the book and did not promote the book as part of a program to cure specific diseases. This opinion is based in part on our understanding that the entity that publishes this book is providing objective information; the authors appear to have a basis for their knowledge in this area; the book conveys the information in an objective manner; and the book does not appear to be promoting specific products (in spite of the fact that many different products are discussed). The fact that we are not objecting to this book—which contains specific product information and contact information—should in no way be interpreted to mean the Commission would not object to other books that conveyed such specific product information." So I highly recommend you get this book. You can buy this book at www.naturalcures.com. However, I have taken many of the product suggestions in that book and they are included in this publication.

E-mails

Many people from around the world send me e-mails, letters, and faxes, and other types of correspondence asking me specific questions about specific things. These questions could be "What kind of mattress do you sleep on Kevin?" or "What type of water filter do you personally use?" or "What bottled water do you think is good and you drink?" or "What type of air filter is in your house?" or have you heard of this product or that product, or this doctor or that doctor, or this treatment or this technique, and what are your opinions Kevin? Well, I was always under the impression that living in America, sharing opinions between two individual people would not be a violation of any law. But just to make sure, I sent a letter to the Federal Trade Commission and told them that I am receiving some letters, e-mails, and telephone calls from people from around the world, and that it was my understanding that I was free to express my opinions and say anything I want in these one-on-one types of communications. Imagine my absolute surprise when the "Gestapo," whoops, I mean the Federal Trade Commission, wrote me back a letter stating that it was their opinion that anyone who contacted me would be doing so because they have seen me on television selling my book. Therefore, my communications are not protected by the First Amendment.

It was the FTC's position that if somebody met me on the street and said, "Hey, Kevin. I've seen you on that TV infomercial selling your book. Let me ask you a question. What type of water filter do you use?" The FTC contends that that person would be approaching me "in connection" with the infomercial. Therefore, according to the FTC I would be prohibited from mentioning a product by brand name. The letter from the FTC is so unbelievable to me it reeks of the KGB. I feel I am in Nazi Germany or Stalinist Russia where if you want to express an opinion you have to look over both shoulders and whisper in somebody's ear. Heaven forbid the Gestapo would be lurking in the shadows and overhear an opinion coming forth from my mouth that they did not like and agree with. I feel like if I state an opinion that the FTC does not like they will swoop in with their federal agents, their guns drawn, screaming to get on the ground, spread-eagle, handcuff me, and take me away for violation of some insane arbitrary dictum that they may have come up with. Well, let me be perfectly clear. It is my opinion that if somebody calls me on the phone, or meets me on the street, or sends me an e-mail or writes me a letter and asks me a question about what type of dog food I give my dog, I am free to mention the product by brand name. I believe that if somebody in any form asks me a question about anything, I am free to express my opinion and state what I want to state without fear of reprisal from the Federal Trade Commission.

Imagine how silly it would be to be on the Larry King show and have Larry ask me, "Kevin, what type of bottled water do you drink?" and have me give this answer: "Well Larry, I would love to tell you the brand of bottled water that I drink, keeping in mind that I am not a paid spokesperson for any bottled water company and I am not compensated in any way if I mentioned the name of a particular bottled water. I have no financial interest whatsoever. I do not own stock in any bottled water company, my friends do not work for any bottled water company, my relatives are not on the board or own stock in any bottled water company that I know of, but even with all that being true Larry, the Federal Trade Commission has said that I cannot tell you the brand name of the bottled water I drink." Can you see how insane? Is it obvious to you that the Federal Trade Commission is overstepping their bounds? Is it obvious to you that they are going beyond the scope and spirit of the agreement that we entered into and was ordered by the court? Can you see how the Federal Trade Commission is suppressing my rights and violating my civil liberties? Can you see how the FTC is going beyond any legitimate interest in protecting consumers and is now into the realm of suppressing the expression of opinions from a U.S. citizen?

In a letter dated October 12, 2004, the Federal Trade Commission states very specifically that I cannot, through letters, e-mails, telephone calls, books, websites, etc., "promote specific branded products." The insanity here is that the FTC's definition of "promote" is simply naming a specific brand name product. The intention of our agreement was I would stop selling or having any financial interest in products. If in fact I owned stock in a particular water company and went on Larry King and mentioned that water company by brand name and told people, "Yes, buy XYZ bottled water. It's the best water in the world. It's the water I drink. It's the water I think everyone should drink, etc., etc., etc." If I had a financial interest with the sale of that product, or in the success of that company, then certainly I would be promoting that product, and I have agreed with the Federal Trade Commission that I will not do that. But what I did not agree to was that I would be stopped from expressing my opinions about products in which I have no financial interest. You see the FTC's position is insane. They actually state very specifically, "If Kevin Trudeau were to provide specific branded product information to people who have communicated with him as a result of his 'commercial speech' [that means from people who have seen my TV infomercial where I am selling my book] ... it is our opinion that Mr. Trudeau would be promoting a specific product and consumers would be purchasing such products based on potentially false and misleading statements in his book, his website, or his newsletter." Can you see how insane the FTC is?

I want to point out a few things that the FTC has said in correspondence to show you just how onerous they are, how suppressive they are, how insane they are, how outrageous they are, and I want to show that it is absolutely obvious that the FTC is retaliating against me for publicly speaking about the FTC in a negative manner. I want to show you that the FTC is inconsistent with their statements, contradictory with their opinions, and make demands that have not been agreed to in the order, are overreaching, and are simply suppressions of First Amendment free speech. The FTC states in its letter that if I were to "promote mattress brands or air freshener brands that I believe are good that would be okay because these would not relate to the content of my book."

So the first thing the FTC said is I couldn't in any way, shape or form even *mention* any product by brand name. Now they have changed their position and have said—well, you can mention a mattress or air freshener because it doesn't relate to the content of your book. Perfect! So then I wrote a newsletter, and in that newsletter I recommended three particular mattresses, the Tempurpedic® mattress, the Select Comfort®, and the Nautilus Sleep System®. I mentioned the products by brand name and I gave the website information in my newsletter. I sent the newsletter to the FTC and said, "Here you go. Here's my newsletter. I mentioned these products by brand name, which was what you said I could do in your letter dated to me October 12, 2004."

The FTC wrote back and said—No, no, no. You can't mention any product by brand name, and you can't put any website in your newsletter if that website mentions a product by brand name! I guess they forgot what they wrote in their October 12, 2004, letter. Again, this shows that the FTC is inconsistent, keeps flip-flopping and changing their position. I then sent a letter, on September 28, 2004, and asked them if I could sell *Consumer Reports* magazine and the *Consumer Reports Buyers Guides*. The FTC wrote back and said yes I can even though these publications give products by brand name, obviously promote and recommend those products for purchase and give ordering information. So the FTC immediately reversed their position, but the reason was because "*Consumer Reports* accepts no outside advertising, no free test samples, and has no agenda other than the interests of consumers." It also went on to say that I could sell these *Consumer Reports* publications that promoted products because "more than 100 testing experts work in seven major technical departments ... with more than 25 research experts working in three different ... and further that the *Consumer Reports* policy is that the ratings, nor the reports, nor any other information ... can be used in advertising or for any other commercial purpose ..." It went on to say that I could sell the *Consumer Reports* publications, which promoted products by brand name, because they are "objective, factual representations that set forth their product testing results." They went on to say that the *Consumer Reports* publications were *not promoting* any branded product and were not directly or indirectly an advertisement for any product, program, or service. Great! So I told the Federal Trade Commission that I was going to write my own buyers guide; I was going to be like *Consumer Reports*! They said categorically no. I guess they don't think I can be objective. Who is the FTC to determine whose results are objective or not?

To show that I am committed to adhering to the order of the court that I agreed to, I sent a lengthy detailed letter asking for clarification of what I can and cannot do in relation to television and radio shows. The reason I sent this letter was so the FTC knew that I was committed to adhering to the order and that I did not want to step on any line. Yes, I do have expert legal counsel who can tell me what I can or cannot do. They could simply read the order, give me their opinions, and tell me what it says and what it doesn't say. The problem is the FTC's attorneys interpret the order quite differently than the rest of the world. The FTC is sitting in hiding, waiting and hoping that I make a mistake so they can pounce. This is evident by their response. Their response to my request of clarification was this, "It is our opinion that our letter of February 18th adequately sets forth our position with respect to television and all radio talk shows and we will NOT provide any further opinions with respect to such appearances." What does this mean? This means the FTC is saying: Look Mr. Trudeau, you do whatever you think is right, whatever your attorneys think is right, but if we think you made a mistake we are going to pounce and sue you and try to bury you.

Let me tell you what this is like. You are driving down a road and there are no speed limit signs. You see a police officer off to the side of the road. You pull over and stop. You are not familiar with this area; you are a law-abiding citizen; you do not want to break any laws. You ask the police officer, who is supposed to be a servant of the people, what the speed limit is. The police officer responds: I'm not here to help you. I'm here to prosecute violators of the law. I can't tell you what the speed limit is, you figure it out on your own and if I deem that you have broken the limit I will prosecute you to the highest extent of the law. Folks, that is exactly what the Federal Trade Commission has said to me. Actually verbatim! I asked the Federal Trade Commission to help me. I told the Federal Trade Commission that I was a law-abiding citizen. I wanted not to break any laws; I needed help and guidance. I told the Federal Trade Commission—you are a federal agency, you are supposed to help the citizens of this country. The FTC's response was the arrogance that permeates the police state–type mentality that these organizations operate under. The FTC's response was, "We are not here to help you Mr. Trudeau, we are here to prosecute you when you make a mistake and break the law." Those were the actual words that were said to me. This letter that the FTC sent me on October 14, 2004, shows that this attitude permeates the organization.

On October 12, 2004, I sent to the FTC *Alternative Medicine* magazine. This is a magazine that accepts advertising for health products. The advertisers obviously encouraged the magazine to write positive stories about their products. The articles in this magazine have stories about particular branded products and how they can cure, prevent, and treat disease. They are written by "reporters." The magazine is full of ads for health products. The magazine is filled with health claims. I sent over several other books including *Don't Snore Anymore: The Miracle of Magnesium*; *Prevention Magazine*; *Tapping the Healer Within*; *Seven Weeks to Emotional Healing*; and also the medical journal *The Lancet*. I asked the FTC if I could sell these books and market these books and magazines.

Their letter on October 22, 2004, was a huge surprise. The FTC said that I could sell these publications on television, even though they mention products by brand name and actively promote and sell products by brand name. Their reasoning was alarming. The FTC states that the reason I can sell *Prevention*, *The Lancet*, and *Alternative Medicine* magazines is because they are "well established informational publications created by unrelated third parties" and even though they do contain advertisements that promote specific branded products such as disease-related advertisements for drugs or alternative health products such as Agresept. As long as Mr. Trudeau has absolutely no involvement directly or indirectly with the content, placement, or sale of the ads I would not be promoting the products and, therefore, I could sell these publications. Now, that sounds great. So, it's pretty clear. But then, they dropped the bomb. If I were to create my own magazine the FTC would have "very strong concerns." What the heck does that mean? That means they are not going to tell me one way or the other. They are going to let me try to hang myself. They are not going to tell me what I can and can't do, they are not going to give an opinion, they are going to let me and my attorneys try to figure it out. Then they will just wait, ready to pounce.

The most alarming statement said in this letter was this: "We would also likely have similar concerns if the publications were created or produced by individuals or entities that were *not known for producing reputable, independent informational publications*." Oh, my god! The Federal Trade Commission now had said that I could sell certain people's opinions on television; however, if the book or magazine or publication is written by somebody they deem undesirable, then I can't sell it. Hello, hello, hello. I am screaming from the top of the mountain. This is Nazi Germany. This is Stalinist Russia. This is book burning. This is censorship. This is a violation of the First Amendment. The Federal Trade Commission has no right to determine who is reputable and who is an independent informational publisher. They cannot deem whose opinions are allowed to be disseminated, and whose opinions must be suppressed.

The letter is also incredibly vague and contradictory. When it says if any of the other books mentioned a brand name product, they would have "concerns." Why would they have concerns? Why did they say that the magazine *Alternative Medicine*, which has ads for products and mentions products in its articles, is okay for me to sell, but if an author writes a book about magnesium and mentions a specific brand of magnesium, for which he has no financial interest, that cannot be sold? None of this makes sense.

Then the FTC states that some of these books would be treated as "programs." The letter states that some of these books could be considered programs. How? What is the criteria? Who determines whether the book is a book, or the book is a program? Oh, the FTC arbitrarily decides what is a book, what is an informational publication, and what is a program. Oh, according to this letter the FTC has the ability to be judge, jury and executioner, and they alone can decide who is reputable, who is well established, who is independent, who is objective, and whose opinions can be heard. The FTC is so all over the board on these issues. This letter went on to state that the book *Don't Snore Anymore* is okay, even though it does mention specific branded products because "it doesn't give ordering information, it talks about a wide range and number of products and provides an objective review of the products by an individual with a clear expertise in the area. Also, the book is written by a licensed healthcare practitioner."

So the bottom line here is the FTC now has stated a bunch of criteria, which it basically reverses in other letters that they have sent to me. But the criteria that they give for the reason why I could sell this particular book is:

1. It doesn't tell people how to buy the product. However, if you remember, I can sell *Alternative Medicine* magazine, which does give information on how to buy products, as well as *Consumer Reports*, which does give information on how to buy products.

2. It talks about a wide range and number of products, and is giving an objective review of those products. So, what the FTC is saying is if somebody talked about one or two products that's not enough, they would have to talk about three, four, five, or six, and those discussions would have to be "objective." Well who on God's green earth is going to determine whether they are objective or not? The FTC?

3. The book is written by a licensed healthcare practitioner with expertise in the subject. What the FTC is saying is it all depends on who the author is. If the author is somebody who they deem to be an expert, or is a licensed healthcare practitioner, then it is acceptable for him to write a book, but certainly not Kevin Trudeau. After all, I am not a licensed healthcare practitioner, and according to the FTC, I am not an expert on the subject. Censorship, censorship, censorship, censorship!

4. The book provides substantial amounts of information about snoring and not just about products. Here the FTC is saying that they have the ability to read books and determine what writing style can be used, and how an author can present information and material. Censorship, censorship, censorship!

5. The author of the book has no financial connection directly or indirectly with any of the products discussed in the book. Hmm, this doesn't make any sense. Obviously, *Alternative Medicine* magazine,

The Lancet, and *Prevention* magazine accept advertising. They have a direct financial connection with the products described, marketed, sold, and promoted in their publications.

The FTC is writing their own rules. They keep writing their own rules and then changing their own rules. They say one thing in one letter they sent me, and then another thing in another letter they sent me.

Here is one of the scariest things that the FTC has done. I sent to the FTC a copy of a letter that I was considering mailing to many friends, colleagues, and customers. I sent this letter to the FTC letting them know that many of the people that I would be sending this letter to were persons that bought my book from television. Therefore, any communication with those people should be reviewed by the FTC since it is the FTC's position (which I totally disagree with) that any communication with somebody who has purchased my book from watching the TV infomercial would be under the scrutiny of the FTC and the order that I agreed to. Although I violently disagreed with their position, I sent them this letter anyway to get their thoughts and comments. My attorneys had reviewed this letter and emphatically told me that it was absolutely 100 percent okay to send. But, for precautionary measures, assuming that the FTC is sitting in hiding waiting for me to trip up someplace, for which they will pounce, we sent this letter to the FTC for review and comments.

Here is what the FTC said. In the first four paragraphs I state my opinions about the Federal Trade Commission, the Food and Drug Administration, the American Medical Association, and other industries and government agencies, and how they are trying to attack me and suppress me. I am giving my opinions about politics and how the system is working. It is 100 percent opinion. It is political speech. Here is what the FTC said: "Some statements in the following two paragraphs strike us as potentially false and misleading and should not be made unless they can be substantiated." Can you believe this? The Federal Trade Commission is now stating that I cannot give my opinions about politics without having a file of substantiated documents. Have they ever told a politician that he cannot make statements about the opposing political party without documentation? Have they ever told Ralph Nader that he cannot make comments about corporate and government corruption without fear of being attacked unless he had boxes of substantiation and backup material? Have any journalists been told that they must produce their sources? Of course not.

Later in my letter I talk about a church in which I am a member, and their spiritual balancing prayer sacrament. The Federal Trade Commission had comments about my expression of my religious beliefs by stating this: "It is our opinion that the following passage reflects a prohibited promotion of programs and/or devices." Oh, my God! The Federal Trade Commission now says I cannot practice my religion. I cannot promulgate my religion. I cannot talk about my religious beliefs.

My next paragraph talked about how I believe the FTC has expanded their suppressive and restrictive orders on me personally. I go on to talk about my opinions about how the FTC is suppressing me. The FTC told me, "The following paragraph is inaccurate. You are falsely representing the issue." Well, excuse me Mr. FTC, these are my opinions of how you are treating me. This is how I am feeling; this is what I believe to be true. You cannot tell me I cannot say that you are attacking me, because I believe you are.

I also stated in this letter what the FTC told me specifically. The FTC told me that I could refer people's questions to a licensed healthcare practitioner. It was in their letter. It is in writing. I then wanted to tell my subscribers that if you sent me an e-mail I would refer it to a licensed healthcare practitioner who would then in turn respond. The FTC then said, "This misrepresents what we have stated and what we envision as acceptable." They go on to state that I cannot refer people's questions to licensed healthcare practitioners (as they said I could), but I can tell the people who wrote the question where they can go to talk to a licensed healthcare practitioner. Folks, this is cutting and splitting hairs. This is insanity.

The FTC's final restrictive and suppressive statement is, "With respect to the following Mr. Trudeau is reminded that there are substantial limits on what 'specifically he can recommend to consumers.'" Well, I have to inform the FTC that there are not substantial limits on what I can recommend to consumers. My First Amendment rights have been protected under this order and the only thing that is being restricted is my ability to sell and market products, not my free speech rights.

The FTC basically does not want Kevin Trudeau to succeed. It is interesting to note that throughout my dealings with the FTC their number one concern has always been about me making money. Their concern was not about consumers being hurt. They were always upset with how much money I was making. When the coral calcium infomercial was running and I wasn't getting any royalties, the FTC took no action. I informed the FTC many, many times. They took absolutely no action and couldn't care less because I wasn't making money. Once I started making money on the show, that's when the FTC took action. I signed the order with the FTC that all infomercials that I shot are prohibited from airing. But the FTC told me as long as I'm not being paid on any of those infomercials they had no issue with me. Surprisingly enough, the FTC has taken no action against any of the companies that are currently running my infomercials. Why? They don't care as long as I don't make any money. When the FTC sued me the first thing they said is, "How much money do you have?" The FTC is not concerned with protecting consumers, they are concerned with bankrupting Kevin Trudeau. It is a personal vendetta. You can soon see all of the actual letters to and from the FTC at www.kevinfightsback.com.

CONCLUSION

When I signed my order with the FTC, my attorney went before the judge and the FTC and said specifically, "Kevin Trudeau's goal is to be a consumer advocate." The FTC has taken a position that even though they agree that I could be a consumer advocate, it was already expressed that that was my intention, that I still could not mention a product by brand name. How can a consumer advocate be a consumer advocate without mentioning a product by brand name? That is insane. When you read all the correspondence between the FTC and me since we signed the order, you see very clearly

1. total inconsistencies of what I can and cannot do;
2. the rules keep changing based on the FTC's desire to stifle me and suppress my First Amendment right of free speech;
3. the FTC is obviously retaliating against me for talking publicly about the FTC in a negative manner; and
4. the FTC has decided that they have the ability to determine who is well established, who is reputable, who is an expert, who can write books, what the books can contain, what the titles can be, what information is objective, what the definition of a program is, what the definition of a book is, and they have decided that they alone can determine what is free speech and protected, and what is prohibited under the order.

Folks, my position is very clear.

1. I do not sell products.
2. I do not promote products.
3. I am not compensated in any way, directly or indirectly, on the sale of products.
4. I have no financial interest in any companies that sell products.
5. I only intend on selling informational publications, newsletters, websites, books, videos, DVDs, audios, CD-ROMs, radio stations and shows, and television stations and shows. I am not producing programs or services, only informational publications as was agreed to in our order.
6. I fully intend to exercise my First Amendment rights as protected by the order and the Constitution.
7. I will fight to the highest court in the land this continued suppression by the Federal Trade Commission and what I believe to be a clear violation of my civil rights.
8. I fully intend on running for political office and believe that this suppression is directly tied in to suppressing my political speech.
9. I am a journalist and investigative reporter and exercising my rights as such.
10. I am an activist.
11. I am "The Whistleblower."

Folks, I intend on yelling as loud as I can from the highest rooftops exposing corporate and government corruption all around this nation and around the world. I intend on giving you my opinions about information that I believe "They" don't want you to know. I know hundreds of thousands of you are waiting for my orders to write letters to their respective government representatives expressing their outrage over the suppression of the free flow of ideas and opinions. I don't know about you, but I'm mad as hell and I'm not going to take it anymore. Thank you for your support, love, and constant uplifting communications. Please know that I will continue to fight this war until total victory is achieved. Remember, it's not over until we win!

With all that said, I want you to know the huge risk I am taking by writing this book. In this book you will get the specific product brand name and ordering information that the FTC censored from my first book. In this book you will read my opinions and theories about what these products do in relation to preventing, treating, or curing disease. Remember, these are my opinions and conclusions only based on scientific research, inside sources, interviews, personal observations, and all other accepted investigative journalist procedures. Other people violently disagree with my statements, opinions, and conclusions. You, in consultation with a licensed healthcare practitioner, have to make your own conclusions regarding these products and your own health. Remember, I actually take all this stuff!

CHAPTER 6

Fighting Back!

Power tends to corrupt, and absolute power corrupts absolutely.

—Lord Acton

This chapter gives you several articles that I have written over the last year that have been published in my newsletter and on the www.naturalcures.com website. If you are not a subscriber I encourage you to become a private member at www.naturalcures.com. You can access all the information on the website ABSOLUTELY FREE for an entire week. During your free week trial you will be able to talk to my nutrition and health experts who can personally answer all of your health questions. Since new information about health discoveries is uncovered on a virtually daily basis, it is important that you consider being a member of the website so that you always have the most current and latest information about preventing, treating, and curing disease without drugs and surgery. Also, during your free trial you'll be able to go to the archive section of the website and read and print every past issue of my monthly newsletter.

Let's first talk about some new natural cures.

THE SUN CAN CURE DISEASE

In the *Natural Cures* book I talk about the fact that the sun does not cause skin cancer. The sun is needed for life. If you do not spend time in the sun you will be sick. The sun is vital for health, longevity, and to be disease free. If you are sick, one of the things that you must do is get out in the sun. I can tell you this, that the sun itself can virtually cure disease. Every living thing on the planet, with rare exception, cannot live without solar energy from the sun. Virtually every living thing on Planet Earth needs the sun to survive. (There are rare exceptions to this, of course.) The human body needs sunlight to function at optimal levels and be healthy. Without sunlight, a whole host of physical abnormalities and diseases become prevalent. Without sunlight, you develop diseases, including depression, lack of energy, poor sleep, poor digestion, weight gain, arthritis, constipation, bad breath, body odor, cancer, high blood pressure, high cholesterol, diabetes, attention deficit disorder, stress, headaches, susceptibility to colds, flus, and viral infections, PMS, male erectile dysfunction, loss of sexual desire in women, infertility, anxiety, and more. The sun can prevent all of these diseases. The sun can POTENTIALLY CURE YOU OF ALL OF THESE DISEASES. This is an example of a "natural cure" that they don't want you to know about! Why would a drug company want you to know that the natural cure for depression is simply getting some sunlight? They don't want you to know this truth. All they want to do is sell you drugs. Think about that long and hard. I'll say it over and over again—drug companies only have one objective and that is to sell more drugs. Drug companies do not want to cure or prevent disease. If they did, they would all be out of business.

Does the sun cause the skin to wrinkle and look old? No. One of the things that the sun does is draw out from the body toxins to the skin. It also stimulates cell re-growth, which actually makes you look younger and keeps your skin wrinkle free. Why is it then that people who spend hours and hours in the sun have a tendency to have dried-up skin and wrinkled skin and look older than they are? The reason is because they are so toxic. When your body is toxic the sun will draw out from that body and bring those toxins to the surface. This is a good thing. It helps you cleanse and detoxify your system, keeping you young, beautiful, and healthy.

However, if you are nutrient deficient, specifically in the good oils and fats that you need in your diet, excessive or prolonged exposure to the sun can cause these problems. The solution? Very simple. You absolutely need sun for health and longevity. However, unless you are pretty much toxic free, have no nutritional deficiencies, are balancing your electromagnetic chaos, and are stress free, excessive exposure over a long period of time can make your skin look leathery, dry, and wrinkly. Therefore, the solution is to first and foremost do the things in

Chapter 6 of the book. This will make sure that you are toxic free, that you do not have nutritional deficiencies, that you are balancing the electromagnetic chaos around your body, and that your stress levels are dramatically reduced. Therefore, you can spend as much time in the sun as you want and it will benefit you. There is a caveat to this, every person's pigment is different and will "burn" at a different level. Obviously, use common sense. If you are pale white and haven't been out in the sun in years, don't go out in the sun in the middle of the day for four hours. You will get sunburned and it will not be a good thing! Build up the time in the sun.

It is important to sunbathe and get sun over your entire body. Remember, never ever, ever use any sunscreen. Do not put anything on your skin that you can't eat. Sunscreens cause skin cancer. Every person is different, but I will give you a good way to start your sunbathing. Bathe your entire body in sunlight for fifteen minutes in the morning, within the first four hours after sunrise, or in the evening within the last four hours before sunset. Fifteen minutes on both sides is a good place to start. Build up and get as much sun as you feel comfortable with.

There is also a very important additional benefit available from solar energy and the sun, and that is called "sun gazing" (www.solarhealing.com). Sun gazing is actually looking at the sun. This can only be done right after sunrise or right before sunset. Other times would be too dangerous for the eyes. However, the health benefits of sun gazing go even beyond that of sunbathing. I would encourage you to go to this website to learn more information on sun gazing. I have seen and heard of hundreds of people that have virtually cured themselves of major diseases by simply sunbathing and sun gazing. This sounds incredible to some people. It sounds crazy and ludicrous to some people. The facts are that you can cure and prevent almost all diseases by sun gazing and sunbathing. That is why it is one of the things in Chapter 6 that can help you cure and prevent virtually every disease. This is another overlooked, simple "natural cure." And the best part is this natural cure is free. Don't think just because it is easy and free that it is not a natural cure. It is a natural cure for disease. Will it absolutely cure the disease YOU HAVE? I don't know, but I do know it will HELP YOU CURE OR PREVENT ANY DISEASE YOU HAVE. I do know and believe that it will make the curing and healing process happen better and faster and more complete.

DMSO AND HYDROGEN PEROXIDE

If there are two miracle products on the planet that can virtually help assisting in you curing virtually every disease it is DMSO (dimethyl sulfoxide) and hydrogen peroxide. The reason you have never heard about these two products is because they are 100 percent unpatentable, and they are incredibly inexpensive. This means that no one will spend any serious money reviewing the effects of these products, and the pharmaceutical industry categorically wants these products to be off the market and the information about them suppressed. These are miracle products. These products help cure herpes, cancer, arthritis, MS, muscular dystrophy, and virtually all virus-type diseases and degenerative diseases. There are volumes that can be written about these two products. Over the next few months I am going to have on my website, www.naturalcures.com, so much information about the use of these two products in the curing of disease it will blow your mind.

What these two products effectively do is get oxygen into your body. Nobel Prize–winning author Dr. Otto Walberg discovered that cancer and all viruses cannot live in an oxygen-rich environment. When your body pH is acidic, there is very little oxygen in your blood and in your tissues. When you flood your body with oxygen, your body pH goes from acidic to alkaline. When your body is flooded with oxygen, viruses instantly die, cancer dies, and your energy levels skyrocket. Using DMSO topically can rid a person of all types of diseases that are virus-based, from herpes, perrones disease, shingles, warts, moles, etc. Hydrogen peroxide can be used topically and, also, taken orally to flood your body with oxygen. It can also be taken intravenously, and is used in medical clinics around the world that specialize in cancer.

I encourage you to go to the internet and type in DMSO and start reading about its powerful effects. Also, type in hydrogen peroxide and start reading about how it is used to cure and prevent all types of diseases. Please know that most of the information is being suppressed and the pharmaceutical industry has set up a host of front websites talking negatively about these two products. I can assure you that all the negative discussion is misleading and untrue. These are miracle products. They can help you cure and prevent cancer and virtually all types of medical diseases. They must be used correctly, and I advise you to use them under the supervision of a licensed alternative healthcare practitioner. They can also be used very effectively in combination with essential oils, herbs, and nutritional supplements. The DMSO speeds the assimilation of these nutrients, making them work quicker and faster. They are also very effective in helping get rid of Candida throughout your entire body, as well as detox your body. These are miracle products. Let me say it again, these are miracle products. Proper use can change your life.

More on DMSO

I mentioned previously that DMSO (dimethyl sulfoxide) is colorless, nontoxic water soluble liquid derived from wood pulp. DMSO comes in very small molecules and has the unique ability to permeate the skin and cells very quickly. It is a powerful solvent of both inorganic and organic material. Its penetrating ability is far superior to most any other substance. It comes in gel and cream form. When applied to your feet, it can within moments cause your breath to smell slightly garlic-like. This is because it penetrates so quickly and travels throughout the body so rapidly, DMSO also pulls in water at an incredible rate. It has such a powerful attraction to water that it can even pull it out of the atmosphere. When you combine DMSO's ability to penetrate and attract water you can see why it travels throughout the body so rapidly. It is important to know that DMSO is used throughout the world as a medical treatment for many afflictions, including arthritis, head and spinal injuries, infectious diseases, cataracts, asthma, sinusitis, diabetes, sciatica, cancer, stroke, herpes simplex, and much, much more. It has been known to inhibit bacterial growth, viruses, and fungi. At Hospital Santa Monica in Rosario Beach, Mexico, Dr. Curt W. Donsbach uses DMSO and hydrogen peroxide intravenously on virtually every cancer patient with reportedly remarkable success. This appears to be because cancer cannot survive in an oxygen-rich environment. Both DMSO and hydrogen peroxide get oxygen into the body very quickly. It helps alkalize the body's pH. As I mentioned before, the FDA will not allow the use of DMSO for the treatment of disease because it is not a patentable drug. This is done not to protect patients, but to protect the profits of the drug companies. There is a great book written by William Fharel which talks a lot about DMSO and hydrogen peroxide. It is called *Never an Outbreak*, and I highly recommend it. It is available on the internet.

GET RID OF YOUR SILVER FILLINGS

I've heard of people who have cleaned their colon, liver, kidneys, wiped out parasites, viruses, stopped eating processed foods and drugs yet still have symptoms and feel they are not at their optimal health levels.

When all else fails, you must address the devastation of toxic dental metals, root canals, and mercury amalgams. This information is still being ignored by the majority of mainstream dentistry and medicine. Holistic doctors (doctors who treat the whole person and not just disease) have looked at this issue for years. It has been recognized as having a devastating impact on your health. Metal simply should not be in your mouth. Researchers in Europe have estimated that perhaps up to half of all chronic degenerative diseases and illness can be linked to the toxic dental metals in your mouth. It most notably causes symptoms like MS, Parkinson's, arthritis, headaches, and lack of energy. It can also cause stress, depression, anxiety, mental confusion, feelings of insecurity, lack of concentration, irritability, kidney, cardiac and even respiratory disorders. Remember, all dental metals are toxic. They contain serious toxins. These toxins adversely affect your liver, thymus, thyroid, spleen, critical organs, and many body functions. This is one constant toxin that can break down the body's ability to perform efficiently, leading to disease and illness. If you are sick in any way, open your mouth and take a look. I would highly encourage you to remove all metal and root canals. Remove all dead and bacteria-infected teeth. Doing this can bring absolutely miraculous healing to many afflictions. You will see unexplained symptoms vanish. Remember, don't go to mainstream dentists, look for alternative dentistry, biological holistic metal-free, or Huggins dentists. Here is a list of references:

Peak Energy Performance
(800) 331-2303   Referrals for Huggins dentists.

International Academy of Oral and Toxicology
(407) 298-2450   Metal-free dentists.

Foundation for Toxic-Free Dentistry
Box 608010, Orlando, FL 32860-8010
Send self-addressed, stamped envelope for more information.

Environmental Dental Association
(800) 388-8124

American Academy of Biological Dentistry
(831) 659-5385 or (831) 659-2417

Matrix Corp.
(866) 949-4638   Huggins Office

www.talkinternational.com
Directory of mercury-free and biological dentists.

EATING FAST FOOD CAUSES CANCER, DIABETES, HEART DISEASE, AND DOZENS OF OTHER ILLNESSES!

My independent observations have shown that eating fast food causes disease in the same manner that smoking cigarettes causes lung cancer. You are reading this right. The fast food restaurants totally disagree with my conclusions and state emphatically that there is no evidence supporting my claims. I disagree with them 100 percent. Let's look at the facts. McDonald's says if you eat in their restaurants once a week you are a "heavy user." People, however, do not frequent just one fast food restaurant. People go to multiple fast food restaurants. I asked people who eat fast food at least three times a week how their health is. Here is what I have found. In the people that I interviewed who ate in fast food restaurants three or more times a week consistently, ninety percent had heart disease or high risks of heart disease. Ninety-two percent had pre-diabetes or diabetes. Ninety-five percent were overweight. Eighty-five percent had food and/or environmental allergies. Ninety-one percent had sleep problems. Ninety-four percent had depression or mood swings. Ninety-seven percent had constipation. One hundred percent had an acidic body pH, which means, according to Dr. Morter, they are prone to get cancer. The list goes on.

The question is why does fast food apparently cause so much disease and illness? There are many factors. I believe the most important factor, which is overlooked and virtually never discussed, is that fast food is loaded with CHEMICALS! Any time you talk to a doctor about fast food they talk about calories, sodium, carbohydrates, fats, proteins, and the like. Doctors never mention the chemical poisons used in the producing of the food, the chemicals used in the processing of the food, the microwaving and irradiation of the food causing it to be energetic toxic, the growth hormones and antibiotics used in the meat and dairy, and the other environmental toxins that get into the food in the cooking, storing, and manufacturing. I believe that in addition to the calories, sodium, carbohydrates, proteins, and fats being in an abnormally proportioned state, I believe the most important reason that eating fast food causes disease are the CHEMICALS AND POISONS in the food.

Let's take it a step further. I went and interviewed 100 cancer patients. All of them, 100 percent, in the last year averaged three fast food or chain restaurant meals per week. I interviewed a little over 100 diabetics and found the same thing. The same thing occurred with patients with heart disease, allergies, constipation, Fibromyalgia, fatigue, obesity, arthritis, and MS. Virtually every one of the people that I talked to that had these diseases ate in fast food or chain restaurants at least three meals per week. Those that didn't ate processed food from publicly traded corporations at least three times or more per week! People disagree with my conclusions, but it seems to be pretty obvious to me. Eating fast food and eating processed food sold by publicly traded corporations causes disease.

How bad is fast food? How could they say their processing methods are sanitary? It's impossible. Did you know that even the government in reviewing the safety and sanitary regulations at fast food restaurants find violations EVERY SINGLE TIME AN INSPECTION IS DONE! That's right; every single time a food inspection is done at a fast food or chain restaurant serious health violations are found in sanitation. This means that the food is poisoned. This means the food is not safe to eat, yet we eat it almost every single day. Did you know that health violations occur in the processing plants of virtually every publicly traded corporation making your favorite brand name food? This means the food is not safe to eat. This means the food is causing disease and illness. This is why eating 100 percent organic food from small companies is a must. I continue to get thousands of e-mails every week from people who tell me they are amazed at how their health has dramatically changed after they stopped eating fast food and processed food, and simply changed to 100 percent food. When you stop putting all the poisons and chemicals in your body you can see dramatic health changes.

CAUSES OF DISEASES

In my book I mentioned that I was treated by Dr. Tang at the Century Clinic in Reno, Nevada. The clinic is now called Sierra Integrated Health, and the medical director is Dr. Tang's son. I was recently at Sierra Integrated Health and had a chance to visit with the patients and healthcare providers. It was interesting to note some of the statistics being shared. Did you know virtually every person who is sick has major food and environmental allergies and doesn't even know it?

Most people think of allergies as coughing, sneezing, wheezing, watery eyes, and things of this nature. This is not the case. When you are allergic to something, all it means is your body reacts negatively to that particular substance, whether it is something you smell, something you eat, or something in the environment, perhaps a toxin in some soap, cleaning fluids, paint, or chemicals in food. When your body reacts negatively (an allergic reaction) it doesn't mean you will sneeze or have a runny nose or watery eyes. It means something in your body is not going to act correctly. It virtually means a suppression of your immune system or a part of your body's function that stops operating optimally. This opens the door for illness and disease. It can make you fatigued, tired, irritable, grumpy, etc. Most people in testing are found to have environmental and food allergies. It is believed that this is caused by Candida, as well as all of the poisons and toxins being put in our food supply today, our water supply, and the air. It is highly suggested and recommended that you address food and environmental allergies. When you do, your body can go back to normal and you are more prone to heal quicker from any disease or ailments you have and prevent sickness from ever occurring.

It is also important to note that a common ailment that is present in people who are sick is Lyme Disease. Lyme Disease is very rarely diagnosed properly. People who have symptoms of MS, Fibromyalgia, chronic fatigue, etc. are never diagnosed as having Lyme Disease. Lyme Disease is prevalent in person after person after person. The percentage is outrageously high to the point of being epidemic. If you are sick I would highly encourage you to check to see if you have Lyme Disease. If you do, the standard protocol that a medical doctor would give you is a round of antibiotics. I would highly recommend against this. Go to a clinic that uses no drugs and surgery, and you can be treated with homeopathics, herbs, nutritional supplements, DMSO, hydrogen peroxide, and things of this nature that have been found to be very effective at treating Lyme. As always, I encourage you to get treatment from a licensed healthcare practitioner who does not use drugs and surgery.

VITAMIN E CURES CANCER!

This should be the headline, but you will probably never see it. Why? Because all-natural vitamin E is such a powerful health enhancing supplement that the drug companies are trying to discredit it every way they can. Here is an article by Dr. Jeff McCombs, the author of the book *Lifeforce*. It describes the most recent "study" and report on vitamin E. This explains and exposes how "studies" are really nothing more than fraudulent reports bought and paid for by the pharmaceutical industry to either falsely make you believe that their drugs are effective and safe, or falsely make you believe that all natural remedies are ineffective and dangerous.

Vitamin E by Dr. Jeff McCombs.   In the movie, Dorothy and her companions shudder in fear when they first confront the great and powerful "Wizard of Oz." Only later on do they come to discover that he's a fake, and that he has been deceiving people for years.

Today, the same scene is used over and over again by companies and agencies who attempt to control others for their own personal gain. Many, once reputable and reliable, companies now use the public perception of themselves to control others and profit from deception, lies, and misinformation. A government that once stood for the people is now being sold over and over again to some of the most powerful and influential money interests on the planet. Four of the top 10 Fortune 500 companies are pharmaceutical companies. They have a lobbyist for every state representative and senator in Washington, with some extras assigned to the public committees of the House and Senate. Your health is being sold on a daily basis by every representative and senator who takes their money as long as there is something written down on paper. It doesn't matter if it's true or not, just as long as the pharmaceutical companies say it is.

Let's analyze a recent example. You may have heard of a study indicating that vitamin E is bad for you. The name of this study is HOPE-TOO (Heart Outcomes Prevention Evaluation—The Ongoing Outcomes) and is an "extension" of an earlier study on vitamin E, called HOPE. The name seems to indicate an innocence and hopefulness about it. This couldn't be further from the truth.

When I first read the HOPE-TOO report, I wondered who had performed it and for what purpose. The best way to discover this information is by looking at the original study and see what took place. The newspapers, magazines, and journals will report whatever is fed to them, so they are unreliable when it comes to discovering the truth.

The first question is who funded the study? It wasn't surprising to learn that both studies were funded by pharmaceutical companies. You may recognize some of the following names: Aventis, King Pharmaceuticals, Bristol-Myers Squibb, Bayer, GlaxoSmithKline, Novartis, Pfizer, Roche, Abbott Laboratories, Genentech, Pharmacia, Astrazeneca,

Natural-Source Vitamin E Association, and several others. These are the same companies that produce drugs that kill hundreds of thousands of people each year. Only these companies have the type of money that could fund such a study, representing their own interests, and not the public's.

The next question is for what purpose was this study funded? The main player in these studies is a pharmaceutical giant called Aventis. Closer examination reveals that the timing of the end of the first study (1993–1999) coincided with the release of a drug aimed at helping to prevent heart failure. This was an Aventis drug called Rimipril, also know as Altace. The ending of the second study (1999–2003) doesn't coincide with anything. However, the second study results weren't released until March 15, 2005, which coincides with the release of another Aventis drug aimed at heart failure, Plavix, on March 10, 2005. If the study was an important study of vitamin E, shouldn't the results have been made public in May of 2003 when it was finished? YES. The study, however, wasn't being done for that purpose. These pharmaceutical giants weren't doing a study to discover the importance of vitamin E. They do not sell vitamin E, they sell drugs. Why do so many pharmaceuticals companies invest so much money to study vitamin E? Is vitamin E that big of a threat to them? YES.

When you read the HOPE-TOO study, you see that "The authors note that the adverse effect of vitamin E was unexpected and UNCONFIRMED the other trials." What do the other trials say? Let's look at a few:

- Cambridge Heart Antioxidant study reported 77 percent lower risk of heart attack with vitamin E.

- Finnish study reports reduced risk of prostate cancers in male smokers.

- Columbia University study reports vitamin E slows progression of Alzheimer's disease when used in high doses (2000 IU a day).

- Animal studies report vitamin E protects against cataracts.

- Other studies show that it protects against colon cancer, cystic breasts, etc.

In other words, vitamin E is a better choice than drugs for many conditions. As a matter of fact, when you read the HOPE and HOPE-TOO studies, you'll note that the authors didn't compare vitamin E to their drugs. They compared vitamin E to a placebo. In other words, some people were given vitamin E and others were given something that they were told was vitamin E, but it wasn't. This way, only the researchers know who is taking what. Since I've been talking about looking at the results of the study, it's time that we did. There were 4 main results.

1. Cancer incidence was less in the vitamin E group.
2. Prostate cancer was less in the vitamin E group.
3. Cancer deaths were less in the vitamin E group.
4. Major cardiovascular events were 1 percent greater in the vitamin E group.

If you read those results, you'll see that the headlines should have read, "Vitamin E cures cancer." Instead, what you read is that vitamin E is bad for you. What you should have read is that the TYPE of vitamin E used in this study created a 1 percent increase in cardiovascular events. The researchers do not explain cardiovascular events, so that leaves it up to the companies who funded the study to interpret it however they choose to.

Let's look at the TYPE of vitamin E that was used in this study. This is perhaps one of the most important considerations of these studies that one addresses. If you refer back to the list of funding agencies, you'll see the Natural-Source Vitamin E Association. Nobody can seem to find this company, however. I've checked many resources, and it doesn't seem to even exist. All that I'm able to determine is that they are listed in every Aventis pharmaceutical study on vitamin E. They are listed as the Natural-Source Vitamin E Association of Washington, DC, but seem to be more closely tied to Ontario, Canada, home of Aventis. Nobody in the supplement industry has ever heard of them outside of these studies. It's important here because it is this "association's" definition of natural vitamin E that forms the basis of the few negative studies done on vitamin E. The Natural-Source Vitamin E Association states that natural vitamin E can only exist in a chemically altered, esterified, form. It is this chemically altered form of natural vitamin E that is used in their studies. This form of vitamin E is known to have no antioxidant function in the body. This is not the form to use when testing the effectiveness of vitamin E. The best and most active form of vitamin E is the un-esterified, all-natural mixed tocopherol form, consisting of alpha, beta gamma, and delta tocopherols. This is also the more expensive form. They would have you believe that the all-natural un-esterified version doesn't exist, but it does.

In the scientific community, the HOPE and HOPE-TOO studies are being cited as examples of bad research. There are many questions about who was excluded along the way and for what reasons. The study itself proves that synthetic, chemically altered forms of vitamin E can produce a very slight 1 percent increase in cardiovascular events, while also decreasing certain cancers and death due to cancer.

A better designed study would be to compare all-natural, un-esterified mixed tocopherols to the Aventis drugs. If we use current information about Rimipril and Plavix, we see that they can cause:

Abdominal hemorrhage, pain, gastritis, and constipation; peptic and duodenal ULCERS; rash and skin disorders; diarrhea and nausea; HYPERTENSION; chest and back pain; CARDIAC FAILURE; heart and nervous system disorders; anxiety; insomnia; arthritis; gout; CATA-RACTS; anemia; edema; eczema; pneumonia; cystitis; allergies; fatty liver and hepatitis infections; LEUKEMIA; fetus death; dizziness; low blood pressure; dehydration; vomiting; kidney disease; pancreatitis; death of skin tissues; hearing loss; tremor; tinnitus; vision disturbances; fever; impotence; weight gain; possible death; and amnesia.

All-natural, un-esterified vitamin E does none of the above and in many cases, according to previous studies, it may help to reverse the above symptoms and conditions.

Now, do you think that you'll ever see a study funded by Aventis comparing their drugs to all-natural, un-esterified vitamin E? NEVER.

So, the next time the great and powerful Oz decides to scare you with his façade and hype, just pull back the curtain to see the truth for yourself. I'll take my vitamin E any and every day!

For more information go to www.acgraceco.com.

MIRACLE PRODUCT

Allicin comes from raw garlic. It is antiviral, antibacterial, anti-inflammatory, and stimulates and boosts the immune system. There are many products on the market that contain high amounts of Allicin. In my opinion, this is a "natural cure" that they don't want you to know about. Why? As with most natural cures, this natural cure is better than virtually any drugs or surgery. In my opinion, you should have some Allicin in your home at all times. At the first sign of a cold or flu, or any pain or inflammation, start taking some Allicin, it should knock it out. For more information go to www.affinitylifestyles.com.

THE NATURAL WAY TO CURE CANCER

If you are not concerned about cancer you should be. In America more people are being diagnosed with cancer than ever before in history. If you get cancer you have a higher chance of dying of cancer than ever before in history. Cancer rates continue to rise. Cancer fatalities continue to rise. The war on cancer has been a dismal failure. Over $250 billion has been spent on trying to allegedly prevent and cure cancer. How in the world can $250 billion be spent, yet cancer rates and fatalities continue to rise? The answer, in my opinion, is cancer is an industry. Billions of dollars in profits are made in the treatment and testing of cancer. In my opinion, the pharmaceutical industry simply does not want cancer to be prevented or cured. The evidence of this goes back over fifty years when Jonas Salk cured polio. Let's think for a moment about how many diseases have been cured in the last fifty years. The answer is no disease has been cured! Every single disease is on the increase. The last disease that was ever cured was polio. How did it get cured? Well, at the time polio was a billion dollar a year business. The treatment of polio was very profitable. The pharmaceutical industry continued to state that they were working on a cure for this dreaded disease. Billions of dollars were being funneled into the pharmaceutical companies' coffers by foundations and the government, all trying to research and come up with a way to prevent and cure the disease of polio.

As I have stated before, any time a pharmaceutical company does research, it is simply conducting research to try to find a patentable drug that it can sell and make millions of dollars. It does not want to cure disease or prevent disease; doing so would put the companies out of business. This was the case with polio. It wasn't until Jonas Salk's wife developed polio that a cure was developed. When Jonas Salk's wife developed polio, Jonas Salk simply said enough is enough. He went into a laboratory and within six months developed the cure for polio. He never made a penny on his discovery. Polio was cured, never to be the horrible menace that it once was. People would no longer fear getting polio and suffering a lifetime of illness due to the horrible disease. The problem was the polio industry virtually went bankrupt overnight. At that time, a secret meeting was held with the heads of the major pharmaceutical companies, the American Medical Association, and past commissioners of the FDA. This "cartel" discussed the financial implications of curing disease. It was at this secret meeting that the decision was made that curing disease was unprofitable and it would not be tolerated. That is why there has never been a cure for any disease since that time. The decision was simply made to convince people that "We are so close to finding a cure," when nothing could be further from the truth.

The fact is there are ways to prevent disease, and there are ways to cure disease with natural means. The most important thing for you to consider is the pharmaceutical cartel wants more people to get cancer. Cancer is the most profitable industry in the entire field of medicine and health. There are major financial incentives to increase the percentage of people getting cancer. In my opinion, this cartel is knowingly producing products that give us cancer, therefore increasing their profits. This cartel has been incredibly aggressive at trying to discredit and wipe out any person who exposes the causes of cancer and educates people on ways to prevent and cure cancer. This is not new. Back in 1972, a book was written called *Cancer: Causes, Prevention and Treatment* by Paavo Airola. In his introduction Paavo Airola states, "First, I want to make it perfectly clear that I do not offer a cure for cancer. I only report how cancer is successfully treated in several of the biological clinics in Europe. I do this mainly to protect myself against prosecution by overzealous government agencies who, in the name of protecting the public, mercilessly attack anyone who not only dares to advise but even to report on unorthodox cancer therapies that work."

The causes of cancer are known yet suppressed. If you ask anyone what causes cancer, no one knows! Ask a man, "What is the cause of prostate cancer?" No one knows. Ask a woman, "What is the cause of breast cancer?" No one knows. Ask anyone, "What causes liver cancer, lymphatic cancer, or stomach cancer?" No one knows. The reason no one knows is the pharmaceutical industry continues to state the lie that the cause of cancer is not known! This is a lie. The cause of cancer is known, and the cure for cancer is also known. The cure for cancer is simply stop doing the things that are causing the cancer! This is an oversimplification, but the fact is that there are clinics around the world that cure cancer in virtually 100 percent of the cases without chemotherapy, radiation, drugs, or surgery. Unfortunately, in many states in America it is a criminal offense to cure someone of cancer without using chemotherapy, radiation, drugs, and surgery. There are doctors in America who are being imprisoned for committing the crime

of curing a patient of cancer without using chemotherapy, drugs, radiation, and surgery. How insane. What causes cancer? Here are the basic
causes of cancer:

1. *Toxins.* As I mentioned in my *Natural Cures* book, the number
one reason people get sick or have any disease is too many toxins in
the body. Toxins are the number one cause of cancer as well. The basic
or main toxins that cause cancer include:

a. smoking;
b. mechanical, physical, and chemical irritation;
c. food additives, such as DES, or diethylstilbestrol, which is used in
   food production—primarily in meat products. Eighty-five percent of
   all meat in the United States contains dangerous residual amounts
   of this poison. This is why many countries around the world refuse
   to import American meat. This particular food additive also speeds
   up sexual maturity in young women;
d. artificial sweeteners, such as saccharine and aspartame;
e. nitrites used in processed meat products;
f. hexachlorophene, which is used in many cosmetics, soaps, and
   deodorants;
g. food dyes;
h. non-prescription and prescription drugs;
i. almost all oil used in cooking in restaurants because it is rancid;
j. chemicals used in cleaning products;
k. and many other types of toxins.

So the number one reason you have cancer is the toxins that are
purposely being put in our food, our water, our air, our cosmetics,
soaps, and cleaning supplies that all wind up in our bodies.

2. *Nutritional Deficiencies.* The second cause of all cancers is nutritional deficiencies. Even the U.S. Government states that at least one-
half of all Americans suffer from varying degrees of nutritional
deficiencies. In hundreds of studies from around the world, it is conclusive that even a deficiency in just one vitamin or mineral, or other
nutritive substance lowers resistance to infection and disease, and increases risk of cancer. From these studies it states that:

• Even a mild deficiency of choline produces cancer of the liver;
• vitamin E deficiency increases the risk of leukemia;
• iodine deficiency leads to cancer of the thyroid;

- deficiencies of various B vitamins result in liver damage, as well as cancers;
- deficiencies in zinc lead to cancer of the prostate;
- vitamin A deficiencies lead to tumor developments;
- and on, and on, and on.

3. *Electromagnetic Chaos*. The next cause of all cancers is electromagnetic chaos. I have mentioned this in previous newsletters, cell phones, microwaves, high-definition TVs, laptop computers, and any and all wireless devices categorically, 100 percent lead to and cause the body to be susceptible and prone to developing cancer.

4. *Emotional Stress*. The last reason people develop cancer is emotional stress, which makes the body turn acidic, creating an environment where cancer can develop rabidly.

• • •

As I mention in my book *Natural Cures*, the natural cure for all disease is simply to stop putting toxins in the body, and cleanse the toxins that are in your body out of the body; handle any nutritional deficiencies you have; eliminate, neutralize, or reduce electromagnetic chaos; and reduce emotional stress. When you do these things the body comes back into balance and you virtually can never be sick.

I want to talk here specifically about some of the toxins that specifically relate to cancer. In my book I mentioned that if you can't eat it you shouldn't put it on your skin. This is something that many people blow off as not that important or significant, but I want you to reevaluate this. Many of the products used in cosmetics, skin care, soaps, detergents, shampoos, etc. contain ingredients that are categorically cancer causing. Here are a couple of examples. DEA, or diethanolamine. This particular ingredient has been found in over 600 home and personal care products. These products include shampoos, conditioners, bubble baths, lotions, cosmetics, soaps, laundry and dishwashing detergents. It is just one of an estimated 125 ingredients used in home and personal care products that have been proven to cause cancer. Dr. Samuel Epstein, author of *The Safe Shopper's Bible*, and founder of the American Coalition to Prevent Cancer, is considered the world's leading authority on toxicology. He believes that DEA categorically causes cancer. Yet even though the FDA knows that this ingredient, as well as many others, leads to cancer, it remains in the products you buy. Why? Because the multinational conglomerates that own these companies want you to get cancer. They need to make their products as cheaply as possible to increase their profits and they know that if you use their products cancer rates will continue to rise and they will make billions more on all the cancer treatments that they have a monopoly on.

Consider this: propylene glycol is the main ingredient in antifreeze, yet go into your household cabinets and look at your toothpaste, underarm deodorant, shampoo, conditioner, lotions, soaps, or what have you and you will be amazed when you see propylene glycol. You will also see something called sodium lareth sulfate. Propylene glycol is everywhere, yet it gives you cancer! It is a colorless, viscous liquid used in antifreeze solutions and hydraulic fluids, and as a solvent. It is not only used in brake and hydraulic fluids, paints and coatings, floor wax, pet food, tobacco products, and laundry detergents, but also in cosmetics, toothpastes, shampoos, deodorants, lotions, and processed foods. You will even find it in baby wipes. Check the labels, you will be amazed. This is why pets are getting more cancer than ever before. Pet food companies are using it in pet food. This is why children are getting cancer at a higher rate than ever before. In addition to causing cancer, propylene glycol also causes dermatitis, kidney damage, and liver abnormalities. It can cause skin rashes, dry skin, and skin damage. It is a major irritant to the skin. It also can cause nausea, headaches, vomiting, depression, and gastrointestinal disturbances. The other big problem with propylene glycol is that it doesn't leave your body. It stays in the tissues and continues to build up, causing more and more damage down the road. Keep in mind that there has never been any long-range testing on the effects of these types of toxins used in various products.

The same holds true with the toxic ingredient sodium lauryl sulfate, or SLS. This is another cancer-causing agent. Go look and find it in the products in your cupboard. Not only does it cause cancer, it can change the genetic structure of cells. It induces mutations in the cells. It irritates skin cells, and impairs ability for hair to grow. It has adverse affects on the heart, liver, lungs, and brain. It affects eyes; damages the immune system; and causes inflammation of the skin. All of these problems arise simply by putting this on the skin because once you put it on the skin it gets absorbed into the body. This also is a toxic substance that does not leave the body, but continues to build up residual effects. It's in your toothpaste, your shampoo, and your soaps. This is just the tip of the iceberg. Ingredient, after ingredient, after ingredient that is commonly used in not only foods that you eat, but in the lotions, shampoos, soaps, toothpastes, deodorants, etc. categorically cause cancer and suppress your immune system, causing all types of other diseases.

One of the reasons why we are sicker today than ever before is that the use of these toxic chemicals is increasing at an astounding rate. We put more poisons in our body today than ever before in history. Some researchers suggest that people today are putting ten times more toxins in their body than they were just ten years ago, and the rate continues to go up. This is why if you want to be healthy, you absolutely must understand that you are loaded with toxins, and that you must clean these toxins out. You must do a colon cleanse, a liver/gallbladder cleanse, a kidney/bladder cleanse, a Candida cleanse, a parasite cleanse, a heavy metal cleanse, and a full-body cleanse—it is imperative. I say this to you again, if you really want to be healthy, do not buy products from publicly traded companies. Do not buy brand name products. You can buy shampoos and conditioners, and soaps, toothpastes, antiperspirants, moisturizers, lotions, cosmetics, and skin care products all without the toxins. They are available. I am looking at a hand soap right now that says right on the label "no lauryl sulfates." It is all-natural and mostly organic. I am looking at a skin moisturizer made with natural oils and emollients. This product is great, it will not give you cancer, and it will not make you sick. If you want to be healthy, stop putting toxins in your body. Read the labels of the food you eat and everything you put on your skin.

CURING ACID REFLUX DISEASE

As I've mentioned in my book, the drug companies and the FDA colluded to create a monopoly for the pharmaceutical industry. The drug companies want to control and have a monopoly on treating any illness. The way that the drug companies and the FDA succeeded in creating this unfair monopoly was achieved when the FDA made its own regulation that states that "Only a drug can cure, prevent, or treat a disease." Keep in mind that the FDA is one of the most powerful government organizations in the entire world. They act as judge, jury, and executioner. They have the ultimate authority and ability to charge anyone with a crime and finding that person guilty of a crime without going to trial. The FDA has the power to charge and convict people without due process of law. The FDA routinely violates individual citizen's constitutional rights to due process. The FDA is incredibly powerful. They raid offices, as they did mine, with federal agents with guns drawn. They use intimidation and Gestapo-like tactics to squash, discredit, and eliminate any individual or group that could adversely affect the monopoly of the pharmaceutical industry. When the FDA passed this "regulation" that "Only a drug can cure, prevent, or treat a disease," it established the absolute monopoly of the drug companies. When the FDA passes a regulation it in effect becomes "law," and as outrageous as it sounds, the FDA itself determines whether or not you have broken the law. If the FDA determines you have broken its law, you are then guilty. You have no right to a trial or the due process of law as was supposed to be guaranteed by the U.S. Constitution.

The reason I mention these things now is acid reflux disease is a perfect example of how the FDA and the drug companies worked together to create a monopoly and to create a "disease," and to create billions of dollars in profits. Let me tell you how it works, and I will tell you the cure for "acid reflux disease." Years ago there was no such thing as acid reflux disease. The reason that today we hear about acid reflux disease is because when the FDA passed the law that "Only a drug can cure, prevent, or treat a disease," it set up a monopoly for the drug companies in treating "diseases." Therefore, immediately hundreds of common ailments started to be classified as "diseases." Once a common ailment was classified as a "disease," it then fell under the FDA regulation. This means that once something is classified as a "disease," the drug companies have a monopoly and create a marketing campaign convincing people they have this "disease" and they need to buy their drugs. This is marketing, pure and simple. This is the pharmaceutical companies' absolute desire for increased profits above everything else and at all costs, adversely affecting the nation's health. Drug companies simply want to make more money. They do not want to cure people; they do not want people to be healthy. They want people to be brainwashed into believing they have "diseases" and need to be buying their drugs. I can't emphasize this point enough because it is the basis for why everything I say is true. Remember, it's always all about the money.

Let's go back to acid reflux "disease." As I mentioned, years ago there was no such thing as acid reflux disease. On occasion, a very small percentage of people would develop a little "heartburn" or "indigestion." This was rare. This usually occurred when somebody was overindulging in rich food and alcohol. It usually was associated with people who were gorging themselves on food that they were normally not accustomed to eating. When this occurred they would develop a little "heartburn." It went away in a few hours, not to return so long as the person did not continue his gluttonous eating and drinking ways. The drug companies had secret meetings discussing ways to increase profits. In those meetings it was discussed how the drug companies in conjunction with the food industry could increase the amount of heartburn and indigestion people were getting. If the drug companies themselves, in conjunction with the food industry, could increase the amount of heartburn and indigestion people were getting, and make this indigestion and heartburn occur on a regular basis, the drug companies could lobby the FDA to classify a new "disease" called acid reflux disease. The drug companies could then market to people around the world a magic pill that would have to be taken every day for the rest of the person's life to cure and solve their dreaded acid reflux disease. This was planned, organized, and constructed by the pharmaceutical cartels in conjunction with the food industry.

Why is it today that so many people are plagued with excessive heartburn and indigestion on a regular basis? The answer is the pharmaceutical companies and the food industry collaborated specifically to increase the amount of heartburn and indigestion you get. I want to point out that I never get heartburn or indigestion. There is no way on God's green earth that I will ever get "acid reflux disease." There is no such thing as acid reflux disease. This is a condition that has been put on you by the pharmaceutical companies and the food industry. I will explain how in just a moment. First, let me point out that if you have excess heartburn or indigestion (today being known as "acid reflux disease") it is NOT BECAUSE YOU HAVE EXCESS ACID, as you are being led to believe. If you have heartburn, indigestion, or an acid reflux problem, it is because you do not have enough acid in your system! The pharmaceutical companies knew this. This is how they created such an epidemic problem. First, they created drugs for pain and cholesterol that would be taken by people on a regular basis. These drugs lower the body's ability to produce acid in the digestive system. Next, the pharmaceutical industry knew that antibiotic use kills all the friendly flora in the person's intestines, creating a Candida yeast overgrowth. The Candida yeast overgrowth reduces the body's ability to produce acid and digestive enzymes in the digestive organs of the body. Next, the pharmaceutical industry knew that if the food people ate contained no living enzymes the body would have an inability to produce enough acid to digest the food. When the body does not produce enough acid, and when a person is eating food that has no living enzymes in it, the body cannot produce enough digestive enzymes or acid to digest the food. When this occurs you have heartburn, indigestion, or what is known as acid reflux.

The way the drug companies' acid reflux drugs work to correct the problem is NOT by reducing EXCESS acid. These drugs reduce ALL the acid in your system. When ALL the acid is reduced or eliminated, the body must turn on its acid-producing pumps massively high, flooding the system with acid, thus eliminating your acid reflux, heartburn, or indigestion. This is why when you've seen me on television talk about this problem I say, "If excess acid was causing your heartburn, acid reflux, or indigestion, then by taking some more acid, such as raw apple cider vinegar, would make the problem or condition worse. If, in fact, you don't have enough acid, then taking a spoon of raw apple cider vinegar when you have the condition of heartburn, indigestion, or acid reflux, would eliminate the problem." Lo and behold, any person who has heartburn or acid reflux, if they take a spoonful of raw apple cider vinegar virtually instantly the acid reflux, indigestion, or heartburn vanishes. You see, the reason it vanishes is because your body does not have enough acid; it does not have enough digestive enzymes. By adding the acid in the form of raw apple cider vinegar, your problem is corrected.

The points I make here are very important for several reasons. First, you must know that the pharmaceutical industry and the FDA have an unholy alliance. They are only interested in increasing profits; they are not interested in the health of mankind; they do not want people to be healthy; they want people to be sick; they want people to be brainwashed into believing they have "diseases"; they want you to believe that you need to take a drug every day for the rest of your life. In the marketing departments of drug companies today meetings go on, and on, and on trying to come up with drugs that have to be taken every day for the rest of a person's life. That is how drug companies operate. They are not looking for "cures." They do not want people to be healthy; they only want people to be buying and using more and more drugs. The ideal business model for drug companies is to produce and sell drugs that must be taken every day for the rest of a person's life. I've said it over and over again, and article after article after article is coming out proving that what I'm saying is true. All nonprescription and prescription drugs cause disease, they do not cure disease. They make the body do something unnatural. They virtually should never be taken. If you are being treated by a doctor who is prescribing you drugs I would encourage you to go to another doctor. Find a healthcare practitioner who does not use drugs and surgery. There are alternatives to drugs. Stop listening to your drug-pushing doctor who is getting paid and getting kickbacks by the drug companies to get you to use drugs. The truth must be told. Stop taking drugs. As always, never do this step unless you are under the supervision of a licensed healthcare practitioner. Drugs are powerful and drugs are dangerous, even over-the-counter nonprescription drugs. Stay away from drugs.

If you are experiencing heartburn, indigestion, or "acid reflux," here are my recommendations:

1. Go to a licensed healthcare practitioner who does not use drugs and surgery. Do not do anything I say unless you are being supervised by a licensed healthcare practitioner. I say this for several reasons. First, because I believe it is prudent; and second, if I didn't, some idiot would sue me for practicing medicine without a license even though I am only expressing my "opinions" and I have the right to do so under the First Amendment of the United States Constitution.

2. The first major reason you have indigestion or acid reflux is the non-prescription and prescription drugs you are taking have reduced your body's ability to produce digestive enzymes and digestive acid. You must get off all non-prescription and prescription drugs. This includes anything, including aspirin, Tylenol, sinus medicine, cough syrup, sunscreens (yes, sunscreens are drugs—read the label!), cholesterol-reducing drugs, etc., etc.

3. The second reason your body does not have the ability to produce digestive enzymes and enough acid to digest its food is you have a Candida albicans yeast overgrowth. This was caused by, first and foremost, the antibiotics you have taken over the years. You have to get rid of the Candida to get your body back to producing enough digestive enzymes and digestive acids which will prevent in the future acid reflux, heartburn, and indigestion. I highly encourage you to read the book *Lifeforce* by Dr. Jeff McCombs. Do that program. There are many other Candida cleanses on the market. Some work better than others. Dr. McCombs' program, as outlined in the book *Lifeforce*, I believe is the most comprehensive and best, although it can be for some people hard to stick with. It is worth the effort; the results will blow you away. However, if you can't stick with that program go on the internet or talk to

your licensed healthcare practitioner, and come up with some other options to eliminate Candida. It is important to note that even if you have taken antibiotics just one time in your life that you do in fact have a Candida yeast overgrowth. It must be addressed because it will continue to get worse unless you correct the problem now.

4. The third major reason people have acid reflux, indigestion, or heartburn on a regular consistent basis is because they are eating food that has the living enzymes destroyed. It is important for you to understand that if you buy any food in a can, a jar, or a box, it has absolutely no living enzymes. If you buy fruit and vegetables that are conventionally grown, anything other than organic, it has virtually no living enzymes. Why? How can this be true? Very simply, when you buy fruits and vegetables that are conventionally grown they are all irradiated. This means they are in fact zapped by radiation waves. This kills bacteria. It also kills all the living enzymes. When you heavily cook food it kills all the living enzymes. When you buy food in boxes it has been irradiated, killing all the living enzymes. The processing used in the manufacture of food in boxes kills all the living enzymes. When you buy food in jars it has been irradiated and probably pasteurized. Pasteurized means the contents have been heated to 220 degrees, killing all the living enzymes. Even eggs today are flash pasteurized, meaning that all of the enzymes in the eggs are killed. You must have and consume food with living enzymes. This is why eating organically grown food and staying away from food from publicly traded corporations, staying away from food that falls under brand names, and staying away from food that has been processed in any way is helpful. If you want to eliminate acid reflux, start eating more food that has living enzymes. Eat organic, fresh, raw fruits and vegetables. Go back to my book. Eat a raw organic apple a day. Eat a fresh salad with lunch and dinner consisting of raw organic vegetables. This will add living enzymes. This is a good start.

Now let me give you some additional suggestions to help with acid reflux.

1. *Raw apple cider vinegar*. Take one tablespoon right before you eat each meal. This should eliminate any acid reflux. If you are feeling any heartburn, indigestion, or "acid reflux," take a spoonful of raw apple cider vinegar. Make sure it's raw and organic.

2. *Go to your health food store or consult with your licensed healthcare practitioner and get some digestive enzymes*. Ideally, digestive enzymes with betaine hydrochloric acid. There are many

brands of digestive enzymes; many of them have different forms of enzymes in them. If you have, specifically, heartburn and "acid reflux," then take an enzyme with betaine hydrochloric acid. If you burp a lot and have gas, this will also be helpful as well. Doing this protocol should reduce or eliminate any heartburn, indigestion, or acid reflux virtually starting from the first or second day. Continue with this for anywhere from two to six months, reducing the amount of raw apple cider vinegar and digestive enzymes you are taking, and you should see a complete correction of the problem, a virtual "cure" in anywhere from three to nine months, depending on the severity of the condition. It is also dependent upon your willingness to get your Candida cleaned out and stop the intake of drugs.

Acid reflux is not a disease, it is a scam. Yes, the condition you are experiencing, the discomfort you are experiencing, the horrible feeling of indigestion, heartburn, and "acid" is real. But this has been put upon you specifically and purposely by the pharmaceutical industry in conjunction with the food industry. They vehemently deny my allegations. However, what I am saying is true. Do these things and you will cure your acid reflux and you will stop being a slave to the drug companies. You do not have to take their "acid reflux" pills every day for the rest of your life. Stop being scammed and stop being taken advantage of by these bloodthirsty, money hungry, evil corporate villains.

CONSTIPATION NO MORE!

If you are not having two to three bowel movements every day, you are constipated! Stop. Read that again! It's hard for most people to believe, but it's true. The human body is designed to have two to three bowel movements every day. Over 90 percent of people in America are constipated. Constipation leads to all types of disease, allergies, illness, lethargy, depression, stress, anxiety, obesity, gas, insomnia, arthritis, heart disease, diabetes, acid reflux, bad breath, body odor, bad hair, skin and nails, and more. I'm going to give you some very specific and simple ways to cure constipation.

Let's first talk about what constipation is. As always, if you have constipation go to a licensed healthcare practitioner who does not use drugs and surgery. It is important to know that the cause of your constipation could be any one of a couple dozen reasons. The best way to handle your constipation needs to be addressed and will vary based on your circumstances. Everyone is different, but I'm going to give you some very basic things here that will work in virtually all cases anyway. Why do you need to have two to three bowel movements a day? Let's just go through the basics. When you eat food what is supposed to happen is the food gets eaten, goes into the stomach, gets digested, goes into the small intestine, goes into the large intestine, and out through the colon in the form of a bowel movement. That whole process should take no more than one hour to four hours. This is important. If that process happens in one to four hours, food cannot convert to fat very easily, food does not stay in the body long enough to become rancid and turn into toxins, nutrients are allowed to get into the bloodstream quicker, and the whole system works as it is designed. But here is what happens to most people. You eat food; it goes into your stomach. As I talked about earlier about acid reflux disease, most people don't have enough digestive enzymes in their stomach; therefore, the food goes into the stomach and sits and doesn't digest properly. Already a problem is occurring. Gas starts to develop; the food doesn't digest properly, starts getting stuck in the stomach, and starts moving through the rest of the small intestines and large intestines in a very slow manner. When the food isn't digested in the stomach first, it then cannot be digested in the small intestine and large intestine. It then begins to get stuck and stay there longer than it should. When it gets stuck and stays there longer than it should it begins to attach itself to the walls of the intestines and colon. It gets stuck there; it begins to putrefy and turn rancid; it begins to put out poisonous gas. Other food comes in and gets stuck with that food. The same process occurs. This makes the small intestine and large intestine actually expand, in some cases five to ten times their correct size. This is one of the reasons people have a big gut, or women have the "pouch."

The food that gets stuck and turns rancid and toxic starts putting these toxins into the bloodstream. When it gets stuck on the inside of the intestine and colon, the nutrients from additional food that comes in that you eat is not assimilated into the bloodstream, so you have several problems occurring. You are having excess gas, toxins being put into the system overloading the kidneys and the liver; you have nutritional deficiencies starting right away. You then have allergies starting to get developed because food that is in the body longer than it should begins to turn into a toxin and the body reads all food that comes in like that as a toxin—thus you have an allergic reaction. This also creates a prime breeding ground for Candida yeast, as well as parasites, which I will talk about further. But Candida yeast and parasites cause a whole host of problems—more than you could ever imagine.

When this clogging up of the intestines and colon continues to occur, all the digestive systems begin to slow down, which means your metabolism begins to slow down, which means you begin to gain weight easier, and easier, and easier. You also begin to crave more carbohydrates and sweets and sugars. Interestingly enough, the food that gets stuck there and turns very rancid and toxic, which you become allergic to, you also crave! So when you eat food that you are "allergic to" the whole body begins to spiral downward. All the internal organs, the glands, the hormone levels get thrown out of balance. You are no longer in a state of "homeostasis" or balance, and everything spirals downward. Your health spirals downward; your energy levels go down; stress goes up; depression and moodiness go up; spaciness goes up; ability to think clearly, or make decisions or concentrate, goes down; food craving goes up; gas, flatulence, burping, acid reflux goes up; circulation goes down; diabetes goes up; pain increases; arthritis becomes more prevalent; insomnia, back pain, all go up. I could go on and on and on, but I hope you get the message. What's the cure? Well, guess what? The cure is not taking a drug! This is another perfect example of how the drug companies have totally brainwashed us and taken over a whole industry all for profit.

Can any one of you reading this remember years and years and years ago what the "cure" for constipation was? Think for a minute. Think hard. Remember Granddad! Some of you may remember prunes! Oh, my God! Is it as simple as eating prunes or drinking fresh prune juice? Yes. Prunes have been for centuries one of the most common ways to cure constipation. Today, you never hear about prunes. You hear about all the drugs, all the potions, and powders, and laxatives that you can buy from the drug companies. You never hear about the simple answer of prunes. Amazing, isn't it?

I'm going to give you some simple ways to cure constipation. By the way, one of the other most common reasons your colon and digestive systems slow down, become sluggish, and constipation occurs is because of non-prescription and prescription drugs. That's right. If you look in the Physicians' Desk Reference (PDR), which is the manual describing all the counter-reactions that drugs have in the body, in other words, all the negative side effects that drugs give to the body, you virtually see on every single prescription and non-prescription drug one of the side effects is constipation. The main reason for this is non-prescription and prescription drugs are so poisonous and toxic that when you take them the body needs to hold on to more fluid to try to dilute the poisons otherwise you will die, and one of the ways it does this is to shut down the digestive system and hold on to more fluid. All non-prescription and prescription drugs also have a tendency to make you gain weight. This is why I repeatedly say if you want to remain healthy, if you want to stay healthy, if you want to cure yourself of disease, stop taking non-prescription and prescription drugs! (Of course, do so only under the supervision of a licensed healthcare practitioner.)

So, here are some basic ways to cure constipation:

1. Prunes and prune juice;
2. Aloe Vera gel, juice, or Aloe Vera leaf capsules;
3. Flax seeds, flax seed oil;
4. Castor oil;
5. Various herbs such as senna and cascara sagrada (there are a host of all-herbal natural "laxatives" that are great at temporarily relieving constipation);
6. Walking;
7. Rebounding;
8. Drinking more water;
9. Psyllium;
10. Any high fiber grain or cereal;
11. Yoga;
12. Enemas;
13. Colonics;
14. Parasite cleanse;
15. Candida cleanse; and liver/gallbladder cleanse.

All of these are great at relieving constipation. One of the items I mentioned above is castor oil. Castor oil and prunes were the two most common methods of curing constipation for eons. They are still the absolute best ways to cure constipation in my opinion. A couple of spoonfuls of castor oil work absolute wonders. I'll give you two other miracles for constipation if you really want to clean yourself out, but make sure you do this under the watchful eye of a licensed healthcare practitioner and stay by the bathroom for at least four to five hours. Do not do these before going to bed!

1. One-third cup castor oil with one-third cup of beer. Stir, and drink. Then drink the rest of the beer over the next half hour. Believe me, your constipation will immediately be healed.

2. A couple of spoonfuls of Epsom salts in some warm water. Drink and lie on your left side for one-half hour and get ready for an awakening experience!

When you consult with your licensed healthcare practitioner or go to your local health food store you will see an array of all-natural constipation cure–type products. The point is this—constipation can be simply remedied with prune juice, prunes, or castor oil in addition to all the other methods. How come we never hear about these today? Think about it. You never ever hear about prunes anymore, or castor oil, or prune juice. You just never hear about it, but there is ad, after ad, after ad on television promoting this product, or this drug, or this laxative. Isn't it amazing that the drug companies have brainwashed you? Think about it. Aren't you mad when you realized that you haven't even thought of prunes or castor oil? Why is it that you haven't thought of prunes or castor oil? Because the drug companies have brainwashed you into only thinking about laxatives. The drug companies have brainwashed you—if you have constipation you go to the drug store, you spend huge, insane money to buy stupid, dangerous drugs called laxatives. Folks, this is the brainwashing of America by the drug companies—all in the name of profit. These drugs called laxatives are dangerous poisons. Yes, they will make you have a bowel movement, but they are dangerous, toxic, poisonous drugs. They are incredibly expensive and they are categorically no more effective than castor oil or prunes and prune juice. In fact, castor oil, prunes and prune juice, and the other methods I listed above do not only work as well or better than any drug, laxative, or powder you can buy at the drug store, but they are less expensive and have a host of other health benefits! Cure your constipation today with natural methods. Cure every disease you have with natural methods and, as always, make sure you visit a licensed healthcare practitioner when doing so. Please tell me your success story. I am curious to hear.

LEARNING DISABILITIES AND AUTISM

Learning disabilities in children and adults is at an all time high. Every year more and more children are being diagnosed with learning disabilities and autism. What is the cause? According to many experts, including Robert F. Kennedy, Jr., a senior attorney for the Natural Resources Defense Council and author of *Deadly Immunity*, our government is to blame. There's growing evidence that shows that a drug called thimerosal is to blame.

This drug is found in vaccines. The fact is the more vaccines kids get, the more autism, learning disabilities, and lifelong illness develops. The drug thimerosal is a preservative that was put in vaccines back in the 1930s. Immediately after the drug was put in, autism cases started to appear. It is important to note that autism had never been known before! There was no such thing as autism. Autism started and was created by this drug used in vaccines. In 1989 the Centers for Disease Control mandated that vaccines increase. Vaccines increased from 10 to 24. This means kids started receiving 24 vaccines as mandated by the government. All of these vaccines have this deadly drug thimerosal in them.

This drug is in fact mercury. Mercury is a deadly poison causing all types of brain dysfunction, moto-neurological dysfunction, learning disabilities, and causes dozens of other ailments to develop. This mercury poisoning is most prevalent in vaccines, but also in farm-raised fish and in the air we breathe. Today manufacturing plants put more mercury in the air than ever before. We are all being exposed to more mercury than ever before. Our water supplies are loaded with mercury, more so than ever before in our history.

According to Robert Kennedy, no one has bothered to do any specific analysis on the cumulative impact that all this mercury is doing to our children and all of us. The fact is, we are injecting our children with 400 times the amount of mercury than even the FDA or EPA considers safe. A child on the first day he is born is injected with a hepatitis B shot. This is insane. According to EPA guidelines, you would have to weigh 275 pounds to safely absorb the amount of poison in the hepatitis B shot all children are given.

As I mention in my book, children today are set up for lifelong problems with their health. From the moment a child is born, he's given these deadly vaccines. These vaccines are filled with poison, including mercury, causing illness, disease, learning disabilities, and other ailments. These vaccines also cause our bodies to be more prone to fighting off virus, thus leaving these children susceptible to bacterial infections. This is one of the major reasons almost all children develop ear infections. When ear infections develop, doctors load up the children with massive amounts of antibiotics. These antibiotics wipe out all the friendly flora in the colon, setting off a Candida yeast overgrowth, which then turns into a fungus permeating the entire body and causing all types of medical problems throughout the child's life.

It is important to note that before 1988 only one in every 2,500 American children had autism. Today, one in every 166 children has autism. One in every six children have some type of learning disability, including neurological disorders, delayed speech, language disorders, attention deficit disorder, hyperactivity, decreased motor skill function, and inability to learn new information, and are more susceptible to disease.

This is all connected to the mercury that is put in the vaccines! And in the Fox TV show *Scarborough Country*, it was stated that there is no "good science." In politics, science always gets diluted. This diluted science is done specifically at the behest of the major political contributors who do not want the truth to be known for fear that it would have an adverse effect on their profitability. According to Scarborough, "There's no doubt in my mind that maybe two years from now or five years from now or ten years from now, we are going to find out what we know intuitively, that thimerosal, the mercury in the vaccines, absolutely causes autism and other learning disabilities."

Robert F. Kennedy, Jr. states, "The fact is the science is out there anyway. Anyone can read it. It's even on my website, RobertFKennedyJr.com. The science is clear. There are literally hundreds and hundreds of studies that connect the thimerosal to these disastrous neurological disorders." When Robert F. Kennedy talked to the federal bureaucrats who were defending thimerosal, he found that these politicians and bureaucrats were doing so at the orders of the multinational corporations that are making the money on the sale of these dangerous products.

He discovered what I had been reporting on for years, that these bureaucrats use the media to perpetuate the lie that these things are safe. They use phony scientists who create junk science. These are Robert F. Kennedy, Jr.'s words. Both Scarborough and Kennedy go on to say that this is the same thing that happened in big tobacco and big oil, and regarding global warming. Both Kennedy and Scarborough state that the idea that this is safe is "junk science." They state that it is fraudulent. You are reading this right. Both Kennedy and Scarborough are stating what I had been stating for years. That the tobacco industry, the oil industry, and the pharmaceutical industry all do the same thing. They create their own fake and fraudulent studies. They pay off government politicians to perpetuate lies. They use the news media to make us believe that these things are safe, when in fact they're not safe, and in fact are causing disease.

Scarborough stated, "Politicians like to get reelected. They are working with the pharmaceutical industry." Kennedy actually has the transcripts of secret meetings that were conducted in Simpsonwood, Georgia, in the year 2000. According to Kennedy, "It's the most horrifying thing you can read. There are scientists there from the government who are reading the reports and saying this is undeniable. There's no way we can ever deny this. These vaccines are absolutely dangerous. I am not going to give it to my children, but we have to hide it from the American people."

Robert Kennedy says that this information is so shocking, that we actually have guys who are supposed to be protecting Americans' health who are actually conspiring to keep this stuff in the vaccines and continuing to knowingly kill people.

Scarborough goes on to say, "This reminds me of a lawsuit we were both involved in a couple of years ago regarding water quality, where the people that polluted the water in our community, left our community, and would never drink the water, but allowed our own children to drink the water. It was a disaster and it is a disgrace." I applaud Robert F. Kennedy and Joe Scarborough for taking such an important subject and telling the truth on national television. This is a huge step in exposing the truth about the dangers of vaccines and all pharmaceutical drugs.

Many of you wonder what can you do if your children have already been given amounts of vaccines, massive amounts of antibiotics, and massive amounts of drugs?

The answer is: you need to do the cleanses they mentioned in Chapter 6 of my book. These toxins that you put in your body stay in your body. You must get them out. Doing the cleanses is an effective way to get these toxins out of the body. Another effective way is to go to a homeopathic clinic and get intravenous chelation, which also is very powerful at removing these deadly toxins from the body. The good news is the body has an incredible ability to heal itself. Once the body is free of toxins and provided that you have proper nutrition, limited amounts of electromagnetic chaos exposure, and limited amounts of mental and emotional stress, your body can easily heal itself.

The good news is every cell in your body completely rejuvenates and replaces itself every seven years. If you clean the toxins out, if you minimize the amount of toxins going in, if you make sure your body has no nutritional deficiencies, if you make sure that you are limiting the exposure to electromagnetic chaos, and if you are reducing or eliminating mental and emotional stress, your body can rejuvenate and heal itself. With powerful positive thinking, your DNA structure can actually change.

Genetic weaknesses and imbalances can be corrected and virtually any illness and disease can correct itself, and you can be cured of virtually all disease.

STUDY LINKS HAIR DYES TO CANCER

According to the BBC, researchers have found more evidence that hair dyes cause cancer. I have repeatedly said that if you can't eat it, don't put it on your skin. I have repeatedly tried to inform you of the fact that toxins cause cancer. More and more evidence is making headline news. This particular study shows that those who regularly dye their hair have a higher risk of developing lymphoma.

Lymphomas are cancers of the lymphatic system, a network of vessels which form part of the body's immune system and carry infection-fighting cells, as well as draining dead cells away from tissues.

When you have cancer in the lymphatic system or any blockages in the lymphatic system, you are more susceptible to coming down with and catching and succumbing to any virus or bacteria, since the infection-fighting cells are blocked from getting to where they need to go.

Also, when your lymphatic system is blocked, the ability for your body to get toxins out on a regular basis goes down dramatically. Again, this increases your chance of succumbing to viruses and bacteria, and also developing other diseases in the body such as diabetes, cancer, heart disease, etc.

STUDY LINKS PAIN RELIEVERS TO CANCER

Study after study after study keeps coming out showing what I have been saying to be true. This study shows that over-the-counter non-prescription painkillers such as aspirin and ibuprofen increase risk of cancer. The fact is that every non-prescription drug and prescription drug increases risk of disease. The facts are clear, all non-prescription drugs and all prescription drugs cause illness and disease to varying degrees.

You cannot cure yourself of disease if you are taking non-prescription and prescription medication. You cannot heal yourself if you're taking non-prescription and prescription medication. If you routinely take non-prescription and prescription medication, you are absolutely assured that you will develop more and more illness and disease. You will become sicker and sicker, you will age faster, your energy levels will diminish, depression will increase, obesity will increase. All aspects of quality of life will decrease for you.

I was recently at a health spa where I met an incredible 93-year-old man and his lovely wife. This gentleman is a lawyer living in New York City. He walks five blocks to work every single day. He is healthy, dynamic, full of life, and incredibly bright and alert. I asked him what kind of medication he was taking. His response was, "I don't believe in drugs!" The fact is he takes no over-the-counter medication and he takes no prescription drugs. On headline news there was the story of a 95-year-old man who broke the world record for sprinting the 100 meter dash. This man is obviously an incredible physical specimen. When interviewed, he stated that he did not believe in medical doctors and has not taken any prescription or non-prescription drugs in over 50 years.

The facts are clear, drugs, both prescription and non-prescription, do not make you healthier, they make you sicker. Drug companies are not interested in your health. Drug companies are only interested in their profits. Drug companies only want to get you to buy and use more drugs. If you want to cure yourself of any disease you have and remain healthy, you must eliminate all non-prescription and prescription drugs.

MAD COW DISEASE FOUND IN AMERICA!

I've stated over and over again that the meat produced in America is at an all-time low in quality. I've stated that the meat produced in this country is dangerous and should not be consumed. The way the meat is produced in America creates meat that is toxic and poison and gives you disease. In the book I go through and explain how cows are genetically modified and bred, how they are fed diseased feed, ground-up other diseased, sick animals, and routinely eat their own feces and urine. Cows are injected with bovine growth hormone, causing the animal to be highly diseased. They are given massive amounts of antibiotics and other drug injections, making them diseased and sick. They do not exercise. And when they are slaughtered, the trauma that the animal experiences during the slaughtering and killing process spews adrenaline into the tissue. The animals routinely die in their own urine and feces. The animals are butchered and produced in a manner where they are full of pathogens, disease, bacteria, germs, and disease-causing agents. The meat itself is not natural, it is unhealthy, it is loaded with drugs, growth hormone, as well as feces and urine. The meat is aged, allowing more bacteria to grow.

The major reason why Mad Cow disease is developing in animals is because of these manufacturing processes. The fact is cows are vegetarians and should not be eating the type of feed given to them. Specifically they should not be eating ground up pigs, horses, goats, and other cows, most of which were sick and diseased and not capable of butchering for human consumption.

In a previous newsletter I recommended the book *Brain Trust*, which exposed this. In my *Natural Cures* book, or on www.natural cures.com, I give you several books that I highly recommend in relation to the meat industry as well as the dairy industry. This problem is more prevalent than you realize. The fact is, the only safe meat products in America are organic, kosher products. You want 100 percent organic beef.

Ideally, you want both 100 percent organic and kosher. This way you are assured that the meat and poultry you're eating is disease free. I can guarantee you, if you continue to eat meat on a regular basis, you will continue to get sicker and sicker and sicker. The meat produced in America is not getting better, it's getting worse and worse and worse. If you do eat meat that is not 100 percent organic and kosher, then you must routinely do cleanses to get the toxins out.

Folks, it's all about being healthy and feeling better. Everything that I suggest is all about waking up in the morning, feeling fantastic, being happy, being stress free, being full of energy and vitality and looking forward to a great day. It's about going through your day with no pain in your body, feeling fantastic and full of energy, having a normal healthy appetite. Having no gas or flatulence. Having no heartburn, no bloating. Being fluid and flexible and strong in your body. Being able to walk up a flight of stairs and not get winded. Having energy and vitality throughout the day, and sleeping deeply and soundly. It's all about living a life where you don't get sick. We are not sneezing or coughing. It's about not having sore throats, not catching colds, not having back pains or headaches, not feeling spacey or depressed. That's what it's all about.

It's not about being fanatical. Heck, I go to restaurants. I eat a steak and I know that steak is probably absolutely poisonous! But I also do a colon cleanse and a liver, gallbladder cleanse, and a heavy metal cleanse on a regular basis to get these toxins out. I also make up for it at my home. It's certainly hard going to a restaurant to eat according to our guidelines. But it is relatively easy eating at home and following these guidelines. It's easy because I go to the store and I buy the right food. You can too.

Remember, it's better to do a little than doing nothing at all. Every little bit helps. Don't think you have to be perfect to get benefits.

BREAST CANCER CURED!

Is there a breast cancer cure? Well, in my *Natural Cures* book I mention how flaxseed oil, otherwise known as linseed oil, is very effective in the fight against breast cancer. This research has been conducted for twenty years and been reported by health experts around the world. Linseed oil, or flaxseed oil, is inexpensive and non-patentable. There is virtually no major research being put into the use of linseed oil or flaxseed oil in the treatment of breast cancer or other types of cancer. This is appalling because all the information points to this oil as being a miraculous cure in the treatment of cancers, specifically breast cancer. I was in NBC studios in Chicago getting ready to do an interview. Every time I do interviews I'm always attacked by the interviewer because I am not a medical doctor. I'm always asked, "How can you talk about natural cures, Mr. Trudeau, when you're not even a medical doctor?" My answer is always the same. I am a reporter, I am a researcher, and I am an investigator. These are not my natural cures. I'm not a licensed healthcare practitioner, I am simply reporting on the natural cures that are being discovered and developed from around the world. I'm simply telling you what other people's research has shown to be true. It's not my research and they're not my cures.

She then said, "Well, there's no scientific basis for any of the cures you're reporting on." I was glad she asked this question at NBC because in the lobby of NBC studios in Chicago there was a magazine being given out to all the NBC employees. It was a magazine about health and a healthy lifestyle. The magazine had a very interesting article about how linseed oil was curing breast cancer! This article pointed out that Canadian researchers gave women with breast cancer muffins containing some linseed oil, and it showed that just by eating one muffin a day breast cancer cells were being killed at a higher rate than chemotherapy. What this showed was that it seems and appears that simply a little bit of linseed oil is more effective in killing breast cancer cells than any type of radiation or chemotherapy, with absolutely none of the negative side effects, and none of the expensive costs. The problem is nobody can patent linseed oil, which means no drug company wants you to know about this because if you did then the chemotherapy business for the treatment of breast cancer would dramatically go down and all the companies out there, and all the clinics that have chemotherapy equipment and drugs would lose hundreds of millions of dollars in sales and profits. People could lose their jobs. How insane. People could lose their jobs? Companies could lose money? But women's lives could be saved; women wouldn't have to go through the horror of chemotherapy treatment. Do you see how this makes no sense? Linseed oil and flaxseed oil is not my cure; I'm simply reporting that Canadian researchers have proven that linseed oil is killing breast cancer cells in women who have breast cancer.

If you are concerned about breast cancer, you need to look at these types of things. In this publication I can't give you every reference. This is why the naturalcures.com website is being developed so that I will have all this information from around the world available right at your fingertips, so that you can get unbiased medical information. Linseed oil and flaxseed oil have other dramatic health benefits—too many to list here. If you are reading this and want to do something for your overall health, for the prevention of disease, for increasing health and vitality, I would suggest going to your local health food store and getting some whole flax, which is a great source of fiber, or some flaxseed oil or linseed oil and adding it to your diet. Talk to some people at your local health food store. Go online and do some searches on flaxseed oil, flax or linseed oil. Get some information; take responsibility for your own health. Consider adding this into your diet. One thing I have known for years is that researchers have shown that by mixing flaxseed oil with soy protein in the form of a "shake," when consumed, it seems to take cancerous tumors and shrink them dramatically. This also works with fibrous cysts as well. Again, this is not a Kevin Trudeau cure, I'm simply reporting on research that I have observed from travels all around the world. I personally take linseed oil and whole flax seeds on a pretty regular basis, not every day, but I have it in my refrigerator, I have it in my home and I do add it into my diet as I see fit.

CINNAMON CURES DIABETES

For those suffering from diabetes, researchers point out the chemicals in food, overeating, genetic weaknesses, lack of exercise, and obesity all contribute to diabetes. Researchers have concluded that if a person were to do all the things laid out in Chapter 6 of the book, most if not all diabetic conditions would dramatically improve if not be "cured" fully. Over fifteen million people suffer from diabetes in just the U.S. It's estimated that over thirty to fifty million are pre-diabetic. It's estimated that perhaps at least fifty million are diabetic and don't even know it. Recent studies on cinnamon suggest that it can help maintain blood sugar levels at a consistent area. I also interviewed Dr. Youngsoo Kim who showed me research from the University of Calgary on an herbal formulation that has been proven to cure diabetes in many instances. If you have diabetes, simply go on the internet and do a Google search under natural diabetes cure and you will see several products and research showing that it can be controlled.

AMAZON FRUIT ANTI-AGING MIRACLE

Acai is a fruit from the Amazon. It boosts energy, has disease-fighting and age-fighting properties, and is one of the most powerful antioxidants on the earth. Celebrities like Oprah Winfrey and Denise Richards sing its praises. It is one of the most nutritious and powerful foods in the world, says a leading anti-aging doctor. This fruit can lower cholesterol and protects against heart disease and stroke. It is also loaded with calcium, which prevents osteoporosis, cancer, and makes you sleep incredibly well. It also repairs damaged tissue to the skin.

CROCODILE PROTEIN PEPTIDE MIRACLE CURE?

As reported on the BBC news, scientists in the United States have isolated a powerful agent in crocodile blood which could help conquer human infections immune to standard antibiotics. The discovery was made thanks to the curiosity of a BBC science producer filming a documentary on saltwater crocodiles in Australia. The producer noticed something that surprised her. Despite horrendous injuries to crocs, their wounds rarely, if ever, get infected. The sample showed that there was an antimicrobial peptide in the crocodile blood. In tests the substance kills strains of bacteria that are resistant to all standard antibiotics. Natural antibiotics are found in various animals, including frogs. The peptide is simply a natural chemical made of amino acids strung together, and it can destroy bacteria by penetrating their membranes. These natural antibiotics do not damage normal cells as manmade antibiotics do, which means they are much more useful than any pharmaceutical drug when treating human infections, but there is a major problem. These natural antibiotics cannot be patented, which means there is no pharmaceutical company interested in researching this further. There is no pharmaceutical company that actually wants any of this information disclosed. There is no drug company that has an interest in people being exposed to this inexpensive, more effective antibiotic. They can't sell it, they can't make money; therefore, they don't want people to know about it even though it's better than any chemical man-made antibiotic on the market. This is the outrage. Of course, the FDA says that only a drug can cure, prevent, or treat a disease. So even though this non-drug, all-natural protein peptide is better at fighting infections and bacteria than any antibiotic, the FDA says it's against the law to make that statement even though it's true!

These peptides are also found in great white sharks and are also incredibly effective. There is a product now on the market that actually has these peptides. It's incredibly inexpensive and is incredibly effective in handling all types of viruses from hepatitis D to even AIDS. I've personally talked to a gentleman who had full-blown AIDS. He took this peptide once a day for thirty days and his AIDS is completely gone. This could be an isolated case. Would this natural miracle work on every AIDS patient or every sufferer of a virus or bacteria? I don't know the answer. We would have to test it on every patient to find out, but the answer is—does it work on many people? Yes, I've personally talked to them. As a matter of fact, I've personally taken this myself. Based on my observations and research it appears that this peptide is also an incredibly effective anti-aging regime and preventative measure against viruses and bacteria. People are scared about the various flu viruses. This could be an effective way to prevent or treat them. The problem with the way healthcare is today is all-natural inexpensive discoveries like this are being suppressed and hidden from us. For more information go to www.liquidmannagold.com and www.biologicalmiracle.com.

ENERGETIC "HEALING" RECEIVES PRAISE!

Throughout history new ideas and new concepts receive violent criticism. As time passes and these new ideas gain acceptance, people forget that those who pioneered new discoveries and technologies, and new ways of doing things, were heavily ridiculed, criticized, ostracized, and persecuted. Originally it was believed that the sun revolved around the earth. When astronomers suggested that the earth actually revolves around the sun, many were put to death for suggesting such heresy! When doctors suggested the importance of washing your hands before surgery, many lost their medical licenses because saying such a thing went against all that medical science believed and knew to be true. When two Australian doctors suggested that bacteria can actually live in the stomach and be a partial cause of ulcers, they were ostracized, bashed, criticized, humiliated, and almost lost their medical licenses. Ten years of ridicule was put to rest when these doctors received a Nobel Prize for proving scientifically, beyond a shadow of a doubt, that in fact they were right all along and medical science was wrong for over 1,000 years. Bacteria do in fact live in the stomach.

The same is true with how the mind affects the body and energetic "healing." For years medical doctors have stated that thoughts, and what you believe, and what you think have absolutely no effect on biochemistry, physiology, sickness, illness, or disease. Anyone who suggested thoughts or beliefs could affect your health was a charlatan, a snake oil salesman, a fraud, and a liar. However, medical science became confused when they observed in their own testing of drugs the placebo effect. The placebo effect, as described by medical science, is when you give a patient nothing, yet they believe they are getting a powerful drug and therefore their illness is cured. There is absolutely no explanation except that the patient's "belief" or "thoughts" actually cured the disease. This placebo effect is not questioned in the medical community; it is factual, documented, and known to be true. Therefore, the medical community has reversed their longstanding position; their own admission that the placebo effect exists means that thoughts and belief can miraculously heal the body. The most interesting fact on this is that medical science cannot explain how this occurs. Their whole theory that drugs and biochemistry are the end-all of how the body works and how illness and disease exist is categorically, fundamentally wrong. The proof is the fact that the placebo effect exists.

Medical science cannot deny that when a patient believes that something will work, it often actually does work. Thoughts can cure even incurable diseases. This is proven.

How do thoughts or beliefs cure incurable diseases? No one really knows. There are lots of theories. There is also another interesting indisputable fact. Faith healers and prayer appear to cure incurable diseases. These do not work all the time. No one really knows why another person's thoughts, prayers, or energetic "healing" cures incurable diseases some times and not others. No one really understands the mechanics yet, but the fact exists and it's indisputable that a person can "pray," send "energy," or use some type of "psychic" "healing" and "heal" the incurable disease in another person. This has been documented and, in many cases, happens instantaneously. Quantum physicists explain that what is occurring is happening at an energetic level beyond what medical science can currently see with its own equipment. This is not surprising since we all know that radio waves exist; they are beamed down by satellites, radio towers, and microwave devices all around the world. We see the effects of radio waves and we use them. But what most people do not know is that scientists cannot see radio waves; they do not understand how radio waves pass through solid steel, glass, and concrete. Scientists do not know how radio waves work, yet we use them. Therefore, it is reasonable to say that energy frequencies from a person or a machine can cure disease, even across hundreds of miles or thousands of miles, while at the same time saying we don't exactly know how it works. The bottom line is the facts prove that energy "healing" works, but at this time no one really understands it. We can only theorize how it works, but we don't know how it works.

With this said, in the book *Natural Cures* I recommend energetic rebalancing or energetic "healing." Some people call this long-distance prayer, thought forms, spiritual "healing," etc. You can call it anything you feel comfortable with. The bottom line is it's "healing" with energy. There are several great books written about this which I suggest you read. The books are listed in *Natural Cures*. Two such energetic distance "healing" centers are www.quantumwellnesscenter.com and www.distancehealing.net. I have personally used these energetic "healing" sessions and have talked to dozens of people that have as well. In every case the response has been miraculous. Miracle "healings," physical, emotional, mental, and spiritual take place—sometimes within minutes, sometimes over days, weeks, or months. Sometimes the "healings" are spectacular, miraculous, and instantaneous; sometimes they are more subtle, but in all cases the response has been incredibly positive.

THE HISTORY OF ROYAL RIFE

I mentioned earlier about energetic "healing." Royal Raymond Rife was one of the pioneers in this area. He is regarded as one of the most brilliant and persistent scientists in history. Rife invented technology before it existed, including the first micromanipulators, microdissectors, and heterodyning microscopes. He won fourteen government awards for scientific discoveries and an honorary medical degree from the University of Heidelberg. Millionaires like Henry Timken financed Rife's work, such as the universal microscope with 5,682 parts. With this superb microscope, Dr. Royal Rife became the first human being to actually see a live virus. After nearly 2,000 unsuccessful attempts, Rife finally isolated and identified the human cancer virus. Rife inoculated 400 lab animals with this virus, created 400 tumors, and then miraculously eliminated every cancer tumor by using an instrument he invented to modify its electronic signature. He was using energy! Some people call it frequencies.

Rife used the same technology for other "incurable diseases." Constructing his own equipment, Rife painstakingly analyzed the precise energetic signature unique to each pertinent microbe. Rife theorized that the smallest virus, microbe, or bacteria each had a unique vibration, or energetic signature, or frequency. He believed that every cell in the body also had a unique frequency, or vibration, or energetic signature. He developed a machine that could emit a very specific frequency. By exposing disease organisms to a highly modified form of their own unique electronic electromagnetic pattern of oscillation (frequency or energetic signature), Rife discovered he could destroy them by the millions. The most exciting part is when doing this, nothing else would be destroyed except that particular organism. Rife's discovery on vibrational or energetic "healing" was simply that every organism at the lowest level had a very specific electromagnetic pattern, or unique energetic signature, or pattern of oscillation, or frequency, or "energy."

This is the same theory that Dr. Samuel Hahnemann discovered when discovering homeopathy. Rife's theory that every biochemical compound oscillates at its own distinct frequency pattern was revolutionary, and it's still revolutionary. The medical community disputes this. Rife believed that every living thing has its own unique electromagnetic signature and this pattern is genetically determined, and is therefore unique and unlike any other species. After decades of research, Rife isolated the patterns, modified them, and used them to kill the microbes that produced them. Just as a wine glass is shattered by a particular frequency, so Rife's frequencies destroy only the disease organism whose oscillation pattern corresponds to the modified pattern he broadcasts. This is how Rife technology, or energetic frequency technology, or energetic "healing," or homeopathy, or electronic frequency generators kill disease, cancer, and tumors without adversely affecting any other part of the body. This is quite unlike chemotherapy. Chemotherapy kills cancer cells and tumors, but also kills everything else as well. Why isn't more research being put into this? Because this technology is free, it cannot be patented. Every drug company on the planet does not want this information to be known and does not want any of this researched or used on a wide-scale basis. Doing so would certainly be for the betterment of mankind, but doing so would also be to the detriment of the drug companies. Imagine if these machines were used instead of chemotherapy. Every cancer clinic in the world would virtually go bankrupt and out of business. The manufacturers of chemotherapy would be bankrupt. Billions of dollars in profits would be lost. Oh yes, millions of people's lives would be saved, but that's the craziness that's going on in today's society—who cares about lives, we're talking about money here.

There are many machines that use this technology. Practitioners who use this technology have to do so underground; they cannot say that they are using it. The FDA has agents that routinely go in and arrest people who use this technology, even on themselves. The FDA, keep in mind, is nothing more than a pawn for the pharmaceutical companies. The drug companies have set up organizations, PR machines, and agents to specifically crush anyone who is informing the public about the truth about Royal Rife and energetic "healing." It simply will cost the drug companies too much money in lost profits for this information to be known. This is the outrage. Go on the internet, do a Google search on Royal Rife, or energetic "healing," or vibrational "healing," or any other words like this and you will get good information. For years, in countries that were suppressed such as Nazi Germany, Stalinist Russia, and even communist China, there have been people who do not succumb to the oppression of the government and large companies. People routinely operate in the "underground." The information is available, the cures are available, but it is your responsibility to go seek it out. I am here to help you get that information.

MULTI-WAVE OSCILLATOR

A Russian engineer by the name of Georges Lakhovsky published a book in French in the late 1920s called *The Secret of Life*. A few years later it was translated into Spanish, German, and Italian. In 1939 it was translated into English. The problem was, this was exactly the same time that Hitler attacked Poland and kicked off World War II. The book received virtually no reviews or attention in medical circles. What Lakhovsky discovered and wrote about in the book was simply mind-boggling. His theory and discovery was that all living cells, plants, people, bacteria, parasites, etc. possess attributes which normally are associated with electronic or electric circuits. These theories, by the way, collate with Samuel Hahnemann, the founder of homeopathy, and Dr. Royal Rife. The attributes include resistance, capacitance, and inductance. These three electrical attributes configured properly will cause the recurrent generation of a sine wave exhibiting an effect of physics known as resonance. Resonance can be described as a frequency, an oscillation, an electromagnetic imprint, or energy. These circuits can be called, additionally, electromagnetic resonators, but more commonly are referred to as oscillators.

Lakhovsky discovered, as did others around the world, that all living cells produce and radiate at oscillations at very high frequencies; but not only do they produce frequencies, but they also receive and respond to oscillations or frequencies from outside sources. If these frequencies or oscillations are in symphony with that of the cell, the strength and vigor of that cell can be reinforced and become stronger. If, on the other hand, these outside frequencies are dissimilar, the oscillations produced by the cell will be weakened and dampened, resulting in a loss of vigor for that cell. The cells of disease-causing organisms produce different frequencies than those of normal healthy cells in plants, animals, or people. For people or plants suffering from disease conditions, Lakhovsky found that if he increased the amplitude, which is the volume, of the oscillations of healthy cells, this increase would overwhelm and dampen the oscillations produced by the disease-causing cells, thus bringing about the demise of the disease-causing cells. If you pumped up the amplitude of the disease-causing cells, their oscillations would gain the upper hand and cause the person or plant to become more ill.

Lakhovsky initially proved this theory using plants. He inoculated ten geranium plants with a tumor-producing plant cancer. After thirty days, tumors had developed in all the plants. He took one of the ten plants and simply fashioned a thin copper tube in a one-loop, one-ended coil around the center of the plant. He held it in place with a wooden stake. The coil acted as an antenna collecting oscillation energy from cosmic rays which we are constantly bombarded with. The diameter of the copper loop determined the range of frequencies which would be captured. He found that the loop captured frequencies that matched the resonate frequency of the plant cells. This captured energy reinforced the oscillations produced by the geranium's healthy cells. This allowed the plant to overwhelm the oscillations of the cancer cells and destroyed the cancer. The tumors fell off in less than three weeks and the plant thrived. All of the other cancer-inoculated plants without the antenna coil died within thirty days. In his book Lakhovsky shows pictures of the recovered plant after three months, six months, and one year. With the original coil still in place, the plant grew into a very robust specimen. What this shows is, again, that energy vibrations and oscillations can cure disease and strengthen the body. There is a machine that actually strengthens the good cells in the human body using this technology. Because of FTC censorship, I cannot tell you the brand name of it, but if you search on the internet under "multi-wave oscillator," you should be able to find it. I have used this personally, and others have as well. This is another "natural cure" that they don't want you to know about.

Everything in my newsletters can easily be attacked by someone in the media. They can claim I'm a snake oil salesman, a charlatan, a fraud, and so forth, but these are not my discoveries. I am simply informing you of research produced by doctors, "healers," healthcare practitioners, scientists and researchers from all around the world. I am the only one who is getting this information out to the masses. That is why I am the biggest threat to the profits of the drug companies and the power of the politicians and government officials in state, local, and federal government.

NEW CANCER CURES

In America the news media is trying to brainwash us into believing that only "medical doctors" using chemotherapy, drugs, and radiation can cure cancer. We are being led to believe that only those M.D.s who receive their M.D. title after being trained by the drug industry are the only people qualified to give us advice or information about cancer or our health. We are being led to believe that only chemotherapy, drugs, and radiation, and those things produced by the pharmaceutical industry in America, are the only things that can treat, prevent, or cure cancer. This is being pounded into our head by the FDA, other government agencies, and the news media. This is a great lie. This is fraud. This is arrogance. Consider the hundreds of thousands of DOCTORS around the world who are not members of the American Medical Association. Consider the hundreds of thousands of healthcare providers who treat patients on a regular basis all around the world who were not trained by the American drug industry. Consider the hundreds of thousands of hospitals and clinics around the world that treat patients who have cancer with methods other than chemotherapy, radiation, and drugs. Consider the fact that these alternative treatments have the same or better cure rate than chemotherapy, surgery, radiation, or drugs.

Why is this information being hidden from us? The answer is very simple. The news media today is controlled by the board of directors, officers, and shareholders. The people on the boards of the major media, the officers, and the shareholders have major financial ties to the oil industry, the pharmaceutical industry, and the fast food industry. They are using the media, including the news, to increase their wealth by brainwashing us into believing that only those products produced by the pharmaceutical industry, to which they have financial ties, can treat, prevent, and cure diseases like cancer. This is the big lie. We live in America, we watch TV and read the newspaper, and we are being simply fed the propaganda line that both the government and the multinational corporations want us to hear. We think we live in a free society with the free flow of information and ideas. We used to laugh at the Soviet Union or Nazi Germany or Red China and how the government would lie to its people through the news media. We used to think that America was transparent in the free flow of information. This is categorically untrue. When you travel to other parts of the world people in other countries know that we Americans are in fact being lied to through the media. What you see on TV, what you hear about in the news, is not the truth. The lies and misinformation are a combination of flagrant, blatant, and purposely delivered untruths, half truths, lies, deceptions, and misleading information combined with a lack of fact checking. The other element is the fact that the producers and newsmen have no real desire to put out true information. Their desire is simply to appear to have exclusive breaking information and produce a controversial news segment or show that will get great ratings and get the producers and news people involved accolades, thus increasing their power, their position, their influence, and their salaries. All these people are simply looking to produce pieces that will get them promoted. They are not looking to share with you truthful information. They have a conflict of interest. If you read my book in its entirety and you listen to anything I say in these newsletters, the bottom line is when there is a conflict of interest, and specifically when that conflict is monetary, you can be assured that people will succumb to greed, therefore compromising the free flow of truthful information.

I have received huge numbers of letters from people that have had cancer, read my book, and followed the suggestions—the first being, of course, to go to a licensed healthcare practitioner who does not use drugs and surgery, and get specialized, customized treatment based on your particular form of cancer and your particular situation. True, holistic healthcare providers do not treat cancer, they do not treat symptoms, they treat the person as a whole, they consider and look at all the factors; therefore, the treatments can be incredibly different person to person to person, depending on a multitude of variables. It is true, if you simply did everything in Chapter 6, in my opinion and based on the opinions of hundreds of healthcare providers around the world, that virtually all people with cancer could possibly be cured simply by doing the things in Chapter 6.

However, that blanket statement does not take into account how far along your cancer is, and other factors in your life which may impede the healing process. One new specific cancer cure, which is a nontoxic breakthrough in cancer, as well as stroke, endometriosis, and psoriasis, with no side effects and no contraindications, is a complex of mineral, vitamin, and amino acid known as a palladium lipoic complex (LAPd). The FTC prohibits me from mentioning the trade name for this complex, but there are over 2,000 articles written about LAPd that you can find on the internet. More information about this is at www.centurywellness.com. Dr. James Forsythe, a board certified oncologist, has just completed a twenty-three month study utilizing this complex. All patients enrolled in this retrospective outcome-based study were stage four cancer patients. As the study progressed and the data began to unfold, Dr. Forsythe presented interim results at the following three enrollment points: 104 patients, 160 patients, and 209 patients. The reported results are so extraordinary that we believe the word spectacular accurately conveys the great promise this protocol holds for millions of cancer patients. The most recent report is available at www.centurywellness.com.

The FDA has been trying for years to stonewall studies on LAPd. They have resorted to the intimidation tactics that they have been employing for the past fifty years. First they try to destroy the product with fabricated accusations in an all-out effort to undermine any research that may support the effectiveness of such a product. If the attempt to destroy the product is not successful, they then resort to attacking the researcher. They use smear campaigns, black PR, false and misleading press releases, and Gestapo-like tactics scaring doctors and patients. They use the media to put forth their false propaganda. Why do they do this? The FDA, as I mentioned to you before, is nothing more than a front for the pharmaceutical industry. The revolving door between people involved in the FDA and the pharmaceutical industry is an absolute joke. The people who run the FDA are paid by the pharmaceutical companies. The drug industry owns the FDA. The drug industry owns the politicians who control the FDA. The FDA does what the drug industry wants. It's all about making money for the drug industry; it's not about protecting consumers, and it's not about curing disease.

BREAST CANCER CURE

Millions of women are frightened about the prospects of breast cancer. Breast cancer is becoming epidemic. The first question that is never addressed is what is causing such an increase in breast cancer. I can assure you that there is study after study after study from healthcare providers around the world that suggest that one of the causes of breast cancer is stress and toxins accumulating in the fatty tissue in the breast. These toxins could include aluminum used in underarm antiperspirants, as well as herbicides, pesticides, and various chemicals used in our food production; cell phones and laptop computers also could be a cause. No one knows or is exactly sure what the cause of breast cancer is. However, if a person were doing the things in Chapter

6, it is my firm belief that the likelihood of you coming down with breast cancer is virtually nil.

One potential way to prevent or reverse cancer is reduction of stress. There are many theories of why stress-reducing techniques reverse cancer. One was discussed in the book *Anatomy of an Illness*. In this book, laughing appeared to put cancer in remission. What are the reasons that reducing stress and laughing can cure cancer? There are many theories.

One of the most promising treatments for breast cancer, and all cancers, seems to be linseed oil, which is flaxseed oil. Canadian researchers gave women with breast cancer one muffin a day which contained linseed oil. Cancers were reduced by over forty-two percent. It appeared to work even more effectively than any form of radiation or chemotherapy. The outrage is why isn't more research being done on linseed and flaxseed oils? The answer is obvious.

As I have mentioned to you before, little if any research is ever conducted on a non-patentable substance. Linseed oil and flaxseed oil cannot be patented; therefore, no drug company will invest any money. When research is allegedly conducted on all-natural non-patentable products, ask yourself who is conducting the research. Who is funding it, and what is the purpose of the research? I can assure you and I can prove that virtually every study done on an "all-natural" product was funded in some way by a pharmaceutical company. The reason the research was conducted was to prove that the natural substance did not work—that was the objective and goal. The studies are set up to prove that fact. The way this is achieved first and foremost is actually changing the definition of a natural product. This was done in the vitamin E study. The organization that conducted the study was owned many times removed, at the end of the day, in effect, by the pharmaceutical companies that sold a drug that competed with vitamin E. The "all-natural" vitamin E that was used in the study was a synthetic form of vitamin E. It was called "all-natural" because the foundation that was doing the study changed the definition of what all-natural vitamin E was. It wasn't all-natural vitamin E at all. This happens all the time. The studies are set up to prove that the natural substances do not work.

If you are concerned about breast cancer, or any cancer, I would highly recommend that you reduce stress; use various stress-reducing techniques as described in the *Natural Cures* book. This also can prevent all types of disease from developing. I would also encourage you to add linseed or flaxseed oil in your diet. Go to your local health food store and enquire. There are many easy ways to include linseed and flaxseed oil in your diet. One particular observation was that when all-natural, not GMO-produced soy protein was added with flaxseed oil and consumed, some cancerous tumors shrunk dramatically.

Additional research has suggested that shark cartilage also would shrink cancers. More research needs to be done. When I make statements like this, many times I am attacked. People say that the studies on shark cartilage do not prove that they shrunk cancers. The response is simple: the studies that were done that show things like shark cartilage not reducing cancers are done with an inferior grade of shark cartilage produced in a way so that it becomes non-effective. This is done purposely by the drug companies to discredit the natural products. The bottom line is there are non-surgical, all-natural ways to cure and prevent cancer; new methods are being developed every day. The key is finding healthcare practitioners who are working with cancer patients on a regular basis, finding out what works and what doesn't work, and are developing the protocols. These doctors are not publishing this information, they are not trying to get on television explaining the truth about this because they know they will be attacked, and they will be in many cases jailed for curing cancer without chemotherapy, drugs, and radiation.

The national media continues to attack me and all those people who are trying to get the truth exposed. It drives me crazy when I see news reports from people who say that natural methods don't work. Where are the news reports talking about the hundreds of thousands of people last year that got chemotherapy, drugs, radiation, and surgery trying to cure their cancer, but died anyway?! How come no one is talking about the hundreds of thousands of people that go to medical doctors and are given drugs or surgical procedures to "cure simple ailments" who wind up dead? How come those stories aren't being made headline news? How come we are not hearing about the hundreds of thousands of people in China and India who are given herbs and using ayurvedic medicine, or herbal medicine, or traditional Chinese medicine and being cured of all their diseases without drugs or surgery of any kind? How come we are not hearing the stories of the millions of people throughout South America who are using plants and traditional Amazon medicine and curing their diseases without any pharmaceutical drugs or surgery? Again, there absolutely is a place for drugs and surgery. The problem is the conflict of interest that the drug companies have. They only want to sell drugs, they do not cure disease, and they can only sell drugs that are patentable. This is why they are hell-bent on hiding the truth about non-patentable, inexpensive, non-drug, and non-surgical ways to cure and prevent disease.

VITAMIN D CUTS CANCER RISK IN HALF STUDY SAYS

The headlines should read: "Revealed—The Pill That Prevents Cancer" and "News Flash—CNN Reports That a Multi-Year Medical Study on 2,300,000 People Shows That Vitamin D Reduces Cancer by 50 Percent." The research is in and of course the news media doesn't report it. When I say it I'm called a liar and promoting quackery, but how can you disagree with the research? Scientists at the University of California found that the natural form of Vitamin D, which comes from the sun, dramatically reduces the chances of developing breast, ovarian, and colon cancer. Report after report after report is now coming in, stating the truth about the benefits of getting natural sunlight. This is a natural cure they don't want you to know about. It's amazing that I am called a person who promotes quackery when I make statements such as natural sunlight is beneficial to your health. I've been called a promoter of quackery because I say eat more organically grown fruits and vegetables. I've been called a promoter of quackery by saying reduce stress, exercise, cleanse your colon, drink pure water without fluoride and chlorine … all these things I say are promoting quackery. The fact is what I expose in the book *Natural Cures* is in fact what millions of people and hundreds of thousands of "doctors" in many disciplines believe, use, and adhere to. These things are in many cases beyond theory and have been "proven" through years of observation.

At one point it was considered quackery to suggest that nutrition played any role in the prevention or curing or disease. It was said that washing your hands before surgery was quackery; it was said that NOT doing bloodletting was quackery. Think of all the things we've done over the years that were accepted medical practices—putting leeches on people's bodies, bloodletting, taking mercury (which we now know kills you)—all common and accepted medical practices. Think of all the drugs that were commonly used that are now off the market because they have been proven to be ineffective and dangerous. Throughout history, those people who rocked the boat about the medical profession, those people who suggested that the status quo needed to be changed, and those people who suggested something that was outside the profitability range of the medical industry were called promoters of quackery. Chiropractors were called quacks, acupuncturists were called quacks, homeopaths were called quacks, massage therapists were called quacks, and even those who prayed were called quacks. Now we know all of those therapies have been scientifically proven beyond any doubt to be in fact workable, effective solutions to disease. The suggestion that exercise was important for health was called quackery. Losing weight to promote health was called quackery. Not smoking for health was called quackery. The list goes on and on.

CHELATION CURES HEART DISEASE
AND OTHER DISEASES

There are two types of chelation, oral chelation and intravenous chelation. Oral chelation can be done at home. There are many oral chelation products on the market. You can go to the internet and search under "oral chelation" and see a host of various products; they are very good. If you want faster results, find a healthcare practitioner in your area that does intravenous chelation. When you do chelation you are putting natural substances into your body that chemically bond with toxic materials that are in your body such as minerals, metals, and chemicals. The chelating agents in either the oral formulation you are taking or the intravenous chelation formula encircle the toxic mineral or metal and carry it from the body via the urine and feces. There are several books written on chelation. Chelation is an inexpensive natural treatment that can cure and prevent disease. It is a natural cure they don't want you to know about. The drug companies cannot make money on oral chelation products or intravenous chelation. It is all-natural and can cause spectacular results. When you chelate the toxins out of your body the most common benefit is opening up the arteries. If you are concerned about blockages in your arteries, chelation could be the answer. You don't need angioplasty or bypass surgery if you do chelation early enough. The increased circulation means you have tremendous other health benefits. Men will not need Viagra in many cases since blood flow throughout the body is dramatically increased. When blood flow is dramatically increased because all the arteries are open, you get more oxygen to the blood, which means your alkalinity pH level goes up, which means you are less prone to cancer or other degenerative diseases. You have more energy. People's skin, hair, and nails look better and healthier. Wrinkles can go away. You look younger. You become more flexible. All of your organs start becoming more vibrant and alive—younger and healthier. It is a tremendous practice that I do myself.

CHAPTER 7

How Governments Around the World Con You

I do not read a single newspaper, and I feel myself infinitely the happier for it. The man who reads nothing at all is better educated than the man who reads newspapers.

—Thomas Jefferson

Once the media touches a story the facts are lost forever.

—Norman Mailer

From my previous newsletters, here are some articles that tell the story exposing corruption throughout our government.

I have done the unheard of. I have sued the big, mighty, and all-powerful Federal Trade Commission! Never before in history has an individual citizen decided to fight the goliath in Washington and stop the misleading of the American public. The Federal Trade Commission is one of the most corrupt political organizations in the world. It was commissioned to protect consumers from monopolies and protect consumers from false and misleading advertising, amongst other things. Unfortunately, today, the Federal Trade Commission does the exact opposite. The FTC actually actively engages in protecting the monopolies that exist, and protecting the companies who are putting out false and misleading advertising. Additionally, the Federal Trade Commission is probably the number one violator of its own false and misleading advertising standards.

The FTC repeatedly puts out press releases that are flagrantly and blatantly false and misleading. Corruption must stop. The government must stop taking advantage of the citizens. The large multinational corporations must stop putting profit above ethics, integrity, and honesty. We, as a society, are being made sick purposely so that large companies can make billions of dollars in profits. This must cease. The FTC is engaged in helping this to continue to occur. They must be stopped. The FTC is supposed to protect us; instead it is protecting the large multinational corporations.

Consider this, the Federal Trade Commission takes no action against large multinational corporations in relation to false and misleading advertising. Isn't it surprising, the large multinational corporations never engage in any false and misleading advertising even though they produce the majority of ads? The reason the FTC takes no action against the large companies advertising is not because they are not false and misleading, they flagrantly are, but because those companies are paying millions of dollars to lobbyists and politicians who are then telling the FTC not to take action against them. The most flagrant example of this is the ad for the drug Celebrex. This ad was so blatantly false and misleading that the FDA actually said that this ad must be taken off the market because it is so false and misleading. The Federal Trade Commission is the agency that is supposed to take action against companies that produce false and misleading advertising and rip off the consumers. Here is an ad that was deemed false and misleading, and deemed to have ripped off consumers of hundreds of millions of dollars, yet the FTC remains silent. The FTC should have sued the manufacturer of Celebrex, required the company to pay millions of dollars in fines, and give one hundred percent consumer redress for all the people who took that drug based on the false misrepresentations in the advertisement, but the FTC takes no action. Why? Because of political payoffs.

The FTC is not interested in protecting the consumers; it is interested in protecting the profits of the large companies. The FTC repeatedly sues people like myself who advertise truthfully and honestly, but whose products and opinions can have an adverse effect on the large companies. This is how the FTC protects the monopolies and protects the profits of the large corporations. This is wrong and must be stopped, which is why I have taken this unprecedented action on behalf of all citizens by suing the Federal Trade Commission. Here is a copy of the press release relating to this action. For more information go to www.kevinfightsback.com.

KEVIN TRUDEAU SUES FEDERAL TRADE COMMISSION FOR "FALSE ADVERTISING"
National Consumer Advocate and FTC Critic
Seeks End to Ongoing Retaliation

Chicago, February 28, 2005　Kevin Trudeau, an author who is fast becoming one of the nation's leading consumer activists, filed today two separate suits against the United States government charging the Federal Trade Commission with publishing false and misleading information.

Mr. Trudeau is suing the FTC for very much the same reason that the FTC sues people—for, in essence, a form of false advertising. According to the suits, the FTC has, by its own standards, committed a flagrant violation of the rules governing deceptive communications.

In an agreement to settle prior to litigation then pending in the United States District Court before the Northern District of Illinois, the government expressly acknowledged that "[t]here have been no findings or admissions of wrongdoing or liability by [Kevin Trudeau]."

Within days, however, the FTC issued a news release maligning Mr. Trudeau in language that directly contradicts the terms of the settlement agreement by falsely implying that Mr. Trudeau was found guilty of false advertising.

Mr. Trudeau is charging that the FTC—again, to use the FTC's own articulated standard—given the "net impression" in its press release that Mr. Trudeau has been found guilty of wrongdoing, is a habitual false advertiser, and was ordered to pay a fine. According to the suits, these are blatant falsehoods, which additionally rob Mr. Trudeau of any benefit of the settlement agreement.

On February 16, 2005, Mr. Trudeau, through his lawyers, wrote to the FTC asking the agency to remove the misleading news release from its website, issue a retraction, post the retraction, and disseminate it to all the news agencies that received the original release.

On February 22, Christian White, Deputy General Counsel for Administrative Law and Ethics, rebuffed this request by asserting that the release does not violate the settlement agreement because "nothing in the press release refers to any 'findings' of fact or law ..."

Astonishingly, the FTC is thus defending its actions related to the settlement agreement by stating that its published allegations about Mr. Trudeau, which are presented in their news release as fact, are indeed unsubstantiated.

"The FTC has played fast and loose with the facts," said David Bradford, an attorney with Jenner & Block who represented Mr. Trudeau in his settlement with the FTC and in his current lawsuits against the agency. "If an advertiser manipulated the truth like the FTC has in its website and news release, the FTC would not hesitate to sue them for misleading the public. The FTC has disregarded their first and foremost obligation—to promote the truth."

Even the headline of the release was misleading, Bradford said. It stated that Mr. Trudeau has been banned from airing infomercials, implying a total ban. In fact, there is no total ban—indeed, Mr. Trudeau is currently airing one of the most successful infomercials of all time, for a book which is critical of the FTC.

The lawsuits accordingly charge the FTC with retaliation against Mr. Trudeau. In his publications, and in a highly popular series of TV infomercials, Trudeau has bluntly criticized federal agencies and the FTC in particular for working with the pharmaceutical industry to stifle discussion and marketing of natural food and medicine alternatives.

Mr. Trudeau is the author of *Natural Cures "They" Don't Want You to Know About*, which discusses natural remedies for common ailments and diseases that don't involve expensive drugs or high-priced medical consultation. The book has become a best-seller.

In one suit, Mr. Trudeau seeks a declaratory judgment that the FTC's news release is false and misleading, that the FTC has exceeded its authority, and that the FTC has wrongfully sought to chill Mr. Trudeau's exercise of his First Amendment rights. That suit seeks an injunctive order requiring the FTC to cease its wrongful conduct and correct its misleading statements. Mr.

Trudeau's second suit seeks unspecified monetary damages for injury to his business.

"This breach of contract is so bald-faced that it can only represent a concerted attempt by the government to put Kevin out of business," said Kimball Anderson, a lawyer with Winston & Strawn who also represents Mr. Trudeau. "Their news release repeats charges that, in the course of litigation, were never adjudicated. And now (in its February 22 letter) the FTC even admits it."

The FTC news release was, the suits charge, additionally designed to maximize negative media coverage of Mr. Trudeau and his business. It is evident from media coverage that the strategy has been unfortunately successful, as the resulted coverage appears to have relied primarily, if not entirely, on the FTC release.

I need your support in this action. You can write the Federal Trade Commission and tell them you are outraged at how they mislead the pubic and that you back me. Send your mail to Federal Trade Commission, 600 Pennsylvania Avenue, N.W., Washington, D.C. 20580; or fax to (202) 326-2012, Attention: Consumer Response Center (CRC); or e-mail by going to www.ftc.gov and clicking on "File a Complaint."

FDA FOUND GUILTY OF
ABUSE OF POWER!

In my book *Natural Cures* I talk about the outrageous FDA ban of the herb ma-huang, a natural source of Ephedra. I have repeatedly stated that the FDA abuses its power. I believe the FDA is not protecting consumers, but rather used by the drug industry to protect the profits of the powerful pharmaceutical cartel. The drug companies spend hundreds of millions of dollars trying to persuade lawmakers to ban safe and effective all-natural remedies. The pharmaceutical cartel spends hundreds of millions of dollars trying to convince the public that natural remedies are dangerous and ineffective, and their pharmaceutical drugs are effective and safe. THE EXACT OPPOSITE IS TRUE! A perfect example of this was when the FDA banned the sale of Ephedra. The FDA claimed that Ephedra was so dangerous that it had to be banned from American shelves. The FDA claimed that there was some evidence that the deaths of 153 people were LINKED to the use of

Ephedra. The FDA did state that there was no conclusive evidence that those 153 deaths were caused even partially by Ephedra, but there seemed to be some potential link. The FDA deemed that this proved that Ephedra was so dangerous that it had to be banned totally. Keep in mind that over ten million people had used Ephedra during this time. I have stated that this is an outrage. The FDA has not banned aspirin even though 2,000 people die every year by taking a single dose of aspirin. The FDA has not banned Vioxx even though it is confirmed that well over 100,000 people have died by taking Vioxx. The FDA has not banned drug after drug after drug even though hundreds of thousands of people have been confirmed dead by the use of these drugs, yet, the FDA bans the all-natural herb ma-huang?! Can you see the flagrant abuse of power? Can you see how the FDA is pandering to the whims of the pharmaceutical industry? Can you see how the FDA does everything it can to protect the profits of the drug companies?

Because of this outrageous FDA ban of the perfectly safe and very effective herb ma-huang, a Utah company sued the FDA. After months in the courts the judge strikes down the ban on Ephedra! The FDA loses! The judge's ruling prevents the FDA from stopping the sale of Ephedra. The judge agreed that Ephedra was WRONGLY being regulated by the FDA as a drug and not a food! This is a great win for all of us. The FDA has finally been put in its place. The judge's statement is now forcing the FDA to follow the rules that Congress set down for it instead of making their own rules and acting as judge, jury, and executioner! The FDA said they will continue to fight this ruling.

The bottom line here is it is now becoming more and more evident every day that the FDA is not protecting consumers, but is in fact protecting the monopolies and the profits of the drug industry. It is more obvious now than ever that the FDA is working in conjunction with the drug companies to try to make you believe that natural remedies are ineffective and dangerous, and that drugs are safe and effective. The exact opposite is true. Drugs are ineffective, dangerous, and cause all disease. Natural remedies are very effective, totally safe, and cause no disease; they help the body cure itself. My newsletter, my book, and the website www.naturalcures.com are at the forefront of making these changes occur. Please continue to support the newsletter, encourage your friends and relatives to subscribe, join naturalcures.com and encourage others to do the same, and get as many people as you can to buy the *Natural Cures* book.

NEW YORK ATTORNEY GENERAL'S OFFICE
TRIES TO DEBUNK ME!

I state in my book that one of the methods that the United States Government and other governments around the world use to stop the free flow of information regarding natural non-drug and non-surgical ways to cure and prevent disease is to start a negative PR campaign against that individual person. I state that government agencies actually have sub-agencies within them that do nothing more than collect information and put out smear campaigns. I mention that these agencies put out press releases, which are false and misleading, but are picked up by the news organizations and presented as fact. This is exactly what is happening to me right now. I was contacted by the New York State Consumer Protection Board. This Board is allegedly a part of the Attorney General's Office. The Director of Marketing and Public Relations, Jon Sorensen, sent us a communication asking some very bizarre and interesting questions. First off, notice Mr. Sorensen's title—Director of Marketing and Public Relations. This appears to be a person whose job is to smear those who try to expose government corruption. He is the "public relations man." My insiders tell me that this sub-organization within the New York Attorney General's Office is nothing more than a debunking campaign organization. They spend their time, money, and efforts collecting information, putting out press releases and smearing people's reputation. They do exactly what I say in my book. They are nothing more than "debunkers." They are like Joseph Goebbels of Nazi Germany. They are the propaganda machine trying to brainwash the public into believing what they want. They use their power, in my opinion, in an unjust way. They are abusing their power and are nothing more than a pawn of the lobbyist groups and organizations that finance the campaigns of the politicians. Since my book is having an adverse affect on the pharmaceutical industry and the food industry, those industries are pouring millions of dollars into public relations firms and lobbying groups, all trying to influence politicians into using their political power and clout to squash and discredit people such as myself. I want to expose this organization and its corrupt nature. Here are some of the outrageous questions that Mr. Sorensen asked:

1. Does Mr. Trudeau own a microwave?
2. Can you tell me what meetings Mr. Trudeau is referring to in his infomercials?

3. In Mr. Trudeau's June 2005 newsletter, we would like to know what proof does Mr. Trudeau have that a meeting took place between the AMA, pharmaceutical companies, and past commissioners of the FDA.

4. In the June 2005 newsletter Mr. Trudeau talks a lot about cancer. What is the cure for cancer; and secondly, what is the cure being suppressed?

As you can see, Mr. Sorensen is asking me questions about the contents of my newsletter and book. The contents of my newsletter and book are clearly defined as my opinions. This member of the Attorney General's Office is now questioning my "opinions." How dare he try to intimidate me and try to suppress my First Amendment rights? Whether or not I own a microwave is irrelevant. Of course I do not and never will. As a matter of fact, there are no microwave ovens in any of the offices that I am involved with. As you can see, this particular organization is doing nothing more than an intimidation campaign, trying to gather information to put out a bad PR campaign against me. I hope you are as outraged as I am.

I would like to ask a few questions of Mr. Sorensen. For example:

1. Does he or any of his family members now or ever have owned stock in any pharmaceutical company or food company?

2. Who are the major contributors to the political campaigns in which he is involved? Could it be the pharmaceutical companies or the food industry?

3. Does he have any friends working within the FDA or any pharmaceutical companies or the food industry, or friends working at the FTC?

This seems to be politically motivated. He is simply trying to stop me from expressing my opinions and exercising my First Amendment rights. This is an absolute outrage and will not be tolerated. I am taking aggressive, immediate action by investigating this organization and the people involved. I am going to get to the bottom of why this inquiry was started. I'm going to find out where these people go and eat, who they are meeting with, where they make their money, and what is behind this. I will not leave a stone unturned. I will expose these people for the frauds and corrupt individuals that they probably are. If I am wrong in my assumption, after my investigative team concludes their mission, I will report to you this fact. I certainly hope I am wrong, but if you are as outraged as I am you can contact Mr. Sorensen at (518) 473-9472, or fax him at (518) 474-2896. His cell phone is (518) 527-4496, or call him toll-free at (800) 697-1220, extension 3-9472. Simply tell him you're as mad as hell and not going to take it any more, and that you support Kevin Trudeau.

I AM RIGHT AGAIN:
FAKE RESEARCH HITS ALL-TIME HIGH

One of the things I state over and over in my book is the fact that research and studies are generally fake, false, and misleading. The FTC, the FDA, and the pharmaceutical companies, as well as the food industry continually refer to "scientific evidence," they refer to studies, research, and scientific evidence. I have contended that virtually all "scientific evidence," all studies, and all research are in fact misleading, false, fraudulent, and in some cases, flat-out fake. I have given hundreds of examples of how this is and has been proven to be true. Now, national headlines are saying the same thing. According to the Associated Press, "Misconduct by U.S. researchers reached record highs last year. Research suggests that the amount of fake studies that are being discovered is but a small fraction of all the incidents of fabrication, falsification, and misleading information. As an example, Dr. Andrew Freidman, on the night of his twelfth wedding anniversary, was terrified. This brilliant surgeon and researcher at Brigham and Women's Hospital and Harvard Medical School feared that he was about to lose everything. His career, his family, the life he built, all because his boss was coming closer and closer to the truth: for the past three years Freidman had been faking, actually making up data, in some of the most respected peer reviewed studies he had published in top medical journals! 'It is difficult for me to describe the degree of panic and irrational thought that I was going through,' he would later tell an inquiry panel at Harvard. On this night, March 13, 1995, he had been ordered in writing by his department chair to clear up what appeared to be suspicious data, but Freidman didn't clear things up. 'I did something which was the worst possible thing I could have done,' he testified. He went to the medical record room and for the next three or four hours he pulled out permanent medical files of a handful of patients, then covered up his lies, scribbling in the information he needed to support his study. 'I created data. I made it up. I also made up patients that were fictitious,' he testified. Freidman's wife met him at the door when he came home that night. He wept uncontrollably. The next morning he had an emergency appointment with a psychiatrist, but he didn't tell the therapist the truth and his lies continued for ten more days during which time he delivered a letter and copies of the doctored files to his boss. Eventually he broke down, admitting first to his wife and psychiatrist, and later to his colleagues and managers, what he had been doing. Freidman formally confessed, retracted his articles, apologized to his colleagues and was punished. Today, he has resurrected his career as Senior Director of Clinical Research of Ortho-McNall Pharmaceutical, Inc., a Johnson & Johnson company. He refused to speak with the Associated Press, but his case, recorded in a seven-foot-high stack of documents at the Massachusetts Board of Registration and Medicine, tells a story of one man's struggle with power, lies, and the crushing pressure of academia."

The Associated Press has done a great job in my opinion of uncovering and exposing in specific terms people that have lied and falsified studies. However, it is important to know that this is not an isolated case. Directly from the Associated Press article there are many, many more examples. I will share these examples with you in future newsletters. The important thing to note here is that "scientific evidence," "studies," and "official scientific research data" are and appear to be, generally speaking, almost always misleading. And, as horrifying as it sounds, it appears that it is also false, deceptive, untruthful, and in many cases, pure and simply fake. It is scary to think that "scientific evidence" and official peer-reviewed "studies" are being doctored, made up, falsified, and are pure unreliable untruths. Remember the movie *The Fugitive* with Harrison Ford? Remember how the doctor was falsifying the study so that his magic drug would be approved and he would make hundreds of millions of dollars? Folks, the scary thing is, based on what I have uncovered, this appears to be the norm! Faking and falsifying studies, creating scientific evidence out of thin air seems to be the standard operating procedure. It appears that these are not isolated instances, but in fact, common occurrences. Every time we hear about a study and I send my crew in and start reviewing and digging and investigating, over and over again the same thing comes up. The information is absolutely misleading and, in many cases, plain and simply fake. I have been saying this all along and now the Associated Press and other organizations are coming forward as well. I thank the Associated Press for producing such a wonderful article, and I will continue to quote from this article in upcoming newsletters.

I WAS RIGHT AGAIN: SCIENTIFIC FACTS
REVERSED OVER AND OVER AGAIN

In the book *Natural Cures* I mention that most "scientific facts" are not facts at all, but rather the opinions of people. I mention that most medical facts and scientific facts are usually changed as time goes on and more information becomes available. I mention that the scientific and medical communities are arrogant when they state things as fact instead of stating, "Based on the information we know at this time we believe [such and such] to be true, but we also know that as more information becomes available this conclusion or opinion will change." Scientists never say this. Medical doctors never say this. What they say is, "This is how it is—period." Obviously, when they make these absolute statements and are reversed later on, they never apologize for being arrogant, they never apologize for being wrong in their initial conclusion, they never apologize or state that boy we made a big mistake—we believed this to be true and we were 100 percent wrong. They never state this. They just pull out a new piece of data, present it as a fact, trying to convince people that they are "God."

Here's what the Associated Press says, by AP medical writer Lindsey Tanner: "New research highlights a frustrating fact about science, what is good for you yesterday frequently turns out to be bad for you tomorrow." This conclusion came in a review of major studies published in three influential medical journals, including forty-five highly publicized studies that initially claimed a drug or other treatment worked. Subsequent research totally contradicted the results of almost twenty percent of the first studies. Here is the scary part: "Contradicted and potentially exaggerated findings are not uncommon in the most visible and most influential original research"! The article goes on to state how prominent journals, including the *New England Journal of Medicine, JAMA,* and *Lancet,* need studies that are breakthrough, revolutionary, and conclusive. These magazines are profit magazines that need to have "content" in the form of studies. This article goes on to verify virtually everything I've said in relation to studies. The fact is studies are manufactured, exaggerated, misleading, falsified and, in many cases, flat-out fake. Whatever a study says today, you could easily produce a study tomorrow that will give you the exact opposite results. These studies are paid for by the people who need the specific result. They cannot be trusted. I'm glad to see, over and over again in the major press, that the things that I have been saying are in fact being verified.

KEVIN TRUDEAU SUES THE NEW YORK STATE CONSUMER PROTECTION BOARD!

I continue to do the unthinkable. As you know, I have filed two major lawsuits against the Federal Trade Commission, one of the most corrupt federal organizations in America. As I have stated in my book, I believe that virtually all state and federal agencies that are "allegedly" in place to protect consumers actually have no interest in protecting the consumers. These agencies actually protect the profits of the large multinational corporations and protect the profits of the companies and individuals who donate to the politicians. I have repeatedly shown evidence that these organizations do not conduct true investigations, but rather spread "negative PR" to suppress individuals' First Amendment free speech rights. This has happened for decades. It has happened to me repeatedly. The Federal Trade Commission and other government agencies have repeatedly deceived and misled the public about me. They do this because I am exposing the corruption in these organizations, and exposing the corruption in the multinational corporations. I am the number one person on these agencies' hit list. My insiders tell me that there are actual "task forces consisting of dozens of individuals, funded by the multinational corporations" whose only objective is to find something on Kevin Trudeau and shut him up. These agencies are desperate to stop me from exposing the corruption that exists at the highest levels of government. I state in my book the fact that government agencies which appear to "protect consumers" have a habit of discrediting people such as me by putting out a negative "PR" campaign. I state in my book that one of the most common methods by which government agencies do this is by putting together false and misleading press releases, which are then in turn picked up by the news media and written as "fact." The important elements here are that these government agencies do not do any type of true investigation. They have an agenda; they know exactly what they are trying to achieve, which is to discredit the individual involved; and they put together a blatantly false and misleading press release. The news agencies take these press releases and present them to the public as if it is factual, when in truth this is categorically not the case. I talk about this at length in my book, and here is a perfect example. The current infomercials I have running for my book were sent to the Federal Trade Commission for review BEFORE they were ever broadcast. The Federal

Trade Commission says they cannot "approve" any infomercial. However, they did fully review the infomercial and wrote back that they have no objections to us running the infomercial. Therefore, even though they cannot "approve" the infomercial, they have fully reviewed it and have determined that the infomercial is protected by my First Amendment right of free speech. The FTC has determined, by not objecting to the infomercial, that the infomercial is not false and misleading in any way. The fact of the matter is none of these infomercials are false and misleading. I tell the truth; I tell what I believe; and I tell my opinions—all things that I have the right to do under the U.S. Constitution. It is insane to think that any of my current infomercials for my book are misleading the public when less than five percent of the people who buy my book ever return it. To put this in perspective, the average return rate of infomercial products is over fifteen percent! Obviously, people who see my show and read my book do not feel they are being "misled."

The FTC got frustrated. They are furious that I am running my infomercials and selling so many books. They are very upset that over five million people have purchased my first book. They do not want people to read my book. They do not want people to believe anything I say. They do not want people to find out the truth that I am exposing in my book and in the newsletter. They are trying everything they can to stop me from exposing their own corruption, and the corruption in the pharmaceutical industry and the multinational corporations. In my book I mention a tactic that the government uses when one agency cannot do the job of silencing a whistleblower or critic. The tactic is that they call upon other agencies or state agencies to do the dirty work for them. The FTC has done this with me on other occasions. They went to the FDA, and they went to another state organization to try to stop me from selling coral calcium. They are doing it again. It appears that the FTC worked in conjunction with this "New York State Consumer Protection Board" to organize a vicious, slanderous attack on me. This Board is not interested in protecting consumers. How do I know this? I know it because this Board had virtually no complaints from any consumers about my book or my infomercials. Why in the world is this Board allegedly spending time and effort to warn people about a book and an infomercial about which nobody is complaining, but virtually everybody is praising? Can you see my point? So, it appears that what happened was the FTC got ahold of this Board and asked them to start a smear campaign and try to get the news media to run negative publicity on me personally, my book, and my ad—all in an attempt to stop people from buying the book, reading the book, and believing the book.

What the FTC and the New York State Consumer Protection Board don't understand is they are not dealing with a normal person. They are dealing with Kevin Trudeau. I refuse to be pushed around, stepped on, and have these government agencies strip me of my constitutional rights. I absolutely will fight back with everything I have. This is why I have filed a massive lawsuit against the New York State Consumer Protection Board and the individual people involved for trying to stifle my First Amendment right of free speech. I have also sued them for producing a false and misleading press release. You can read the entire lawsuit by going to www.kevinfightsback.com. Let me point out a couple of interesting things so you can see firsthand how outrageous these people are. It is important that you see right in front of you, in black and white, that these organizations are corrupt, lie, deceive, and mislead the public. It is important that you see in black and white that these organizations produce fraudulent documents, and are doing nothing to protect consumers, but doing everything they can to smear me and discredit me by putting out false and misleading information.

- The press release states that my book does not contain natural cures. This is categorically untrue. When you read the book I repeatedly state over and over again "this is the natural cure." I specifically say what the cures are; I specifically give you what my opinion is as to what the cures are; and I specifically say what the cause of disease is and how to cure it.

- The press release states that I am misrepresenting the contents of my book. This is categorically untrue. How could the New York State Consumer Protection Board come to that conclusion without allowing me due process of law or trial by jury? How can they come to that conclusion when the FTC itself has reviewed my infomercials and came to a completely different conclusion?

- The press release states I am using false endorsements to encourage consumers to buy the book. This is categorically, 100 percent untrue. Every endorsement for the book is 100 percent real, legitimate, and unscripted. Not one person has been paid a cent to endorse my book.

- The press release states, "From cover to cover the book is a fraud." Obviously, this is a lie, and this is nothing more than an attempt to discredit me and try to stop people from buying the book.

- They state my infomercial with Tammy Faye Baker gives the impression that she is endorsing the book and opposes chemotherapy. This is categorically untrue. Tammy Faye Baker was paid to interview me for my infomercial. I met her briefly before the taping. We never talked beforehand. I had no idea what questions she would ask. She read the book before the interview. We sat down and did an unscripted, live-to-tape interview for 28 minutes and 30 seconds. The show was not edited. Everything that Tammy Faye Baker said, she said out of her own volition. She was not coached, coerced, or encouraged to say anything. She asked questions and made her own comments.

- The press release says consumers in New York and across the country are complaining that the book is just another commercial for Trudeau's website. This is categorically not true. Over five million people have purchased the book. As with anything, you cannot please all the people all the time, but over 90 percent of the people that purchase the book absolutely love the book. Anyone that doesn't gets a complete refund, no questions asked.

- The press release states on the back of the book I list endorsements with a quotation from Dr. Herbert Ley. They claim he could not have endorsed the book because he died in 2001. This is false and misleading. The New York Consumer Protection Board is trying to deceive you. On the back of the book I do not list endorsements. On the back of the book I give quotes from people whose opinions or thoughts agree with what I say in the book. I could have quoted Albert Einstein, which I did in the first chapter. He died before the book was written too. I could have quoted Abraham Lincoln, or George Washington, or anyone else for that matter. They are not endorsing the book by reading it, they are making a comment which is truthful and documented, and those comments verify and back up what I say in the book.

- The press release states people with real illnesses are being misled. That is his opinion. My opinion is people with real illnesses are being misled BY THE DRUG COMPANIES!

It goes on to talk about how many times the Federal Trade Commission has levied fraud charges against me for the various products that I have sold. What it does not state is that in all of those ridiculous, outrageous cases, the FTC could never find any wrongdoing! In other words, all of these charges were trumped up and fraudulent themselves. The FTC continues to attack me over and over again on baseless grounds. So what. I'm suing the FTC too. The fact that the FTC is suing me when there are no consumers complaining about any of my products proves the fact that these organizations are only trying to discredit me and not protect consumers at all.

- The press releases state that I tell the joke about a doctor who says to his patient, "If it hurts to lift your arm, don't lift your arm" three times in the book. That's categorically untrue. What I say in the book is, "If a person walks in to a doctor and says every time I hit my foot with a hammer it hurts. How do I cure the pain? The answer is stop hitting your foot with a hammer." That's radically different because lifting your arm is a normal function that the body should be able to do. Hitting your foot with a hammer is not. The press release is false and misleading. They go on to state my opinions about the fact that natural remedies can virtually cure any disease are preposterous; therefore, no one should read the book and I shouldn't be allowed to sell the book. This is a flagrant violation of my First Amendment rights. Certainly he has an opinion to believe that my opinions are preposterous, but he does not have the right as a U.S. Government official to state publicly that my opinions are preposterous and therefore, no one should read the book and I should not be allowed to write the book or sell the book. That is a violation of my civil rights and constitutional rights. When the government puts out opinions they are picked up by the media as fact. They hold more weight than any other group in this country. The government has a responsibility to put out information that is fair and balanced. The government also has a right to protect individuals' constitutional rights, not suppress them.

- The press release states that I claim I don't profit from products and information in my book, but I can see that I do make profit from books sold on my website; therefore I am misleading the public. This is outrageous. On my commercial and in my book I am very clear that I make no money on any product that I talk about; I only make money on the books that I sell. I am very clear and very straightforward about how I make money and how I don't make money. This organization is outrageous.

Immediately, this press release was picked up by the Associated Press and picked up by the news media all across the country. The news media routinely reads these press releases as fact. The news media, magazines, and newspapers do not want you to read my book either. As a matter of fact, *Time* magazine will not run ads for my book. Why? Because *Time* magazine receives too much money from the pharmaceutical industry for all the ads the drug companies run. *USA Today* will not run ads for my book, although I was number one on their bestseller list! They also ran two articles about me, but they refuse to allow me to run ads for my book and tell my side of the story. Why? Because the people involved in *USA Today* make too much money from the drug companies. My book really should be called *The Book "They" Don't Want You to Read!*

This is why I am suing the New York State Consumer Protection Board and the individual people involved personally. I will attack anyone who tries to take my First Amendment rights away from me. I will attack anyone who tries to suppress my freedom of speech. I will attack anyone who tries to slander or defame me. I know the drug companies are spending tens of millions of dollars trying to put negative PR against me and trying to get people to stop buying and reading my book. They cannot succeed. Over five million people now have purchased the book. Virtually everywhere I go people come up to me, hug me, and thank me for the information in the book. I get tens of thousands of bits of correspondence from people who tell me that the book has changed their life, opened their eyes to the truth, and about how doing the things in the book has given them more energy, reduced their stress, relieved depression, eliminated pain, cured them of diabetes, or given them hope against major degenerative disease. I get so many letters from people who say their acid reflux is gone and they are off the stupid drugs! People are telling me how their cholesterol is in check, and their energy levels have skyrocketed since doing the things in the book. I know what I'm doing is right; I know I'm having a positive impact.

I need your help. Why don't you call the New York State Consumer Protection Board and tell these people that you are outraged at their press release! Tell them you like my book, that you do not feel deceived, and that your life is better because of it. Let them know how you feel. The two people involved are Jon Sorensen, Director of Marketing and Public Relations, New York State Consumer Protection Board, 5 Empire State Parkway, Suite 2101, Albany, NY 12223, www.nysconsumer.gov, phone number (518) 473-9472, fax (518) 527-4496, and Teresa A. Santiago, Chairperson and Executive Director, phone number (518) 474-3514, and fax (518) 474-2474.

VIRTUALLY ALL "SCIENTIFIC STUDIES" ARE FALSE, MISLEADING, AND FRAUDULENT

Earlier I pointed out the fact that virtually all "scientific studies" are, at best, misleading. Most of these can be deemed to be flat-out lies, fraud, and pure deception. On my website www.naturalcures.com I will be listing many of these in great detail. Let me point out a few more examples proving this statement to be true. These examples come directly from the Associated Press, Martha Mendoza, national writer.

- Eric Poehlman, a once prominent nutrition researcher, was sentenced in federal court for fabricating research data to obtain a $542,000 federal grant while working as a professor at the University of Vermont College of Medicine. He made up research between 1992 and 2000 on issues like menopause, aging, and hormone supplements to win millions of dollars in grants from the federal government. He additionally received a $1 million chair at the University of Montreal.

- Dr. Gary Kammer, a Wake Forest University professor and alleged lupus expert, was found to have made up two families and their medical conditions in grant applications to the National Institutes of Health—all in an attempt to get federal grant money.

- Dr. Ali Sultan, an award-winning malaria researcher at the Harvard School of Public Health, was found guilty of plagiarizing text and figures, and falsifying data in an attempt to receive federal funds to study malaria drugs for the pharmaceutical industry. Amazingly, he is now a faculty member at the Cornell Medical School in Qatar.

The AP article goes on to state that scientists have been cheating for decades! Examples:

- Dr. William Summerlin, a top-ranking Sloan-Kettering Cancer Institute researcher, actually used a magic marker to make black patches on fur on white mice in an attempt to prove that his new skin graft technique was working!

The list goes on, and on, and on—study after study, after study, after study. It shows that virtually ALL studies are misleading and, in many cases, fraudulent, falsified, and fake. "Scientific studies" can never be trusted.

Just as significant is the fact that information that is known is in many cases never told. Example: I have as an informant, one of the top-ranking insiders at Sloan-Kettering Cancer Institute. The information that is being suppressed is the absolute fact that in every single cancer tumor that Sloan-Kettering takes out of a patient there are massive amounts of pesticides. That's right. There is known evidence that is being suppressed that all cancer tumors are loaded with pesticides. Not 99 percent, but all. Does it mean that pesticides cause tumors and cancer? Well, it certainly would appear that pesticides are at least a contributing factor, although most people can now conclude that pesticides are a significant cause of skin cancer. This is another reason why you have to do the things I say in the book, such as stop eating regular fruits and vegetables and eating only organic. Pesticides cause skin cancer.

The fact is scientific studies can't be trusted because all of this information that is being put out is put out based on the financial interests of the people putting out the information. Remember, it's all about the money. You can believe me because I have no financial interest in anything I say. I'm telling you the information is truthful because I don't care one way or another whether you believe it or don't, it won't make me one red cent one way or the other. I'm giving you the information that's pure, honest, and true. There is virtually no one else that can say that.

The amount of advertising that drug companies do on television, radio, and in print is at an all-time high and growing. Drug manufacturers have only one goal, that is to increase profits. The only way they can increase profits is to convince people that they need to use more drugs. Drug companies simply want more people taking more drugs more consistently. Drug companies are not interested in health, they're interested in increasing sales and profits.

In order to make this happen, drug companies are producing very sophisticated advertisements for television, radio, and print. Additionally, drug companies are producing direct mail pieces. All of these ads are designed to convince you that your life will be better if you take drugs. Millions of dollars are spent using the most sophisticated brainwashing and advertising tactics to produce advertisements that actually are not only false and misleading, but are specifically and purposely designed to get you to believe something that is categorically not true.

Drug companies hire advertising agencies to produce these ads. The drug companies and the advertising agencies come up with the specific "hot buttons" that they must get you to consciously or subconsciously believe when you watch the ad. The drug companies and the advertising agencies know that these "hot buttons" are untrue. An example is they may want you to believe that you'll have more energy if you take their drug, even though the exact opposite is true. The drug companies know they cannot state that you will have more energy because that is a flagrant lie. That would be blatant false and misleading advertising. So they used sophisticated techniques to produce advertisements that get you to consciously or subconsciously, subtly believe that their drug will increase your energy. This is manipulation. This is flagrant and blatant false and misleading advertising. The drug companies have produced so many of these flagrantly and blatantly false and misleading ads and so many complaints have been filed that the FDA actually has stated on multiple occasions that drug company ads are false and misleading.

This is important. Let me state this again, there are so many complaints being filed that the FDA had to actually state that many of these drug company ads are false and misleading. The outrage is the drug companies are allowed to keep the hundreds of millions of dollars in profits that they have received by lying and deceiving consumers. The drug companies have not been penalized.

The Federal Trade Commission is the agency that is supposed to file lawsuits against companies that produce false and misleading advertising and rip off consumers. Here is a flagrant example of corporate and government corruption. The FDA has stated that the drug ads are false and misleading. The FDA has stated that millions of consumers were ripped off and lied to and bought products under false pretenses. The drug companies have made hundreds of millions of dollars by selling products under false and misleading pretenses and flagrantly breaking the law. Yet, the Federal Trade Commission takes absolutely no action against the drug companies. There is no penalty. This is the outrage. This is why you cannot trust the FDA or the FTC to protect you. The FDA and the FTC are only protecting the profits of the big multinational corporations.

THE FLU VACCINE SCAM

Vaccines are a scam. Getting vaccinated is one of the worst things you could do to yourself, your children, and your loved ones. Vaccinations do not prevent illness, they cause illness. The mercury in the vaccines cause autism, brain damage, and disease. The vaccines themselves cause the body to be in an unnatural state and set you up for major disease. In the *Natural Cures* book I give you several other books that I recommend to discuss vaccines. They are: *A Shot in the Dark*, by Harris L. Coulter and Barbara Loe Fisher; *Vaccines: Are They Really Safe & Effective?*, by Neil Z. Miller; and *What Your Doctor May Not Tell You About Children's Vaccinations*, by Stephanie Cave, M.D., F.A.A.F.P., with Deborah Mitchell.

Let me give you the historical facts exposing the dangers and ineffectiveness of vaccines.

In 1871–72, England, with 98 percent of the population aged between 2 and 50 vaccinated against smallpox, it experienced its worst ever smallpox outbreak with 45,000 deaths. During the same period in Germany, with a vaccination ratio of 96 percent, there were over 125,000 deaths from smallpox. (The Hadwen Documents.)

In Germany, compulsory mass vaccination against diphtheria commenced in 1940 and by 1945 diphtheria cases were up from 40,000 to 250,000. (*Don't Get Stuck!*, Hannah Allen.)

In the USA in 1960, two virologists discovered that both polio vaccines were contaminated with the SV 40 virus which causes cancer in animals as well as changes in human cell tissue cultures. Millions of children had been injected with these vaccines. (*Medical Journal of Australia*, March 17, 1973, p. 555.)

In 1967, Ghana was declared measles-free by the World Health Organization after 96 percent of its population was vaccinated. In 1972, Ghana experienced one of its worst measles outbreaks with its highest ever mortality rate. (Dr. H. Albonico, *MMR Vaccine Campaign in Switzerland*, March 1990.)

In the UK between 1970 and 1990, over 200,000 cases of whooping cough occurred in fully vaccinated children. (Community Disease Surveillance Centre, UK.)

In the 1970s a tuberculosis vaccine trial in India involving 260,000 people revealed that more cases of TB occurred in the vaccinated than the unvaccinated. (*The Lancet*, January 12, 1980, p. 73.)

In 1977, Dr. Jonas Salk, who developed the first polio vaccine, testified along with other scientists that mass inoculation against polio was the cause of most polio cases through the USA since 1961. (*Science*, April 4, 1977, "Abstracts.")

In 1978, a survey of 30 states in the U.S. revealed that more than half of the children who contracted measles had been adequately vaccinated. (*The People's Doctor*, Dr. R. Mendelsohn.)

In 1979, Sweden abandoned the whooping cough vaccine due to its ineffectiveness. Out of 4,140 cases in 1978, it was found that 84 percent had been vaccinated three times! (*British Medical Journal* 283: 696–97, 1981.)

The February 1981 issue of the *Journal of the American Medical Association* found that 90 percent of obstetricians and 66 percent of pediatricians refused to take the rubella vaccine.

In the USA, the cost of a single DPT shot had risen from 11 cents in 1982 to $11.40 in 1987. The manufacturers of the vaccine were putting aside $8.00 per shot to cover legal costs and damages they were paying out to parents of brain-damaged children and children who died after vaccination. (*The Vine*, no. 7, January 1994, Nambur, Qld.)

In Oman between 1988 and 1989, a polio outbreak occurred amongst thousands of fully vaccinated children. The region with the highest attack rate had the highest vaccine coverage. The region with the lowest attack rate had the lowest vaccine coverage. (*The Lancet*, September 21, 1991.)

In 1990, a UK survey involving 598 doctors revealed that over 50 percent of them refused to have the hepatitis B vaccine despite belonging to the high risk group urged to be vaccinated. (*British Medical Journal*, January 27, 1990.)

In 1990, the *Journal of the American Medical Association* had an article on measles which stated, "Although more than 95 percent of school-aged children in the US are vaccinated against measles, large measles outbreaks continue to occur in schools and most cases in this setting occur among previously vaccinated children." (*JAMA*, November 21, 1990.)

In the USA, from July 1990 to November 1993, the U.S. Food and Drug Administration counted a total of 54,072 adverse reactions following vaccination. The FDA admitted that this number represented only ten percent of the real total, because most doctors were refusing to report vaccine injuries. In other words, adverse reactions for this period exceeded half a million! (National Vaccine Information Centre, March 2, 1994.)

In the *New England Journal of Medicine* July 1994 issue a study found that over 80 percent of children under five years of age who had contracted whooping cough had been fully vaccinated.

On November 2, 2000, the Association of American Physicians and Surgeons (AAPS) announced that its members voted at their 57th annual meeting in St. Louis to pass a resolution calling for an end to mandatory childhood vaccines. The resolution passed without a single "no" vote. (Report by Michael Devitt.)

For more on the dangers of vaccines and the flu vaccine scam I would like to give you information from Dr. King's website, whose non-profit mission is to "reduce the level of mercury in all drugs, and end the knowing addition of mercury, in any form, to vaccines and other drugs." For more information you can go to www.mercury-freedrugs.com for other valuable articles and information published on topics critical to the health of all Americans. You can also go to www.dr-king.com.

Influenza Viruses and Governmental Fear Mongering:
The "Avian Flu" Scare a Repackaged & Updated "Swine Flu"!
Today's Influenza Vaccines Are NOT Effective!

Based on the current published studies on influenza effectiveness and the CDC's actual reported "influenza" illness and mortality data during the period 1987–2000:

- The current influenza vaccines are NOT effective for children two and under or adults over 65.
- For all other groups, the current influenza vaccines are less than 50 percent effective in a good year and not effective in years where there is a "strain mismatch."
- For the past 20 years, the CDC's claimed 36,000 people die each year from "flu" or "flu-related pneumonia" is a knowingly false claim. When called on the truth of their statements concerning vaccines, CDC officials have admitted (in their "sworn" testimony before Washington State and Delaware legislators) that they knowingly lie about various aspects of vaccines because their "job" is to promote vaccination at all costs, and count the people who die of pneumonia during the "flu season" as "flu-related" deaths even though most are not confirmed to be infected with the "flu" virus.
- The factual approximate "flu-related" pneumonia deaths per year for the CDC data available to the public in the period from 1997 to 2000 are as follows:

a. About 600 to 3,000 deaths each year, which translates into a death rate of about 1.7 to 8.3 persons per 1,000,000.

b. The range of influenza cases is from 34 to 130 million per year or, in percent of the population, 24.4 percent to 50.8 percent.

c. Between 13,000 and 44,000 people were hospitalized for "flu" or "flu-related pneumonia" in the years data was reported by the CDC.

d. There is/was no correlation between the percent of the population inoculated for "flu" and either the "attributed" deaths or the percent of population getting the "flu."

When it comes to children, the available CDC data indicate that:

- For the 1–4 year age group, "flu attributed" deaths were six to 16 each year, and

- For the 5–14 year age group, "flu attributed" deaths were one to 14 each year.

Based on the preceding facts, the CDC's "36,000 deaths per year" is a 12- to 60-fold inflation of their own data on "flu deaths" and an obvious fabrication. Thus, today's "flu" vaccines are not effective in preventing you from getting the "flu"!

Influenza Viruses and Governmental Fear Mongering: The "Avian Flu" Scare a Repackaged & Updated "Swine Flu"!

Next, the bird flu vaccine boondoggle.

Since: a) the current influenza vaccines are not effective, b) the exact "bird" flu influenza (H5N1) virus that will "cause" the alleged "bird-flu pandemic" is not known because the H5N1 virus is rapidly mutating, c) the current experimental vaccines are already a mismatch for the current strain infecting chickens and people in Asia, and d) it takes months to convert a detected viral strain into a vaccine, but only weeks for a "flu" to spread to a significant portion of a population in America. Why, *except to fatten the "flu" vaccine-makers pockets and fund their new facilities and research efforts*, would any sane government of the people, by the people, and for the people fund any similar "bird-flu vaccine" boondoggle?

Just Like the Last "Animal" Influenza Threat!!!
History 101: The Great "Swine Flu" Fiasco

They say that people who do not learn from history are doomed to repeat it. Has everyone forgotten the last flu SCARE: The "Swine Flu" a pandemic that never was!

Like the small contained "Avian flu" outbreaks occurring in China in 2004 and 2005, a small, contained "swine flu" outbreak (which the Centers for Disease Control and Prevention [CDC] investigated and confirmed had been caused by a swine-type influenza A virus) occurred in the U.S. in February of 1976 at Fort Dix in New Jersey.

Like the current "sky is falling" reaction, the Department of Health, Education and Welfare, as well as numerous medical experts, became concerned that a major flu epidemic was imminent for the coming fall. Fear of influenza deaths in numbers similar to the 1918 flu epidemic led to a recommendation that the federal government vaccinate all Americans. When insurance companies refused to provide coverage to the vaccine manufacturers, the government agreed to accept liability for claims of adverse events. This obstacle having been cleared, the National Influenza Immunization Program (NIIP) officially started in October of 1976. The number of vaccinations given each week increased rapidly from less than one million in early October to more than four million in the later weeks of the month, and reached a peak of more than six million doses a week by the middle of November 1976. The NIIP was unique in the annals of epidemiology: an organized surveillance effort was in place from the very beginning, and over forty million people were vaccinated during the short time the NIIP was in effect. However, on December 16, 1976, the NIIP was suspended following reports from more than ten states of Guillain-Barré syndrome (GBS) in vaccines. By January of 1977, more than 500 cases of GBS had been reported, with 25 deaths. Millions of dollars in lawsuits and many years later, the only "epidemic" was an epidemic of vaccine injuries as the "swine flu" pandemic never appeared.

Influenza Viruses and Governmental Fear Mongering:
The "Avian Flu" Scare a Repackaged & Updated "Swine Flu"!

Yet, today, our government is *again* fear mongering about another influenza, the "avian"/"bird" flu, and pursuing the same stupid path to create a vaccine for a disease that may never exist and, like the swine-flu vaccine, is likely to damage thousands, even though there are drugs that are effective treatments for treating those who contract any influenza virus and other drugs and treatments for the symptoms and post-infection diseases, mainly pneumonias, which tend to become active in those infected by an influenza virus.

Wake up America! Stop the lies! Stop another unsound vaccine! Stop the "avian flu" vaccine! Demand this obviously unsound "avian flu" vaccine program be stopped! Also, demand that:

- The current ineffective influenza vaccination program should be stopped immediately!
- The current antiviral "flu" drugs be stockpiled and used to treat those who contract any influenza virus!
- An immediate program for developing better antiviral drugs for the influenza and other viruses that are currently being addressed by vaccines with serious side-effect risks!

Respectfully,
Paul G. King, Ph.D, MS, BA
Founder, F.A.M.E. Systems
www.dr-king.com

MERCK HID THE TRUTH ABOUT DEATHS IN VIOXX STUDIES

Drug companies and all pharmaceutical manufacturers are hiding the truth about the dangers of both their prescription and non-prescription drugs. These publicly traded pharmaceutical companies are only interested in making money, and only interested in getting more people around the world to be using more and more of their drugs. These companies are repeatedly lying about the safety and effectiveness of their drugs. Drug companies hide facts that prove that their drugs cause disease and death. Drug companies lie about the fact that their drugs do not do what they claim to do. Non-prescription and prescription drugs do not cure disease. Non-prescription and prescription drugs only temporarily suppress symptoms. Non-prescription and prescription drugs actually cause disease, make you sick, and even cause death.

When I say that the drug companies are lying in their studies, falsifying their data, and misleading the public about how dangerous their drugs are and how ineffective they are, people claim that it is impossible that these things are happening. Let me point out some interesting facts that can easily prove that the drug companies are in fact hiding the truth that all non-prescription and prescription drugs are causing disease and killing people, and these same drugs are not as effective as the drug companies would make you believe. First, this type of corporate misleading of the public is not isolated to the pharmaceutical industry. Let's ask ourselves, "Have other corporations been found guilty of misleading the public, lying about the safety and effectiveness of their products, and proven in court to falsify information, produce fake documents and data, and purposely lie to and mislead the public?"

Remember when Ralph Nader, the great consumer advocate, wrote the book *Unsafe at Any Speed*? In this book, Nader exposed how General Motors lied about the safety of the Corvair. It was proven that General Motors knew that the Corvair was a dangerous car and many people would die if they did not recall the vehicle. The book pointed out and proved the fact that the corporate executives knew that people would die, but decided to let those people die—all in the name of profits. It was also proven later that Ford knew that thousands of people would die with their "exploding Pinto." The executives of Ford made a business decision that it was okay for people to die because the company could not afford to lose the millions of dollars by recalling the Pinto. It was a more cost-effective business decision to handle lawsuits from the dead people's families than to recall the vehicle and fix the problem.

Let's fast-forward and look at the front-page story that was later buried about how a pharmaceutical company shipped blood tainted with the HIV virus overseas to be sold. It was proven that a pharmaceutical conglomerate knew that the blood was tainted with the HIV virus and decided to sell it anyway. How many hundreds of thousands of people received blood transfusions and are now HIV positive, all in the name of profits for the drug companies? This was front-page news reported on major television networks.

The tobacco industry knew as early as 1950 that cigarette smoking would cause disease and deaths. They hid this information and lied about it, even in front of Congress, for over fifty years. The tobacco industry hid the truth that they knew about the dangers of their product, falsified documents, and lied about it for almost fifty years.

Enron had senior executives lie about the company's profitability and allowed millions of people to lose their entire pensions and life savings—all in the name of profit.

WorldCom's senior executives were proven to have lied to the public in a blatant and flagrant scam in a greedy desire to increase their own personal profits.

Executives from Tyco lied to investors and shareholders and virtually operated the corporation as their personal piggybanks, all so they could line their own pockets.

Fast food companies have been found guilty of lying to the public about the cleanliness of their restaurants and the ingredients used in their products. Major food manufacturers are being found guilty every year of lying to the public about the ingredients that are being put into their mass-produced food that is being sold throughout the world.

This brings us to the pharmaceutical conglomerates today. Two years ago a gentleman won a Nobel Prize for developing a technology that can test a drug's effects on all the known body receptors. This test allows drug manufacturers, for the first time, to see all the negative side effects that non-prescription and prescription drugs will have on the body. It also tests the long-term effectiveness of these drugs. I have personal firsthand knowledge of this individual and the company he works for. This technology proves for the first time that every single over-the-counter non-prescription drug and every single prescription drug simply temporarily suppresses symptoms. This test proves that there is not one single drug manufactured that actually cures any disease. This test proves, without any question, that every single non-prescription and prescription drug is much less effective than the companies advertise. This technology proves that every single non-prescription and prescription drug actually is ineffective and does not do what it is promised to do. Most importantly, this test proves without any question that every single non-prescription and prescription drug has adverse effects on multiple receptors in the body. This means that for the first time we have a test that proves that every single prescription and every single non-prescription over-the-counter drug is actually causing the body to become sick, ill, and develop disease, and even causes death. The drug companies are spending hundreds of millions of dollars trying to suppress this information. The drug companies have inside data proving that their drugs cause disease, cause illness, and cause deaths.

How do we know this is true? First, as I mentioned earlier, this is common practice amongst corporations all around the world. The tobacco industry, the auto industry, the food industry, the fast food industry, and the drug companies have all been proven in court to repeatedly, and on a regular basis, falsify documents, falsify research, lie in producing data, mislead the pubic, and completely provide false and misleading information regarding the safety and effectiveness of their products. If we go back over the last fifty years, this happens in virtually every industry on a consistent, repeated basis. This is not new. We also know that this is happening in the pharmaceutical industry today by the fact that dozens of scientists working for the United State Government's National Institutes of Health and Centers for Disease Control and other government agencies have come forward, stating from personal knowledge and experience that this information that the drug companies are producing is false and misleading, and full of lies. These scientists are stating the fact that the drug companies' nonprescription and prescription drugs are causing disease, illness, and death, and are not as effective as the drug companies are leading us to believe. These whistleblowers are telling the truth and are being repeatedly attacked, suppressed, and debunked. Even members of the FDA itself have come forward in congressional hearings stating that information is being falsified and doctored, and the truth about the drugs is not being revealed. Scientists and researchers from the drug industry itself are coming forward and blowing the whistle. Just like insiders from the tobacco industry and insiders from the auto industry are coming forward blowing the whistle, and have blown the whistle, on the falsifying of documents in those industries, insiders from Big Pharma are coming forward and blowing the whistle on all the falsification of documents in the pharmaceutical industry. There are thousands of doctors around the world who are prescribing drugs and seeing that these drugs are not doing what they are advertised to do, and are causing massive negative side effects in the patients. These doctors are livid and very upset that their reports that they are submitting to the pharmaceutical companies are being hidden, suppressed, and squashed. These doctors are rising up because they know firsthand that the drug companies are lying about the safety and effectiveness of their drugs.

This leads us to the most recent case against the pharmaceutical industry relating to the drug Vioxx. Remember, Vioxx was a pain medication. This was not a drug designed to save anyone's life. There isn't a single person whose life would be saved by taking Vioxx. It was simply a pain medication that the drug company Merck wanted to sell because its "marketing department" knew that it could produce billions of dollars in profits by convincing people that this was the best, most powerful pain medication in the world. The fact is it was not the best, most effective, or powerful pain medication in the world. The fact is that there were dozens of other non-prescription over-the-counter and prescription pain medications that suppressed pain much better. There are other non-patentable very inexpensive ways to reduce or eliminate pain that were even more effective than the non-prescription and prescription drugs currently being sold. This was not about producing a drug that would save people's lives; this was about producing a drug that could be sold, marketed at a huge markup, and make Merck billions of dollars.

That's where we have a problem; that's where we have a major conflict of interest. We have a drug company that's not interested in saving lives, or increasing the quality of someone's life. Their interest is in simply producing a pill for a penny, selling it for $150 and through a strategic, sophisticated marketing campaign to convince the "stupid public" that this is a needed drug that could make their pain go away better than something else. This was a flagrant lie. The facts are shown and proven now that Vioxx was an ineffective pain remedy, that there were much more effective pain remedies available, prescription, non-prescription, and all-natural, all of which were much less expensive and much more effective. So why did Merck want to sell this drug? Because it could make billions of dollars in profits. The fact is over 100,000 people are dead today because they took Vioxx. In court documents it has been proven that the executives at Merck knew as early as five years ago that tens of thousands of people would die if they sold the drug Vioxx. But just like the executives at General Motors in relation to the Corvair, and just like the executives at Ford in relation to the Pinto, and just like the executives at Big Tobacco in relation to cigarettes, the business decision was made to "let the people die" because it's cheaper to handle the lawsuits than to not sell the drug and make the profits.

Now we find front-page news in the *Wall Street Journal* that Merck executives not only knew and hid the information, but actually falsified documents and didn't report known deaths in the clinical trials of Vioxx. This is unthinkable to the general public; however, it is not unthinkable or amazing to me. I have said this happens. People have harassed me because of that claim, but it is true and believe me this is not an isolated case. I know firsthand that there are other pharmaceutical companies that have people in their clinical trials that died where the documents are falsified and those deaths are never reported—all in the name of profit. People always ask me today, "Is there a place for drugs and surgery?" The answer is in my opinion, I believe yes there is a place for drugs and surgery, but drugs and surgery should only be used as a last resort to save a person's life or dramatically increase the quality of their life before they die. The drug companies' marketing departments do not want drugs to be used only to save someone's life or to increase the quality of their life. The drug companies' marketing departments are interested in getting people as early as possible in their life to start taking drugs and to take those drugs every day for the rest of their life. This is the only way drug companies can increase their sales and increase their profit and increase their market share. Remember, drug companies are publicly traded corporations. They only have one legal responsibility, and that is to increase shareholder value. That means drug companies have a legal obligation to increase sales and profits above everything else. This means drug companies have only one mission and that mission is to get more people taking more drugs on a regular basis on planet earth.

Drug companies categorically do not want to cure a disease or see people healthy. If every person was healthy, then all the drug companies would be bankrupt. Drug companies years ago wanted to create drugs and surgical procedures and methods that could save someone's life or treat a disease bringing it to a cure. The business model of drug companies has changed over the last fifty years. Now the business model is let's create a disease that can be established early on in someone's life, such as acid reflux, then let's create a drug and convince the patient that they must take this drug every day for the rest of their life. This is the mission of drug companies. The problem is all nonprescription and prescription drugs cause disease, cause illness, and cause death; they only suppress symptoms, and they only do so in the short term. Remember, the Nobel Prize–winning gentleman for medicine's revolutionary technology proves that every single over-the-counter non-prescription drug and prescription drug causes illness and disease and is not as effective as the drug companies would allow you to believe. All these highly toxic chemicals do is temporarily suppress a symptom, making the body do something unnatural, while at the same time putting other areas or other parts of your body into a disease-prone state or completely out of balance where disease and illness can develop. All non-prescription and prescription drugs cause disease; they do not cure anything. If you want to be healthy, if you want to never get sick, if you want to have more energy and vitality, if you want to look younger, if you want to live longer and have more vitality, strength, stamina, and happiness in your life, it is vitally important to eliminate or dramatically reduce non-prescription and prescription drug use. As always, never do this unless you are doing so under the care of a licensed healthcare practitioner. This is the first most important step to a healthy long life.

THE DRUG COMPANIES
CONTROL THE MEDIA

You get information from newspapers, magazines, the radio, and television. Think about it. Everything you pretty much "know" you learn from what you read in a newspaper, what you read in a magazine, what you heard on the radio, or what you heard on television. Think about this—what if all of those places where you get your information were actually owned by a company trying to sell you a product? Let's assume that the newspaper, the magazine, the radio, and the television that you get your information from were all owned by McDonald's Corporation. Do you think that McDonald's would use the newspaper that they own, the magazine they own, the radio station they own, and the television network that they own to convince you to eat more food at McDonald's? Of course they would. That's how business operates. This is what people don't know today. People don't know that major corporations have figured out that the easiest way to sell their products and services is to take control over newspapers, magazines, and radio and television stations.

If a big company or a big industry wants to get the masses to buy their products, all they have to do is control the flow of information, control the media. Let's take *Time* magazine as an example. Pick up a *Time* magazine, flip through it and see how many ads there are for drug companies. Ad after ad after ad in *Time* magazine is for drugs. When you look at all the advertising revenue *Time* magazine receives from the drug industry would it surprise you that the drug industry controls much of the content written in the articles in *Time* magazine? Would it also surprise you that the drug companies also control what other ads are placed in *Time* magazine? Let's take it a step further. Let's look at the board of directors of *Time*. Isn't it interesting that one of the senior board members is also on the board of the drug company Eli Lilly. Hmm ... interesting, isn't it? The plot thickens. Let's investigate further and see how many other board members, as well as officers and directors of *Time* own large amounts of stock in pharmaceutical companies. Hmm ... the plot thickens. Let's find out how many friends and relatives of the senior executives, officers, and board members of *Time* work for or are heavily invested in the drug industry. Hmm ... the plot thickens even more! Now, let's ask ourselves why would *Time* magazine do negative articles about Kevin Trudeau? Why would *Time* magazine forbid Kevin Trudeau from advertising his book? Why would *Time* magazine attack Tom Cruise when he bashed the use of psychiatric drugs? Interesting, isn't it? Open your eyes folks. *Time* magazine is nothing more than a tool that the drug industry is using to brainwash you. This happens with radio stations, newspapers, and television, as well as magazines.

The pharmaceutical companies today are some of the most profitable, powerful corporations on planet earth. They are sitting on hundreds of billions of dollars in cash and they are specifically going in controlling the media. This way they can use the media; they can use television, radio, newspapers, and magazines to brainwash you. And what are they trying to brainwash you into believing? Very simply this: they are brainwashing you into believing that drugs are effective and safe. They want to brainwash you into believing that all-natural remedies are ineffective, worthless, and dangerous. They are trying to brainwash you into believing that your life will be better if you are popping pills and taking drugs every single day. They are trying to brainwash you into believing that your health will be better, that you will be happier if you are taking pills every single day. They are trying to brainwash you into believing that you are sick, that you are ill, that you have some "disease," and that you "need" to be taking a drug every single day for the rest of your life. This is what is happening today. You are being misled, you are being lied to, you are being deceived, and you are being brainwashed by the drug companies, as well as the fast food industry. They are taking control of the media. They are taking control of the newspapers, magazines, television stations, and radio stations. This is happening all around the world.

My television commercial for the *Natural Cures* book was put on a station in a foreign country outside of America. Immediately, the show was pulled from the air. Why? Because that television station is controlled by the local pharmaceutical company and the local fast food companies. They do not want people reading my book. In one foreign country my books were bought by a local pharmaceutical company and destroyed. Imagine, a local pharmaceutical company went around with trucks buying every single one of my books, taking them off the shelves and then destroying them. The drug companies don't want people to read my books. The drug companies are spending millions of dollars in getting people to write crazy things all over the internet about me and my book. The fact is the people who read the book and do the things in the book are getting healthier. I was just with a group of people who had read my book and they were all telling me how their diseases were cured by simply doing the things in the book. Asthma was cured, acid reflux was cured, periodic depression was cured, breast cancer—cured in sixty days, migraines cured, allergies cured, obesity cured. The natural cure for your disease is doing the things in Chapter 6 of the book. Do not be deceived by the media. Remember, the media is controlled by the pharmaceutical companies as well as the fast food industry. It is also controlled by the petroleum industry, which I will get into later in another book. The bottom line here, though, is these three industries, petroleum, which is big oil, fast food, and pharmaceuticals are pretty much all working together. They all feed off one another; what's good for one is virtually good for all. So go back, read Chapter 6 again, and start doing all the things that I recommend and you will start feeling better than ever before.

GOVERNMENT OFFICIAL CRITICAL OF "NATURAL CURES" BOOK ARRESTED FOR CRACK COCAINE POSSESSION!

As many of you know, my book exposes the corruption in government and big business. It exposes how government officials routinely lie and mislead the public. It exposes the motivations and reasons why government officials lie and mislead the public. It explains how the lobbyists get money from corporations and illegally and routinely funnel that money to politicians who in turn order other high-ranking government officials in regulatory agencies to lie and mislead the public and persecute and prosecute those people and companies that could hurt the profits of the major international corporations that are donating all the money. This pipeline of money from corporations to lobbyists to politicians is now being exposed on a major scale in the national media.

My book explains that politicians use government agencies such as the FTC, the FDA, and various consumer protection boards to spread misinformation, false information, and lies about individuals and companies that are affecting the profits of the large multinational corporations. These agencies do this under the guise of trying to "protect the public." Nothing is further from the truth. These agencies are not interested in protecting consumers or the public; these agencies are nothing more than politically appointed people who work for their politician government elected officials and do their bidding. Throughout history, politicians appoint and put their own cronies in their administrations and government. The politicians use the government employees and agencies to help their own political aspirations, increase their own power, and make sure they are returning favors to their major donors; therefore getting reelected, increasing their power and influence base and putting more money in their pocket.

This is not a cynical view or a conspiracy theory, this is factual. It hasn't been reported as much as it should, but it has been reported in newspapers, magazines, and by independent journalists and investigative reporters for hundreds of years. This is how politics work, not just in America, but all over the world. Throughout the world politicians who are earning meager salaries live in multimillion-dollar homes and drive the most expensive cars. How can these politicians have such great wealth when they earn such meager salaries? No one questions this. It's like the mafia boss who says he earns $100,000 a year as a waste management contractor, but lives in a $10 million mansion! It's obvious he's getting money from somewhere. Politicians are the same way.

Because I am exposing for the first time, from personal knowledge, and from direct sources in Washington, the pharmaceutical industry, and the fast food industry, and throughout government I have been viciously attacked. The government officials in Washington know that I know the truth. They know me personally because I have been there. I am blowing the whistle on what I personally know and what my direct sources tell me. This is why in the last twelve months since my book came our there has been a major increase in stories and outings of corruption at the FDA, the pharmaceutical industry, the food industry, and in political government organizations in Washington and throughout the country. My book and my exposing of why I know is causing this. This is good for the country, it's good for democracy, and it's good for the people.

One of the most vicious attacks that I received over the last few months was from the New York State Attorney General's Office, Department of Consumer Protection. The Office of the Attorney General in New York has an organization called the Consumer Protection Board. This Consumer Protection Board is headed by nothing more than politically appointed cronies of the major politicians in the state. These politically appointed cronies do the bidding of the politicians in the state of New York and Washington. The Consumer Protection Board is nothing but a front. It has no interest in protecting consumers. It has never done anything to protect consumers. The only thing this Board does is act as a black, negative PR machine that does the bidding of the politicians. I have exposed this scam and fraud. Because I exposed the corruption, this Board started a massive negative campaign against me. The Consumer Protection Board put out flagrantly false and misleading press releases about me and my book. The Consumer Protection Board was led by a crazy fanatic named Caroline Quartararo. This woman was appointed by the governor. She has never had any interest in protecting consumers; she is simply a pawn of the politicians. Our inside sources have e-mails from Quartararo's office to other officials showing, in black and white, that this organization was deliberately putting out false press releases filled with lies. The e-mails show that the agency was doing nothing to protect consumers, but was simply on a mission to discredit me and stop people from buying my book. The agency was relentless in attempting to contact Oprah Winfrey to do a negative story on me. The agency called various people and tried to get them to lie about me and my book. We have this documented.

When I heard of Quartararo's outrageous actions and read her flagrantly false press releases I said to my attorney, "This woman must be on crack!" Well, come to find out, I was actually correct. Ms. Quartararo was arrested for possession of crack cocaine. You see, I will not be attacked without fighting back. When this woman and this agency started this flagrant violation of my First Amendment rights, and flagrant violation of the law, and flagrant misrepresentation of me, my book, and misleading of the public I organized my team of insiders and investigators to do every bit of research we could on Ms. Quartararo and other members of the Consumer Protection Board. Our investigators assured me, based on their surveillance, that this woman was using crack cocaine and was potentially a dealer of crack cocaine. We passed this information on to the officials, who were informed of the exact location of the crack cocaine purchase. She was arrested. Information obtained from my sources indicates that other members of these agencies also appear to be involved in similar activity. I fight back. These criminals in government are not going to continue their fraud and deception of the American public. They are not going to stop the free flow of ideas and expression of my First Amendment rights under the Constitution of the United States. The corruption in government is going to be exposed and will stop. I am leading the charge. There is more information on the story at www.kevinfightsback.com.

WASHINGTON CORRUPTION EXPOSED

In my book I talk a lot about how the corruption works in Washington. Up until now people like myself who have exposed and blown the whistle on how the corruption and money flows in Washington have been ridiculed and called "conspiracy theorists." We've been mocked, laughed at, and criticized. My book has been the most up-front about exposing how the money flows and the corruption works in Washington. I expose how big corporations give millions of dollars to the lobbyists in Washington. These lobbyists then turn around and funnel this money directly to the politicians in various forms such as trips around the world to golf resorts and luxury resorts, fancy meals, no-show jobs for friends and relatives, political contributions, etc., etc., etc. In some cases the payments are more overt. A prime example is a politician who owns a house worth $500,000, sells it to the lobbyist for $2 million, thus getting $1.5 million more than the house is really worth. That's a $1.5 million payoff. The lobbyist, a few months later, sells the house for half a million, taking the $1.5 million loss. These types of transactions are very common. I have exposed them; other people have exposed them. We have been laughed at and mocked, as I have mentioned.

Finally, my insiders have put enough pressure on Washington by exposing the truth that finally for the first time in history a major lobbyist has come forward, been charged, and has pled guilty to this incredible crime of corruption. Jack Abramoff has pled guilty to federal charges of conspiracy, tax evasion, and mail fraud. He faces thirty years in prison. He is admitting to doing exactly what I have said goes on in Washington. He has admitted that he has in fact received tens of millions of dollars from corporations and funneled that money, illegally in the form of bribes, to over sixty members of the Senate and Congress in Washington. This is unbelievable. This is like Joe Valachi, the first member of the mafia to come forward and actually admit that a mafia exists, godfathers exist, crime bosses exist, organized crime exists, mafia hits exist, and payoffs from the mafia to politicians exist. It was unheard of up until the time that Joe Valachi, an insider, blew the whistle. Now, one of the most powerful lobbyists in Washington admits what we all know, and all knew all along—that corruption in Washington is flagrant and blatant; that the corporations own the politicians. The Constitution starts "We the people," it doesn't say "We the corporations." Unfortunately, today we have lobbyists in Washington.

There are thousands of lobbyists in Washington. We have one lobbyist saying that he has paid off over sixty members of Congress, both senators and congressmen. Do you think he is the only one? Let's be realistic. Of the thousands of lobbyists, there are hundreds and hundreds of people just like Jack Abramoff. There are hundreds of lobbyists who have been doing, and are doing, the exact same thing that Jack Abramoff has now admitted to and pled guilty to. The corruption in Washington is out of control. Money and power always corrupt. This is major because it acknowledges that everything I'm saying in the book *Natural Cures* is absolutely true. I can assure you I am working diligently on exposing more and more corruption in both corporations and government. Every time you see a news article written about something that's going on at the FDA, or with the drug companies, or with the fast food companies, or with various corporations that are advertising, or with politicians, when you start hearing about corruption and fraud, always wonder, "Humm, did Kevin Trudeau play a part in getting this exposed?" I can assure you there is a very good chance that the answer is yes. That's why subscribing to my newsletter and being a subscriber to www.naturalcures.com is so vital. Those are the resources that I am using to help change America for the better.

YOU CANNOT BELIEVE THE MEDIA

As I mentioned in my newsletters, television stations, radio stations, newspapers, and magazines are being gobbled up and controlled by large multinational corporations, primarily in the pharmaceutical industry, the fast food industry, and the oil industry. The heads of the pharmaceutical industry, fast food industry, and oil industry work closely together. All three industries are intertwined. The small group of multibillionaires that controls these three industries knows that if they control the media, including television news, radio, newspapers, and magazines, they will be able to control the information that the public receives. This is similar to what happened in Stalinist Russia and Nazi Germany. In those regimes and in regimes around the world, information is controlled. It's called the propaganda machine. It is very powerful and very effective. It is the most effective way of controlling the masses.

Controlling what you believe to be information, truth, and news is how the oil companies, drug companies, and fast food companies brainwash you. A perfect example was the recent major breaking news story of the author of the book *A Million Little Pieces*. This author appeared on *The Oprah Winfrey Show* and Oprah recommended this book and it became a part of her book club. The book became a runaway best-seller. It is a book about a man's drug and alcohol addiction and how he turned his life around. It is a page turner and a great read. It is a book about overcoming; it is a book about redemption. It is an inspiring book and an entertaining book. However, the book was portrayed as a biography or a memoir; therefore, it was suggested that the book had to contain 100 percent verifiable, documentable facts. It was suggested that nothing in the book could be embellished, altered, changed, or juiced up to make the story a better read, more compelling, and emphasize certain points. A website called *The Smoking Gun* allegedly "broke" the story that the book contained some information that was not provable, not capable of verification and, in some cases based on the review of documents only, appeared to be false. *The Smoking Gun* alleged that their research of documents suggested or proved that some of the things said in the book were in fact lies. This became headline news all over CNN. This was the number one news topic in America.

It's amazing to me that such an unimportant issue was the number one news story for over a week. I began to wonder why this was such a huge news story. It was picked up by all the networks, but primarily by CNN. Larry King had the author on his show for the entire hour. It was talked about, talked about, and talked about over and over again. The amazing thing was that the journalist from *The Smoking Gun* was also all over the news. He was doing a major media tour, he was everywhere, and prominently displayed was the fact that he represented *The Smoking Gun* website. I began to be curious. It was almost as if CNN was actively advertising and promoting *The Smoking Gun* website. I began to smell a rat. So I sent my team of investigators in to find out what the real story was. Lo and behold, AOL Time Warner, the parent company of CNN, is also the parent company of *The Smoking Gun*! *The Smoking Gun* revenues are based on the number of hits it gets to its website. I had my investigators track down sources at AOL Time Warner, *The Smoking Gun*, and CNN. My sources tell me that this was a specifically planned way not to expose a major news story, but rather make a major news story out of virtually nothing simply to promote *The Smoking Gun* website, to increase the number of hits to its website, therefore increasing the revenue it could generate from its advertisers. Remember folks, it's all about the money. You can't believe the media. You can't believe what you read in the newspapers, what you read in magazines, what you hear on television, or what you hear on the radio.

In today's journalistic world we are not being told the truth. News organizations and the media are not reporting the facts. They have an agenda, they have a story and an angle they want to present, and then they go out and create that story and create that angle. They are not reporting factual information. They are simply propaganda machines to brainwash you into a certain way of thinking, to get you to vote a certain way, to get you to believe that certain companies and organizations are good, and that certain legislation is good, that certain products are good. The oil industry, drug industry, and fast food industry control the media. We live in a propaganda land. We don't have free access to media like we used to, and we don't have free access to information. We are becoming more and more like communist China, Stalinist Russia, and Nazi Germany in how we get information, and how it's filtered by the government, and filtered through the multinational corporations.

YOU CAN'T BELIEVE THE GOVERNMENT

The United States Government lies to you on a regular basis. State government, local government, and the federal government consistently and routinely mislead the people and lie to the public. When you see a government agency put out a report you can almost always be assured that the information is misleading, untrue, false, fabricated, or a flagrant lie. All information that comes out of the government is filtered through political advisors. The political advisors filter the information that you get from every aspect of government—every agency in government and every politician. These political advisors tell politicians what to say, how to say it, and what words to use. All of this information is run through focus groups to find out which words are positively received by the public. All of this information is run through the political advisors who talk to the lobbyists who are paid by the multinational corporations, and it is determined what message the companies are the happiest with. When you receive information from a politician or government agency, at every level you can be assured that it's specifically designed to make sure that the politician stays in office and that it benefits the donors to those politicians, the large multinational corporations. All the information you get, virtually every press release and every speech, has been run by lobbyists, who are paid for by the multinational corporations, and the political advisors who are reviewing how this is going to impact reelection, and how it is going to impact the politician's rise in power within the government.

In the last twelve months since my book came out and I exposed the corruption in government and I exposed this fact, we have seen record numbers of stories about politicians and government officials who have been caught lying. A few good examples of the government's flagrantly lying are:

- The New York State Consumer Protection Board, led by Caroline Quartararo, put out false and misleading press releases about me and the *Natural Cures* book. I sued the agency for violating my First Amendment rights and putting out a press release full of misinformation and lies. We won a preliminary injunction against the agency and the judge basically said that the agency violated my First Amendment constitutional rights.

- I sued the Bureau of Prisons, including the warden and assistant warden of the correctional institution that I was in. We proved that the warden, the assistant warden, and the food service administrator blatantly lied under oath and committed perjury. These are members of the Department of Justice! They should be in jail themselves.

- A major researcher from the government of Korea put together a study on stem cells. The study was reported all around the world for months. It was then discovered that the study was a complete fabrication and 100 percent false. The researcher and the government

admitted that they made up all of the research. When asked why, the answer was to get more grant money and to increase power and prestige. Remember, it's always about the money.
- The government works with the auto industry to produce mileage ratings. These ratings are listed on the sticker of every car. It is now discovered that all of these mileage ratings have been false and nothing but fabrications. Lies, lies, and more lies.

Many people are familiar with the Roswell incident regarding the alleged crash of a UFO where the government actually had in its possession a crashed UFO, including alien bodies. At the time of this incident the headlines read, "U.S. Government in Possession of Crashed UFO." Within twenty-four hours the government changed the story and said, no, there was no UFO, there were no crashed alien bodies, and it was only a weather balloon. How anyone could confuse a flimsy weather balloon with a large, solid UFO containing alien bodies is beyond me. For years, and years, and years the U.S. Government held by the story that there was no UFO spaceship, and there were no alien bodies—it was only a very small weather balloon. Investigation after investigation by our government continued to report that the case was closed; there was no flying saucer, there were no alien bodies—it was only a weather balloon.

Who is telling the truth? Is our government telling the truth? Did they tell the truth the first time when they admitted it was a flying saucer and they had alien bodies, or did they really make a mistake and just correct their mistake? Were they telling the truth in the beginning or are they telling the truth now? We finally have an answer. When the government changed their story and said it was not a flying "disk," and there were no alien bodies, but rather only a weather balloon with no bodies whatsoever, the government released a series of photographs with two military officers holding some flimsy scraps of a weather balloon, suggesting that this is what was found. These flimsy scraps of thin weather balloon do not match any of the earlier descriptions of a large, solid craft that was originally seen, and they made no attempt to talk about the alien bodies.

The interesting thing is that in all of the pictures that the government released, one of the officers was holding in his hand what appeared to be a letter or a telegraphed message. It appeared to be some type of communication on paper that he was holding. In virtually all of the photos you only see the blank backside of the paper; however, in one of the photos you actually see blurred typing. He actually is holding the letter or telegraphed message so that you can see the typing. Within the last few years photo imaging technology has become so advanced that it is now actually possible to read the letter. We now have the evidence that the government has been lying to us all along relating to this incident. This was reported on national television. The story, however, has never made headline news. The imaging technology shows that the letter came from a general to the officer holding it, telling the officer to ship the crashed flying "disk" and the alien victim bodies to Houston! So, there you have it. The government is saying to the public: there is no alien spacecraft and there are no alien bodies. Yet, right in the hand of the military officer are the orders from his general, on the very same day, to ship the alien spacecraft and the alien bodies to another facility.

I am not a conspiracy theorist, I am simply an insider who has been there and knows how the government works. The government and large corporations routinely lie and mislead the public. They do so for very simple reasons, to increase their own power, prestige, and money. That's really what it's all about. When you look at what's happening to politicians in Washington, such as Tom DeLay being indicted for corruption, we see how fearful and frightened these politicians get when they are threatened with loss of power and prestige. It was reported that this senator was totally upset about the fact that he would lose his corner office and his large staff of secretaries! For those of you reading this, you really may not have any idea of how important power, image, prestige, influence, and personal accolades are to these people in government and corporations. The corner office with the bathroom, the extra amount of secretaries, and the private table at the country club are as important as the money. Power and influence and money are the motivating factors the higher you get up. There are many, many people who pass on money as long as they have more power and influence. These are the motivators that make men lie, cheat, steal, and take advantage of you and me.

Great Book

There is a great book which talks at length about how politics, the press, and special interests are targeting your rights to vitamins, minerals, herbs, and true information about health. The book is entitled *Ephedra Fact and Fiction*, authored by Mike Fillon, and published by Woodland Publishing, (800) 777-2665.

Richard Kreider, Ph.D. from Baylor University says, "The book is fascinating, a classic example of how misinformation stemming from various special interest groups and broadcast by the media can cause a political and legal firestorm regarding a supplement."

The American Association for Health Freedom says, "The book is a disturbing look at the political and financial agendas, media hype, and ulterior motives surrounding the wrongly accused supplement industry. A sound and thorough argument."

The book investigates every avenue from behind-the-scenes deals between lawmakers and pharmaceutical companies to using the media's ability to misinform the people. It explains how front PR firms are used, including the blatant dismissal of legitimate research supporting supplements safety. The book's discoveries and explanations of the scenarios are not simply about Ephedra, but rather expose the entire supplement industry, the legislation that governs it, and how lobbyists, special interests, the drug companies, and media are all working together to hide the truth about nutritional information from the public. I highly recommend this book. It goes into great detail and validates everything I've been saying in my book and in my newsletters.

The Disease Conspiracy: The FDA Suppression of Cures

Robert Barefoot has recently written a new book, which he has dedicated to Oprah Winfrey. This is a spectacular book, a quick and easy read that contains suppressed actual clinical studies documenting how vitamins and minerals inhibit the growth of cancer and prevent heart disease, diabetes, MS, lupus, and dozens of other ailments. The book provides the actual scientific evidence that reporters, journalists, and M.D.s say do not exist. Disease can be quickly wiped out in America in spite of the hundred-year conspiracy by the FDA and drug industry to suppress this information. The book also addresses the epidemic vitamin and mineral deficiency in the United States and explains why black Americans suffer from the highest disease and mortality rates due to these deficiencies. The book is available at www.cureamerica.net. Highly recommended.

What People Are Saying

In October 1996 I was diagnosed with prostate cancer. The diagnosis was confirmed by biopsy. In October of that year I started following Robert Barefoot's calcium regime. In July 1997 I had another prostate biopsy in which no evidence of malignancy was found. The regime outlined in the book *The Calcium Factor* improved my immune system to where the body could heal itself without intrusive measures like surgery, chemotherapy, or radiation.

S. Ross Johnson, Retired President of
Prudential Insurance Company of America

I've been an attorney involved in very complex litigation involving natural supplements and their ability to treat or cure various types of illnesses including cancer. I am well known in Maryland as a litigator, repeatedly being named as one of the outstanding trial attorneys specializing in complex matters of all natures and have written concerning trial techniques. Robert Barefoot was engaged as an expert in the use of natural supplements, specifically minerals and their affect on various forms of cancers. He is a renowned author in the field. There have been many occasions when I have found him to be extraordinary in this field of expertise. My professional opinion is that Robert Barefoot's knowledge and experience with minerals and other natural substances and their application for the treatment of illness is quite unique. In fact, I am not aware of any other individual who possesses the knowledge and expertise in this very important and expanding field as Mr. Barefoot.

David Freishtat, Attorney, Freishtat & Sandler,
Baltimore, Maryland

A Closing Thought by Robert Barefoot

Every decision that the Food and Drug Administration, the Federal Trade Commission, and the American Medical Association make will ultimately result in billions of dollars in profits or losses for the drug industry. The management of each of these organizations intertwines with the drug industry to the point where there is an enormous conflict of interest. Every year the drug industry has several drugs recalled because people are dying. Hundreds of thousands have been killed to date and nothing is said or done by these organizations that are supposed to protect the public. Instead, they spend enormous amounts of time and money trying to suppress the nutrient industry even though no one has ever been killed by a nutrient. Also, even though their own best scientists are advocating that certain nutrients can indeed prevent and cure the worst diseases, they refuse to discuss or evaluate their own findings even though the drug industry itself has on occasion called a nutrient a drug, such as Vitamin D, and sold it for a profit. Instead, they try to incarcerate those advocating the use of nutrients to prevent disease even though there is staggering evidence that the nutrients work. These actions to suppress the truth about nutrition by these organizations make their efforts a conspiracy against the American public, as most diseases can be cured by natural nutrients. They also spend fortunes advocating that nature made a mistake when it created the sun as it causes cancer. This concept is disputed by our best medical researchers who advocate that the sun is crucial to good health, thus it's what occurs in nature versus the FDA coalition, which includes the major medical organizations. You will have to choose who is right—your doctor or what nature intended—it's your choice. Today, we are at the beginning of a new millennium. All major diseases can be wiped out. We can create a disease free America and world. To do this we will have to break the back of the FDA, FTC, and AMA conspiracy with the drug industry. To help accomplish this, get on the internet and read books like *Disease Conspiracy* and others. You will be amazed and dumbfounded by the enormous amount of information that is available about the FDA conspiracy to keep you from knowing about the clinical studies and scientific evidence that prove that you can live a much longer and disease-free life.

Bob Barefoot

CORPORATIONS AND THE GOVERNMENT REPEATEDLY LIE—HERE'S THE PROOF

For years, people like me have been saying the mercury in your fillings is causing all types of disease. The media, the FDA, and the medical community have called us charlatans, snake oil salesmen, and liars for saying such things. Now, finally, on the front page of the *Chicago Tribune*, the headline reads "Are Your Teeth Toxic? The mercury in silver fillings would be hazardous waste in a river, yet it's sitting in your mouth." I made this statement to a reporter, and I was told I was a liar. The article goes on to talk about the fact that the silver in your mouth can and does make you ill. Go back and read my newsletter article where I said if all else fails and you still have symptoms that cannot be cured, clean out all the amalgam fillings in your teeth. There are hundreds of thousands of testimonials from people that had incurable symptoms that are now living happy, healthy lives without disease, illness, or sickness simply by taking the toxic material out of your mouth.

Here is another example. Our friends in the drug industry and the FDA said that an ingredient that has been used for years called phenyl-propanolamine is safe and effective. This is outrageous, but happens all the time; you never hear about it in the news. The FDA repeatedly says drugs are safe and effective. The FDA categorically lies on a regular basis. They say that drugs are safe and effective because of pressure from the politicians who are paid off by the drug executives and the drug companies themselves who are putting the executives at the FDA on their payroll. The FDA also says these drugs are safe and effective because many of the studies they are looking at are fake, and false, and misleading. This has been proven over and over again throughout the world. They also say these drugs are safe and effective because of the review boards of medical doctors. Keep in mind that the review boards only consist of medical doctors, members of the American Medical Association, and no other type of healthcare provider such as a chiropractor, a holistic doctor, a homeopathic doctor, an oriental medicine doctor, or an ayurvedic doctor—no other doctors are allowed, only M.D.s trained by the drug industry. These review boards contain doctors who are on the payroll of the drug industry that is submitting the application for drug approval—again, conflict of interest. So, routinely the FDA says drugs are safe and effective when in fact they are not safe and they are not effective. That means the FDA routinely approves drugs to be sold that cause disease and kill people, and do not do what they are alleged to do. They are not effective at all, and they cause disease, illness, and sickness, including stroke, heart attack, liver damage, fatigue, depression, and death. Then, after hundreds of thousands of people are adversely affected, these drugs are recalled—taken off the market. But no need to worry, the drug companies still made billions of dollars in profits. Who cares about the hundreds of thousands of people who died or have permanently been made sick by these drugs that didn't even do what they were supposed to do. The most recent drug to be recalled is this phenylpropanolamine. It has now been shown that this drug increases stroke, bleeding in the brain, as well as a host of other medical problems. This is a dangerous drug and causes illness and disease. What is this drug in? You wouldn't believe it. Here is a list of medications containing phenylpropanolamine.

- Acutrim® Diet Gum Appetite Suppressant
- Acutrim® Plus Dietary Supplements
- Acutrim® Maximum Strength Appetite Control
- Alka-Seltzer® Plus Children's Cold Medicine Effervescent
- Alka-Seltzer® Plus Cold Medicine (cherry or orange)
- Alka-Seltzer® Plus Cold Medicine Original
- Alka-Seltzer® Plus Cold & Cough Medicine Effervescent
- Alka-Seltzer® Plus Cold & Flu Medicine
- Alka-Seltzer® Plus Cold & Sinus Medicine
- Alka-Seltzer® Plus Night-Time Cold Medicine
- BC® Allergy Sinus Cold Powder
- BC® Sinus Cold Powder
- Comtrex® Flu Therapy & Fever Relief
- Day & Night Contact® 12-Hour Cold Capsules
- Contact® 12 Hour Caplets
- Coricidin D Cold, Flu & Sinus
- Dexatrim® Caffeine Free
- Dexatrim® Extended Duration
- Dexatrim® Gelcaps
- Dexatrim® Vitamin C/Caffeine Free
- Dimetapp® Cold & Allergy Chewable Tablets
- Dimetapp® Cold & Cough Liqui-Gels
- Dimetapp® DM Cold & Cough Elixir
- Dimetapp® Elixir
- Dimetapp® 4 Hour Liquid Gels
- Dimetapp® 4 Hour Tablets
- Dimetapp® 12 Hour Extentabs Tablets
- Naldecon® DX Pediatric Drops
- Permathene Mega-16
- Robitussin® CF
- Tavist-D® 12 Hour Relief of Sinus & Nasal Congestion
- Triaminic® DM Cough Relief
- Triaminic® Expectorant Chest & Head
- Triaminic® Syrup Cold & Allergy
- Triaminic® Triminicol Cold & Cough
- Triaminic® Orange 3D Cold & Allergy Cherry (Pink)

- Triaminic® 3D Cold & Cough Berry
- Triaminic® 3D Cough Relief Yellow 3D Expectorant

Look at this list and ask yourself, have you ever taken this or have you given it to your children. You should be outraged. The FDA is not protecting you and me. The FDA is protecting the profits of the drug companies. I can guarantee you that this over-the-counter medication that you innocently gave to your children or took yourself has caused you to become sick. It may have caused permanent damage. I will say it over and over again, prescription and over-the-counter non-prescription drugs all cause illness and disease. More and more drugs are going to be recalled and pulled from the market. The drug companies and the FDA and other government officials lie on a regular basis.

Another outrage showing that the FDA, the government, and the drug companies lie to us on a regular basis is cough syrup. I have said for years that the research shows around the world and thousands of healthcare providers and doctors agree that over-the-counter cough syrups do not do what they say and are dangerous. I have been called a liar, and a charlatan. It has been said that statements like this that I make will stop people from taking needed medications and therefore I should be silenced. Well, here we go. Front-page news "Cough Syrup Practically Worthless Doctors Say." That's the headline. Who is saying this? Real medical doctors, members of the American Medical Association. Dr. Richard Irwin, chairman of a cough guidelines committee for the American College of Chest Physicians, says over-the-counter cough syrups contain combinations of drugs that have never been proven to treat coughs! How on God's green earth then have the drug companies been able to market these as ways to treat coughs? Answer: they paid off the politicians and the people at the FDA. Open up your eyes folks, this is happening every day. Again, the FDA lies to us and the drug companies lie to us.

Another headline proving that the government officials do not want to tell the truth, but rather increase their own power, prestige, and income is the new DNA technology that has been developed. DNA technology is now one of the most effective ways to prove guilt or innocence in a murder or rape case. There are hundreds, if not thousands, of people in jail today who were convicted of murder, rape, or other crimes that may be cleared of any wrongdoing or proven guilty beyond any doubt if this new simple DNA technology was used to review the evidence of their case. If prosecutors were interested in the truth, and if they were interested in true justice, they would want this DNA test run on all those people in jail. The prosecutors should want to know for sure if the person that they prosecuted and put in jail is in fact the guilty party. If that person is in fact innocent, the prosecutors, in the name of justice, should want that information known so that the person wrongly accused can be released and, just as importantly, so that the investigation on finding the guilty party can continue. Prosecutors do not want this DNA test used on past cases! This is unbelievable to me. I asked prosecutors why this was the case. The answer was prosecutors are not interested in justice; they are interested in winning cases. They only want to get a conviction. These prosecutors are scared to death that the people that they put in jail are innocent. If it is proven beyond any doubt with this new DNA technology that these people that they prosecuted are in fact innocent, it could ruin these prosecutors' careers; therefore, the prosecutors do not want this test run. This is the most unbelievable and outrageous thing I've ever heard. There are people in jail whose lives are destroyed because these prosecutors put them there. The prosecutors do not care if the person is guilty or innocent; they just want the person to stay in jail because if the person was innocent their own careers could be adversely affected. How can these people sleep at night? This shows you that the people in government are not interested in anything or anyone else except themselves and their own power, prestige, careers, money, and influence.

YOU CAN'T BELIEVE THE MEDIA

The news media simply lies to you. The news media cannot be trusted. They lie to you and mislead you in several ways. First, they do this purposely because the officers and directors and stockholders of the television, newspaper, radio, and magazine media want to use that media to help their other investments and businesses and industries that they are a part of. They are simply using the media as a propaganda tool. The second way you are misled and lied to, as I mentioned earlier, is the producers want to create sensational programming to get great ratings; therefore, they can get promotions, increase their national influence, power, prestige, and incomes. And thirdly, national news organizations simply do not do a good job of fact checking information. This happens all the time. Most recently, it happened to me. ABC News, which repeatedly attacks me, because the directors of the news organization have major ties to the pharmaceutical industry, did a story on *Nightline*. The interview with the *Nightline* person lasted over an hour and a half; they edited it down to make me look bad as they always do. Here is a major news organization that can't even get the facts right. They mentioned that I put on a pool tournament in Chicago, Illinois. It was amazing because the film crew was actually there for around six hours at the pool tournament filming me. The pool tournament was in Orlando, Florida; the film crew was there in Orlando, Florida! But the *Nightline* piece said on their website and on the television that it was in Chicago. They can't even get their facts straight. *20/20* did a piece and said lie after lie after lie about me. They said I never sent them the report on the University of Calgary study on the combination of herbs that has been used in treating diabetes. The fact is that studies have been done on this combination of herbs (the FTC prohibits me from mentioning its trade name). You can go to their official website, which I sent to ABC News, showing all the information from the University of Calgary and the various diabetic associations in Asia. They simply lied to the public about the truth about the fact that there is an herbal all-natural way to cure diabetes.

I sent them the information from the *New England Journal of Medicine* where the American Medical Association was quoted saying that 900,000 people died by taking pharmaceutical drugs. They said that that statement was untrue. The statement is true. I sent them the information. They simply blatantly lied. The question that some of you ask is how come I can't sue ABC News for this misleading fraudulent piece on both *Nightline* and *20/20*? The answer is under the free speech laws they can pretty much get away with anything as long as they prove that they "thought it was true when they made the statement and did it without malice"; therefore, I would have to prove that they did this maliciously! Now that is pretty hard to prove in court. This is how the news media gets away with lies. You can go to www.kevinfightsback.com and I will soon have all of the *Nightline*, *20/20*, and various pieces that have been put out, and I give you fact by fact rebuttals, showing you how these organizations are full of crap, mislead, and lie to you.

WEBMD IS PROPAGANDA MACHINE
FOR BIG PHARMA!

Thirty million people visited WebMD last month. They went there to get information about health. Unfortunately, what they didn't realize is

WebMD is nothing more than a front organization for the pharmaceutical industry. It is a propaganda machine designed to sell you things that the pharmaceutical industry sells. They want to sell you drugs and surgery. They want to bash any natural, inexpensive, non-drug and non-surgical way to cure and prevent disease. WebMD is full of lies and misinformation. There should be a disclosure stating that this is nothing more than a front by the pharmaceutical industry, and in fact owned by the pharmaceutical industry. Here are excerpts of an article about WebMD. Robert Davis, Ph.D., writes, "Do both types of medicine deserve media coverage, alternative and conventional?" Many people who go to WebMD ask about dietary supplements or other alternative therapies. Many of these people express disappointment and even anger over what they regard as WebMD's inadequate attention to such topics. For example, one user weighing various options for relieving back pain inquires why WebMD's treatment section on back pain barely mentioned chiropractic care. Would it not be reasonable to at least touch on the subject? Likewise, another WebMD user observes that in WebMD's cholesterol information section there is no discussion at all about fish oil supplements, a therapy that has been proven to reduce cholesterol.

The outrage is that WebMD gives false and misleading information about these alternatives. It's as if they are trying to get you away from believing that inexpensive non-drug and non-surgical ways to cure and prevent disease are effective and safe. It appears that WebMD is simply trying to get you to believe that drugs and surgery are the only answer, that they are all safe, and that they are all more effective than anything else you could choose. WebMD's health guide reference on back pain goes into great detail about medications, surgery, and even experimental therapies like botox, but devotes just two sentences to chiropractic care saying that it's unproven! This is a flagrant lie. The Chiropractic Association sued the American Medical Association in the state of Illinois over the statements made by the American Medical Association that chiropractic care was unproven, unsafe, and ineffective against back pain. In the courts it was proven the exact opposite is true. It was proven in court that the chiropractic care and options are actually more effective than anything the American Medical Association doctors could provide in the form of surgery or drugs. Chiropractic care is proven and more effective than any drugs or surgery. WebMD is simply lying to you.

Likewise, studies show that omega 3 fatty acids found in fish oils lower levels of blood fats and triglycerides. But WebMD's cholesterol health center refers only to the benefits of eating fish, but never discusses the inexpensive alternative to the lipitors, which are fish oils.

This is why www.naturalcures.com is so needed. Www.natural cures.com will be the only place in the world where you can get unbiased health information. At www.naturalcures.com we will give you the drug options and the surgery options, we will give you all the options that are available to medical science, but we will also go into depth and tell you all the true information about herbs, homeopathy, naturopathy, energy healing, chiropractic, acupuncture, supplements, foods, stress reduction, etc., etc., etc. At www.naturalcures.com if you went to back pain or cholesterol you would see all the choices without any bias. We take no advertising and we sell no products. We only want to provide you true information. My website www.naturalcures.com is in its infancy and needs your support to become what I envision it to be. Please go to www.naturalcures.com and become a member and encourage all of your friends to become members as well.

CHAPTER 8

The Insider Secrets They Don't Want You to Know

The perfect bureaucrat and politician is the man who makes no decisions and escapes all responsibility.

—Brooks Atkinson

ABC'S *GOOD MORNING AMERICA* ATTACKS ME!

ABC's *Good Morning America* television show, at the time of this writing of this chapter, is putting together what I believe to be a one-sided, false, and misleading story on me and my best-selling *Natural Cures* book. By the time you are reading this there is a good chance that the story may have already run. Without seeing the final story, I will give you the interesting facts as I know them up until this point. As you all know, the drug companies do not want me selling my book and exposing the fact that drugs are ineffective and unsafe, and that there are in fact natural "cures" for virtually every disease. The drug companies do not want you to know that they are only in business to make money and sell you more drugs.

The major food companies want my book off the market because they do not want me exposing the fact that the major food companies are secretly putting chemicals and ingredients in the food purposely to increase your appetite, get you physically addicted, and make you fat. Both the powerful pharmaceutical industry and food industry are spending millions of dollars in public relations campaigns and funneling millions of dollars to lobbyists in Washington, putting pressure on

169

Washington politicians to use agencies like the FDA and the FTC to stop me from selling my book.

The FTC uses "news organizations" and TV shows such as ABC's *Good Morning America* to spread their anti–Kevin Trudeau propaganda. ABC's *Good Morning America* show is heavily sponsored by both the drug companies and the major food industry. Therefore, ABC does not want me selling my book either. They have a major conflict of interest. Here is what I believe has happened.

The Federal Trade Commission sent out false and misleading press releases to news organizations all around the country trying to get people to run negative stories on me and my *Natural Cures* book because it became the fastest selling book in American history where tens of millions of people were exposed to the shocking truth and dirty little secrets about the drug industry and the food industry. Both of these industries started using the millions of dollars that they have available to spread misleading and false information about me and my book. The major television networks that get hundreds of millions of dollars in sponsorship money from both the food industry and the drug industry have pressure put on them by those industries to run negative stories about me and my book. The individual reporters doing these stories, and producers of these stories, probably own stock in fast food companies, major food industry companies, and pharmaceutical companies. My book is probably having an adverse affect on their own stock portfolios, so they have a major incentive to run negative stories about me and my book.

It appears the FTC covertly worked with ABC's *Good Morning America*, giving them false and misleading information about me and my book. ABC's *Good Morning America* called me asking for me to do a taped interview. We all know that when a news organization does a taped interview they have the ability to edit that interview and make you look like a complete idiot. Their selective editing also twists and misleads the facts and truth. Therefore, most prominent people do not do taped interviews, they will only do live interviews. This way, there can be no editing and you can hear the complete information in an unedited form. I told ABC News that I would be more than happy to go to New York at my own expense and do a live interview. They categorically denied my request. They only wanted to do a taped interview so that they could butcher my comments and produce a piece that was one-sided, biased, false, and misleading.

Even though they knew that I declined doing a taped interview, they arrived at my home unannounced at 7:15 A.M. with TV cameras and reporters. I was still in bed sleeping. At 7:15 A.M., totally unannounced, the ABC News film crew started banging on my door and ringing the doorbell nonstop for thirty minutes! How unprofessional, rude, and an invasion of privacy. Why did they show up at 7:15 A.M.? So that they could make it appear that I was unwilling to answer the door and answer their questions. This is false and misleading.

I would like to send a film crew of my own to the individual reporters' and producers' houses, as well as the president of the ABC *Good Morning America* show and bang on their doors at 7:15 A.M. demanding a personal interview. I would like them to see how it feels!

The reporter started yelling through the door that my book did not contain natural "cures." This is false and misleading. In Chapter 6 of my book it specifically says that the "cure" for every disease is doing the things in Chapter 6. The book does give you the natural cure for every disease. Any statement otherwise is false and misleading. The reporter also started yelling through the door that many people were unhappy with the book because they felt that the book did not contain natural cures. This is false and misleading also. I get over 500 e-mails a day. The vast majority of these people absolutely love the book and for those people who are smart enough to do the things in Chapter 6, those individuals are seeing their diseases and illnesses diminish or be totally cured.

The fact is, if ABC portrays any of these false and misleading situations I will take massive and immediate action against this organization. For example, if ABC's *Good Morning America* show tries to make you believe that I denied doing an interview or would not come to the door when they came to do an interview, this is false and misleading. I absolutely accepted doing a live interview. If ABC News does not clearly state that they came to my door at 7:15 A.M. and banged on it for thirty minutes, and they try to suggest that I was unwilling to answer the door, that is false and misleading. They woke me out of bed and, of course, I would not answer the door. These reporters were so belligerent and rude, they would not leave when requested to do so. I had to call the police and the police escorted them off the property for trespassing. If ABC's *Good Morning America* segment suggests that the book does not contain natural cures, this is flagrantly untrue as the book does contain the natural cure for every disease and clearly says so. If ABC News suggests that huge percentages of people are unhappy with the book, this is flagrantly untrue as the vast majority of people who buy the book, who read the book cover to cover, absolutely love the information that is in it and are benefiting greatly from it.

You need to know that news organizations do not provide you with accurate, truthful "news." You have to know that organizations like ABC's *Good Morning America* are not news organizations giving you facts. They are propaganda machines that are in effect owned by the sponsors. ABC's *Good Morning America* show is nothing more than a propaganda machine for the drug companies and the food industry. The drug companies and the food industry hate my book and hate me blowing the whistle on their deceptions and lies. They use these organizations to stifle people's First Amendment rights. You can be assured that I am taking the leading role in this country at fighting these news organizations from false and misleading portrayals of information.

A good example of this is the boxing promoter Don King. The TV network ESPN produced a segment about Don King. This segment gave the impression that it was giving the viewer "facts" about Don King. It gave the viewer the impression that it was reporting "news" about Don King. This was not true. This segment was merely giving the opinions of the producers. It portrayed information that may have been untrue and false, and at least was misleading. It did not give you the entire true, honest, clear, balanced picture of Don King. This happens all the time in the news media. It happens in newspapers, magazines, television, and radio. These news organizations are no longer presenting factual news. They are nothing more than propaganda machines for the publicly traded companies that own them. Don King was so furious that he surprised the world by filing a $2.5 billion lawsuit against ESPN. I support Don King's action 100 percent. We have to stop the television stations, the radio stations, the newspapers, and the magazines from having the ability to twist facts and present information that is false, misleading, and deceiving. People need to know the conflicts of interests with these stations in relation to the stories and viewpoints that they express. People need to know that when a TV station says something is bad, that there may be a financial incentive for that station to say that something is bad. People need to have full disclosure. Honesty, truth, and fairness in the media should be something that people everywhere should demand. If not, then TV, radio, newspapers, and magazines will continue to be nothing more than the propaganda outlets of those who own them, using them for their own personal financial self-interests.

Please support me in my fight against this injustice. Write ABC's *Good Morning America* and tell them that you love this book and you love the work I'm doing. Tell them you are upset with their one-sided, biased, unfair portrayal of me and my book. Tell them you are upset; that the sponsors of their show, the drug companies and the food industry, have such an ability to dictate the content of their programming. Tell them you think it was unfair for the reporters to be banging on my door at 7:15 A.M. Tell them you're mad as hell and are not going to take it anymore. Please know that this will not be the first battle. I thank you for your support as I fight this battle—not for me, but for you. Remember folks, I don't need to be doing this. I know all this information. I have it. My family has it. We enjoy spectacular health. We don't take drugs; we don't get sick. We know this information. I'm doing this work for you, and believe me I am taking massive amounts of heat and abuse because I have chosen this mission. Please continue your support.

ABC'S *GOOD MORNING AMERICA* PUTS OUT FALSE AND MISLEADING STORY ON ME AND MY *NATURAL CURES* BOOK

ABC's *Good Morning America* did a story on me and the *Natural Cures* book. The story was flagrantly false and misleading in the net impression it left on people watching it. This is standard operating procedure by the news media. Why would the news media do a negative story on my book? Very simple. The majority of advertising money that ABC gets is from the pharmaceutical industry and the large food companies. These are the two industries that I expose the most in my book for their fraud and corruption and how they are in fact making us sick and fat on purpose so that they can make more profits. I believe that the sponsors put pressure on ABC to put this misleading story on.

The most obvious example of how they misled the public in their story was when they showed the reporter knocking on my door and made it appear that I was unwilling to answer the door and answer their questions. What they failed to mention was that they came to my door at approximately 7:00 A.M. in the morning unannounced. This way, they knew that I could not answer the door since I was still sleeping. This is misleading. It is also misleading because I repeatedly told them that I would do a live interview at any time. They denied my request. I also repeatedly told them that I would do a taped interview provided that I could view how they edited my comments. They denied my request again. You see, it is obvious that they wanted to mislead you into believing that I had "something to hide" or was unwilling to answer their questions. I need your support. Please write ABC's *Good Morning America* and tell them you are outraged at their false and misleading representation in their story. Tell them how much you benefited from the book and my newsletters and how the information is in fact changing your health for the better. I need your support now more than ever. You can write ABC at ABC, Inc., 500 S. Buena Vista Street, Burbank, CA 91521-4551, or call (818) 460-7477, or e-mail netaudr@abc.com.

I AM NOT ALONE!

Medical doctors now are backing up what I say!

The *New York Times* ran a public health notice, which was published on January 23, 2005. This public health notice was put out by Dr. Matthias Rath, M.D.

NO AMNESTY FOR MAKERS OF DEADLY DRUGS!
PROTECT YOUR HEALTH! ACT NOW!

Largely unbeknownst to the American people there is a war going on that has claimed victims in every family. This war is escalating and threatens every human life. It is a war being waged in the interests of the multibillion dollar pharmaceutical industry, which is not a health industry but rather an investment business built upon the continuation and expansion of global diseases. Your health and the health of every person in America is threatened in several ways:

1. *"The business with disease" as the basis of the pharmaceutical industry.* The pharmaceutical industry is a multibillion dollar investment business that has orchestrated the largest fraud in human history. It promises health, but in fact thrives on the continuation of diseases. This fraud scheme is easily unmasked. Most pharmaceutical drugs are designed to merely cover disease symptoms, but are not intended to cure or eradicate diseases. As a direct result of this multibillion dollar fraud business, no cure has ever been found for cardiovascular disease, cancer, diabetes, or any other chronic disease. On the con-

trary, these diseases continue in epidemic proportions, killing about 5,000 Americans every day. This compares to the annihilation of a city the size of San Francisco every year.

2. *The epidemic of dangerous side effects caused by pharmaceutical drugs.* The dangerous side effects of Vioxx, Celebrex, Lipitor and Prozac are not the exception, they are the rule. Due to their synthetic nature, most pharmaceutical drugs are toxic to our bodies, causing organ damage and other serious side effects. According to the American Medical Association, one million American suffered disabilities from taking pharmaceutical drugs and more than 100,000 of them die as a result of this every single year.

3. *Legislation that protects the expansion of the deadly business with disease.* For decades drug companies have used their giant profits to manipulate the public and influence legislation, including that from the U.S. Congress and the White House. Now that the deadly consequences of the pharmaceutical fraud business have been unmasked the survival of this industry depends on the protectionist laws. The current push of the Bush administration for so-called "medical liability reform" is not about protecting gynecologists and medical doctors from medical liability lawsuits. The centerpiece of the proposed medical liability legislation is to prohibit punitive damage awards and liability lawsuits brought by injured patients against drug companies. This medical liability legislation is being used as a cover to grant amnesty to drug manufacturers, protecting them from having to compensate millions of patients for the harm their drugs have caused. It is payback for the pharmaceutical industry, which was the largest corporate sponsor of the Bush election campaign. The people of America and their political representatives have to realize that the proposed medical liability legislation is a "Trojan Horse." Passing it means granting immunity to the drug makers, allowing them the unrestricted expansion of their deadly business with disease at the expense of patients. As the direct consequence of this law, tens of millions of Americans will suffer disability and die from preventable diseases within the next decades.

4. *Withholding life saving information about the health benefits of vitamins and natural therapies.* A precondition for this "business with disease" based on patentable synthetic drugs is

the suppression of effective and safe, but non-patentable and therefore less profitable, natural therapies. For decades the pharmaceutical industry has strategically expanded its influence on medical education with devastating results. It has deliberately blocked any information about the essential role of vitamins and other micronutrients in maintaining health contained in every textbook of biology, biochemistry and natural science from entering medical school teaching and medical practice. Through their strategic influence, the pharmaceutical industry has established a global monopoly on medicine. As a direct result, generations of medical doctors have not received adequate training in nutritional and other natural therapies. Doctors and patients alike have become victims of the pharmaceutical industry's efforts to monopolize human health. As a result, tens of millions of Americans have died unnecessarily over the past decades because this life-saving health information has not been available to them.

5. *Suppressing effective natural therapies by law.* Effective, safe and non-patentable natural therapies threaten the very basis of the pharmaceutical investment business. They target and correct the underlying cellular deficiencies of today's most common diseases, thereby preventing and even eradicating them. The elimination of any disease inevitably destroys a multibillion dollar drug market for the pharmaceutical industry, thus the pharmaceutical industry has launched a global campaign to protect its patent-based "business with disease" by outlawing natural non-patentable therapies at the national and international level. This is the background for the Bush administration's attack on the Dietary Supplement Health and Education Act. The key legislation protecting the rights of the American people for free access to natural therapies and to freedom of health choice. If this fundamental human right to natural health is taken away the health of billions of people will be compromised and tens of millions of them will pay the ultimate price for generations to come.

This public health notice was written by a medical doctor! I wholeheartedly support Dr. Rath's work and courage.

I WAS RIGHT! FDA CALLS LEVITRA® AD FALSE AND MISLEADING!

In my newsletter a few months ago I had mentioned that the ad for the drug Levitra is false and misleading. Obviously, someone at the FDA is reading this newsletter. Obviously, your letters and calls of outrage are making a difference. The FDA now has stated that the ads for Levitra and Zyrtec® are false, misleading, and full of unsubstantiated claims. The federal regulators have ordered the ads be pulled. The FDA says that the ads make unprovable claims and fail to highlight side effects and FDA warnings as to the dangerous nature of the drugs. The ads for Zyrtec compare two people—one obviously sick, sneezing and wiping her nose, and another who looks perfectly healthy. The captions of the ads imply that the healthy and alert person has taken Zyrtec; the sickly and unhappy one has taken a different medication. The FDA says this is giving the wrong net impression to the consumer; it is false and misleading.

This is good news, but one obvious action is missing. The outrage is the FDA "asks" the companies to stop running the ads. The FDA is not ordering the companies to stop running the ads! But the most obvious outrage is where is the FTC?! The Federal Trade Commission is supposed to prosecute companies that mislead the public in their advertising. The FTC routinely files lawsuits against companies who they claim are running ads that are false and misleading, or contain unsubstantiated claims. In every single case, the FTC files lawsuits against these companies, demands a complete asset freeze of the entire corporation, as well as a personal asset freeze of all directors and officers of those corporations. This happens time and time again. However, we'll note that the FTC takes this action virtually only against companies that sell all-natural products. Here, the drug manufacturers have produced advertising that has already been deemed to be false and misleading, and contain unsubstantiated claims. Where is the FTC?

The outrage is why the FTC isn't prosecuting these companies in the same aggressive manner that the FTC goes after companies that sell natural products. Why isn't the FTC suing these drug manufacturers, demanding a complete asset freeze and a complete freezing of personal assets of the officers and directors? The answer is political payoffs. Every one of you reading this should be mad as hell. This is an outrage to the highest degree. The corruption in both the FDA and the

FTC is beyond belief. I have personal investigators reviewing all of the workings at these organizations. I have inside moles telling me the secrets. We are looking at the individual people involved at both the FDA and the FTC. I can tell you that these people are making millions of dollars through buying and selling stock on insider information, as well as potentially other illegal activities. My sources are telling me this and I believe it to be true. I will be writing a complete book about the workings of the FTC and the FDA. In this book I will name names. When you start investigating the individual people involved in these organizations and you look at how much money their friends and relatives are making, who they work for, their stock transactions, their secret meetings, etc., you find fraud, deception, and corruption all the way up and down the line.

The FTC needs to take action against the drug companies for producing false and misleading advertising, yet it does nothing. It must demand 100 percent consumer redress. That means it must demand that the drug companies give back all of the money to every single person who bought those drugs under false and misleading pretenses. This is what the FTC does when it sues companies that sell all-natural products. It demands that every consumer get all of their money back because those consumers purchased the product on unsubstantiated claims or were misled and misrepresented by the advertising. This is exactly what has happened in the case of these drug companies. They produced ads that were false and misleading and contained unsubstantiated claims. People purchased these drugs based on these false pretenses. The companies should be penalized, the individual officers and directors should be penalized, and the customers should get all their money back. The FTC does nothing. This is an outrage. Folks, we are a major force that is effecting change. Please pick up the phone and call the FTC, or write the FTC, and tell them "I'm mad as hell and I'm not going to take it anymore. I support Kevin Trudeau." The FTC's fax number is (202) 326-2012, Attention: Consumer Response Center (CRC), their mailing address is Federal Trade Commission, 600 Pennsylvania Avenue, N.W., Washington, D.C. 20580, and to send an e-mail go to www.ftc.gov and click on "File a Complaint."

STAY AWAY FROM ASPARTAME!

Aspartame is marketed as NutraSweet®, Equal®, and Spoonful®. If it says sugar-free on the label, don't even think about it! Aspartame is so dangerous that when the temperature of this sweetener exceeds eighty-six degrees, the wood alcohol in aspartame converts to formaldehyde, and then to formic acid, which in turn causes metabolic acidosis. Formic acid is the poison found in the sting of fire ants. The methyl toxicity mimics, among other conditions, multiple sclerosis and systemic lupus. This is why MS is being diagnosed more than ever before. This is also why lupus is being diagnosed more than ever before. In my opinion, these symptoms are being misdiagnosed and the problem is simply aspartame. Aspartame also gives you symptoms of Fibromyalgia, spasms, shooting pains, numbness in your lungs, cramps, vertigo, dizziness, headaches, tinnitus, joint pain, depression, anxiety attacks, slurred speech, blurred vision, memory loss, and leads to other major diseases.

Keep in mind that diet products use aspartame so that they can claim that these are good to help you lose weight. The exact opposite is true. These chemically altered products make your body crave carbohydrates. When you are eating or drinking diet products using aspartame you are almost assured to gain weight. The poison in aspartame stores in the fat cells, particularly in the hips and thighs. When the poison stores in the fat cells, the fat cells need to dilute the poison by retaining fluid. This is why people who drink lots of diet sodas have bigger hips and thighs. Aspartame is also extremely dangerous for diabetics because it drives the blood sugar out of control. This also causes the body to convert food to fat much more easily. Children, pregnant women, and diabetics are especially at risk for neurological disorders and should never be given artificial sweeteners, particularly aspartame.

Somebody will ask, "Why isn't something being done about this?" The answer is for you to remember "it's always all about the money." Here is a prime example of how the money flow works to keep the truth hidden from you. Monsanto, the leading manufacturer of aspartame and the patent holder, funds the American Diabetic Association, the American Dietetic Association, and the American Academy of Family Physicians. This means that Monsanto in effect owns these associations. Because these associations are dependent on the money they receive from Monsanto, they have made a deal with Monsanto to not criticize aspartame to the food industry and, more shockingly, they are actually required to endorse Monsanto's products! Can you see why you can never believe anything you hear from any of these "associations"? Every single association, from the American Medical Association, the American Cancer Society, the American Heart Association, the American Diabetic Association, and on and on and on all receive money from special interest groups. When they receive the money from these special interest groups they are told what products to endorse and which ones to criticize. These associations are nothing more than mouthpieces for the multinational corporations that are secretly giving them the money to operate. Stay away from aspartame and every artificial sweetener. Stay away from Splenda. I will write more on Splenda later, but if you want to get the inside scoop on Splenda go to www.thetruthaboutsplenda.com. The bottom line here is, as I always state, do not buy any product from a publicly traded corporation. Do not buy any name brand products. Every product that you want is available from a small independent producer who is making a good quality product that will not make you sick.

NATURAL CURES BOOK MAKES
FRONT PAGE OF *USA TODAY* NEWSPAPER!

The *Natural Cures* book was mentioned on the front page of the newspaper *USA Today*. It was also on the front page of the *Life* section of *USA Today*, and another article was on page 2 of the *Life* section of *USA Today*. According to *USA Today*, the *Natural Cures* book is the number two best-selling book in the whole United States, second only to *Harry Potter!* That makes it the number one nonfiction book in America. The sales of *Natural Cures* in bookstores and via the infomercial are unprecedented. This is a testament to the fact that people are telling people, are telling people, and are telling people about the book. It shows that people are reading the book and positively experiencing results from the information in the book and telling their friends, relatives, and neighbors about it. It's amazing to me when I go to places I see people reading my book. The most exciting thing, however, is when people spot me and tell me the positive effect my book has had in their life. Folks, when just one person comes up to me and hugs me and says that the information in my book has made their life better that makes all the criticism I am receiving, and attacks that I get, all worth it. Why is it that the news media and the government can't see the positive effects that this book is having? The answer is they do know that people are being positively influenced by my book. They also know that my book is having a negative influence on the drug industry and the pharmaceutical industry, and is exposing the corruption in government agencies at the highest level. This shows the government agencies are not interested in the people, they are only interested in their own money, power, and influence. They are only interested in protecting the profits of the multinational corporations, and protecting their own corrupt organizations. I am interested in what benefits the people—that's the difference.

The important thing about these *USA Today* articles is that *USA Today* refuses to allow me to run ads for my book. This is significant. This shows exactly what I say in my book about how the news media controls the free flow of information. In my book I point out the fact that newspapers such as *USA Today* are in fact publicly traded companies or owned by publicly traded companies. These publicly traded companies are owned and controlled by people who have major financial ties to the pharmaceutical industry, the food industry, and the oil industry. My book, therefore, is something that the people who control *USA Today* do not want you to read. Let me say that again. The people who control *USA Today* are heavily tied to the drug industry; therefore, they do not want you to read my book. They want to do everything they can to discredit my book. Therefore, they will write articles about my book, but forbid me to run advertising promoting my book. This should be illegal, but it's not. Why? Because the power rich who control *USA Today* also give millions of dollars to the politicians who make laws. That's how it works.

Let me point out, in *USA Today*, what was written and the inaccuracies. The first thing that happens any time any news organization writes about me or my book is they point out something that I totally think is irrelevant. They keep bringing up the fact that I have no medical training, am a convicted felon, and the FTC has repeatedly sued me. These are three issues that have no relevance to the book. Everyone knows I'm not a doctor, and everyone knows that a medical doctor could never write the *Natural Cures* book because they are too tied to the drug industry. Everyone knows that in my early twenties I pled guilty to applying for a credit card incorrectly and have a felony conviction. I talk about it in my book; I've talked about it for years; I've turned my life around; I took responsibility for my actions, and I'm one of the great American success stories for it. And everyone knows that I have constantly exposed the corruption at the Federal Trade Commission and because of that the Federal Trade Commission has repeatedly sued me. What is never brought up is that these suits have been baseless and there has never been a finding of any wrongdoing. In other words, the FTC is repeatedly filing frivolous lawsuits against me in an attempt to discredit me. What they don't mention is that there are no consumer complaints for any of my products. They don't mention that I have over 25 million customers and that over 95 percent of them absolutely love my products and the way we conduct business. I have one of the highest customer satisfaction rates of any business in the world.

So let's point out some inaccuracies. First they call me a former used car salesman. Categorically not true. I used to be in the new car business, not used car business, for six months when I was nineteen years old. The article says much of the book's success hinges on my infomercials. That's debatable, but the fact is people are telling people, are telling people, are telling people, and that's why the book is selling so well. They talk about the fact that the FTC sued me for selling coral calcium. What they don't say is that in every lawsuit filed by any attorney general or the FTC that there has never been a finding of any wrongdoing. What they don't say is that these charges are trumped up and frivolous. What they don't say is that there are no consumer complaints.

The second article, on page 2, was laughable. The whole article basically says that "medical experts question much of [my] advice." It then goes on to quote "medical doctors, pharmaceutical paid representatives, drug company representatives, and government officials." Of course these people are not going to believe what I say in the book. They have financial interests if you do not believe what I say in the book. Do you understand that? It's important when a medical doctor or any member of government says something negative about my book. They have a financial interest in you NOT believing what I say. I, on the other hand, have absolutely no financial interest if you DO believe in what I say. See the difference? I'm telling you to do things that I have no financial interest in. A medical doctor is telling you to do things from which he makes money if you do them. Remember, it's always about the money.

I would encourage you to write these reporters and tell them that you bought the book, liked the book, and tell them your success story. The two reporters at *USA Today* are Liz Szabo, phone number (703) 854-5455, e-mail address Lszabo@usatoday.com, and Gary Strauss, phone number (703) 854-3420, e-mail address gstrauss@usatoday.com, and *USA Today*'s e-mail address editor@usatoday.com.

NATURAL CURES DISCUSSED ON
THE BILL O'REILLY SHOW

The O'Reilly Factor, starring Bill O'Reilly on FOX News television cable network, had a featured segment on the *Natural Cures* book. Originally, O'Reilly's office called and asked me to appear on the 10th of August. I was unavailable as I was doing a seven-day fast at the We Care Spa outside of Palm Springs (yes, I actually do all the things I say to do in my book!). I explained that I would be available on the 17th of August. This was confirmed. However, someone dropped the ball somewhere and the O'Reilly people had me inadvertently scheduled on August 10th. I could not make the personal appearance, so my lead attorney, David Bradford from the law firm of Jenner & Block, made an appearance on my behalf. Bill O'Reilly was there with a reporter who wrote a negative article about me, and Stephen Barrett, who is the gentleman that runs the website *Quack Watch*.

Stephen Barrett is a disgraced ex-psychiatrist who was proven in a Wisconsin court to lie and defraud the public about natural healthcare. He is nothing more than a pawn for the pharmaceutical industry and bashes anything to do with natural or alternative medicine. This man is nothing more than a spokesperson for the drug companies. In his view there is no natural remedy for anything, and the only way to be well is to take drugs, take drugs, take drugs, take drugs, take drugs— and if that doesn't work, have surgery, have more surgery, and have more surgery. In my opinion, he is a complete idiot. He doesn't believe chiropractics works, acupuncture works, or anything works. He only believes that drugs, drugs, drugs, and surgery, surgery, surgery are the only answers. Looking at his financial background, it would not surprise me if this guy was being paid millions of dollars into Swiss bank accounts by the pharmaceutical industry to put out this Joseph Goebbels–type propaganda against alternative natural remedies. On the air he appeared like a bumbling buffoon and a complete idiot.

The reporter had nothing at all to say, mumbled, and could only come up with the fact that I was sued by the FTC on various occasions with alleged fraud.

My attorney, David Bradford, was brilliant. Even Bill O'Reilly came to my defense on several occasions. We exposed the fact that I have never been found guilty of any wrongdoing or any false and misleading advertising. We exposed the fact that all the press releases and lawsuits by the FTC were frivolous, lies, misrepresentations, or outright attempts to discredit me. We exposed the fact that over three million people have purchased the book, and the book is well-balanced, tells people to visit licensed healthcare practitioners, and gives people all kinds of options to consider. The book clearly states that everything in it is my opinion, that people have to be exposed to various ideas, and that no one has a monopoly on the truth. I want to personally thank Bill O'Reilly for talking about my book on the show. I would also like to thank Bill O'Reilly for taking a very fair and balanced approach to discussing the book and letting all sides be heard. I happen to enjoy Bill O'Reilly's show and think he does a great job and this segment was no exception. If you want to write Bill O'Reilly personally and let him know that you benefited from my book, you can do so by writing Bill O'Reilly at oreilly@foxnews.com. Any comment to Bill about the fact that you purchased the book, liked the book, and benefited from it would dramatically help. However, as I wrote earlier in the newsletter, if you simply send me the letter in a "To whom it may concern" format, I will send it to Bill O'Reilly for you, as well as other reporters around the country and the world.

In relation specifically to the Bill O'Reilly piece I would like to mention the following. Immediately upon conclusion of the show I was inundated with phone calls, letters, and e-mails from people who saw the show and told me how much they supported me and my work. The outpouring of support was overwhelming and I want to thank all of the people who took the time to write and call expressing their belief in my mission. One particular person called and I would like to summarize what she had to say.

> I contacted Mr. O'Reilly to let him know I was not happy with him. I had a son who was diagnosed with terminal brain cancer in 1991. I did not want him to have chemotherapy and radiation so I took him to Mexico for alternative treatment. I was arrested and charged with child neglect and child abuse because I did not give my child chemotherapy and radiation. How insane. The charges were eventually dropped. My son never got chemotherapy or radiation and only used alternative natural treatments. My son is cancer free and currently lives in Austin, Texas. I believe the government does not want a cure for cancer. I believe Kevin Trudeau is doing a wonderful job and that Americans

should have the freedom of choice for health care. Kevin keep up the good work.

VF, Michigan

These are the type of comments that make all the difference because people are being saved by the information available in the *Natural Cures* book.

FIND THE CAUSE TO CURE YOUR DISEASE

I can't harp on this enough. People are always saying what's the natural cure for this Kevin? What's the natural cure for this disease? What's the natural cure for this ailment? The answer is always the same. You must find the cause, you cannot treat the symptom! Medical doctors today never ask what the cause of a symptom is. Medical doctors today simply treat symptoms. This is the problem with medical treatment today. If you have a pain in your hand and you go to a doctor, the doctor says "Hmm … what can I do to reduce or eliminate the pain? Hmm … maybe this cream will numb the pain. Maybe this pill will numb the pain. Maybe this injection will numb the pain." Maybe cutting out a part of your anatomy will numb and stop the pain. All the doctor is trying to do is treat the symptom. He's trying to get the pain to be reduced or go away by giving you some synthetic chemical drug, cutting out parts of your anatomy, or some other abnormal treatment. The problem with this approach is he's never asking, "What's causing the pain?" He's never asking what the cause is; he's never treating the root cause. Without treating the cause, you'll never solve the problem, you're never really fixing the situation. If you go to your doctor and you have heartburn the doctor says, "Hmm … what can I do to stop the heartburn? What can I do to suppress the symptom of heartburn? Maybe take this pill, maybe cut out a part of your anatomy." All he's thinking about is trying to come up with something that will stop the symptom of heartburn. What he should be asking is, what is causing heartburn in this patient? Why is this person developing heartburn? What is going on inside that is making this person's body be abnormal? What is causing it? Could it be his body is out of balance? Could it be something he is eating? Could it be some non-prescription or prescription drug he is currently taking or has taken in the past? Could it be some emotional difficulty the patient is going through? Could it be some structural issue such as his spine is out of balance? Could it be a genetic heredity situation that needs to be looked at? Could it be that the food this person's consuming is all microwaved or pasteurized with no living enzymes? Could it be that this particular person is deficient in some vitamins, minerals, or other nutrients? The doctor never asks for the cause, he never tries to find the cause.

If you truly want to be healthy, you cannot be treating symptoms. You can't just try to suppress the symptoms. You must ask what the cause is. By doing this you will eliminate or reduce symptoms in the future. When you just suppress a symptom what occurs is something else is going to develop later on, and it will probably be much more serious and much more severe. People ask me all the time, "Kevin, what do you do when you have a headache?" My answer is, "I don't know because I've never had a headache." This is true. I never have a headache, but if I did have a headache I wouldn't say to myself, "Hmm … it must be an aspirin deficiency." I wouldn't ask myself what pill can I take to numb the pain. What I would ask myself is what has happened in the last twenty-four hours that is causing pain to be in my head? I would ask, what could be the cause? The first thing I would do is suggest it could be some buildup of toxins and I would probably do a fast, do a colonic, or do some gentle cleanse for the next twenty-four hours. I would probably also rest. I may use Biotape; I may use some magnets to help stimulate my body's own ability to heal itself. I wouldn't try to suppress the symptom; I would try to help my body cure itself. I would stimulate my own body's immune system. If you want to be healthy it's important that you not suppress symptoms, but ask what the cause is. Always, always, always seek professional care from a licensed healthcare practitioner. I recommend getting two or three opinions and going to people who do not use drugs and surgery, this way you'll get more information and more options.

ASSASSINATION ATTEMPT!

People always come up to me on the street, shake my hand, and thank me for writing the book. They have seen and read the blistering attacks. They come up to me and thank me for the book, thank me for the information, and tell me how their lives are better because they are starting to do some of the things in the book to improve their health and quality of life. They thank me for opening their eyes to the truth about the corruption in government, the FDA, the pharmaceutical industry, and the fast food industry. They can't believe I'm naming names. They can't believe a former insider is actually coming forward and saying, "Yes, I was there and I know the truth." People always ask me if I'm scared for my life. It's a good question. I can honestly say I am not scared for my life, but I do know my life is in grave danger because I'm exposing people that will be going to jail. What I am doing is blowing the whistle on such incredible corruption that people are going to lose their power, lose their influence, lose their jobs, lose their positions and, in many cases, go to jail. Corporations are going to be exposed for their fraud and their stock values will plummet and people will lose tens of millions of dollars. Because of this there are many powerful and wealthy people who are scared and fearful of what my exposing will do. These same people would like nothing more than for me to shut up or simply vanish.

It is absolutely true, factual and documented that there are hundreds of whistleblowers who have simply vanished over the years. It is absolutely true and documented that there are hundreds of biochemists, scientists, and researchers who were talking about breakthroughs in medicine that could cure and eliminate disease with inexpensive natural remedies that have simply vanished or mysteriously died. I have an author who is putting together a book documenting the mysterious deaths of over 100 medical researchers who were all on the brink of announcing a cure for various diseases with non-drug and non-surgical methods. All of these medical researchers mysteriously died under the most bizarre and suspicious circumstances. This author is also documenting all of the mysterious disappearances and deaths of people in Washington and other political organizations when secrets and truths were about to be exposed. This is eerily similar to the witness in the mafia trial who is about to go on the stand and tell the truth about the workings of the mob and then is found dead from an alleged heart attack, or is shot and killed, or simply vanishes never to be seen again. It is obvious to everyone that the person was "whacked" or "rubbed out."

So what about me? Well, I recently bought a car. The car was in my garage. I went to take the car for a drive and as I was driving down the road, something sounded funny with the wheels on the front of the vehicle. My intuition told me something was dreadfully wrong. I immediately slowed the car down and pulled into a gas station. The moment I pulled into the gas station the front right wheel fell off the car. It appeared that someone had replaced the lug nuts on the wheel with much smaller lug nuts so that the front wheel at high speeds would fly off the vehicle, thus causing an accident, severe injuries to myself, or even death. Did someone actually change the lug nuts, or was this just a mistake when I purchased the vehicle? When I purchased the vehicle I had the car fully inspected. Was not noticing the difference in lug nuts on the front right wheel simply an oversight on our part, or was it deliberately done? We may never know. I do know from my sources that the drug companies are actively involved in discussions about what to do with Kevin Trudeau. I do know from my sources that there are tens of millions of dollars being put in to specifically find ways to publicly discredit me and use negative PR against me and the book. Are there also covert operations being done to "eliminate" me? We may never know, or time will tell. As I've said before in the newsletters, if you ever see a headline that says, "Consumer Activist Kevin Trudeau Commits Suicide," please be assured that it was absolutely, positively not a suicide!

TOXINS IN AIR AND FOOD CAUSE DISEASE

Many headlines are coming out showing that toxins in what we eat and in the air are causing disease. Many of you may not be familiar with chemtrails. If you look up in the sky on occasion you will see these white trails that come from planes. They linger in the air for a long time. What are they? There are many theories, but my insiders and sources tell me that the United States Government is testing various forms of biological and chemical warfare, and one of the ways they are doing this is by releasing chemicals in the air. These chemtrails are now being confirmed by various government officials. We are told that there is no harm, they are safe, but for some reason I don't believe our government. Can chemicals in the air cause disease? I believe so. A report came out of Canada showing that a particular town had an abnormally high amount of pollution. There were oil slicks in the creek, odors in the air, and a funny smell from water coming out of the faucet. An interesting observation was made in this community. The ratio of boys to girls being born is completely out of wack. It indicates a serious environmental contamination issue by many of these harmful chemicals. The article goes on to talk about how deadly these chemicals are and what other health-associated issues are being forced on these poor people in this community. This reminds me of the Erin Brockovich story. The Erin Brockovich story shows that pollution can cause cancer in a community, and it also showed beyond any doubt that corporations will lie and deceive the public and try to cover up their misdeeds.

When you read the Erin Brockovich story or watch the movie with Julia Roberts, you are absolutely amazed that a major corporation can be so evil in the way that it tries to cover up what it's doing to the people. It amazes everyone who watches the movie or reads the book at the way the executives' attitude is basically to hell with the people, let them die, we're talking about profits here! The executives couldn't have cared less that their actions were killing people and giving them cancer, all they cared about were the profits and the bottom line.

Another study shows that farm-raised salmon is causing disease. Farm-raised salmon has contaminate levels that increase cancer risk and other horrible diseases. Many kinds of farm-raised fish are also injected with coloring and other chemicals to preserve them and make them look more attractive. Go back and read the *Natural Cures* book, specifically Chapter 6. Do the things in Chapter 6 and I believe you will cure yourself of disease.

CHAPTER 9

Weight Loss Secrets

Patterning your life around other's opinions
is nothing more than slavery.

—Lawana Blackwell

My definition of a free society is where it is safe
to be unpopular.

—Adlai Stevenson

If you want to lose weight, it is absolutely imperative that you eat a substantial breakfast. The facts are clear. The vast majority of people who are thin eat breakfast, the vast majority of people who are overweight eat no breakfast or a very light breakfast. People who are overweight generally have a slow metabolism. In order to get your metabolism moving, one of the most important things you can do is eat a substantial breakfast.

There are two elements here: (1) you must eat a substantial breakfast, and (2) you must eat the right kinds of food that make your metabolism go up and get your body burning fat instead of eating food that causes your body to retain fat and gain weight. Is there a best breakfast? Well, let's start with this basic premise: everything you eat for breakfast must be organic and unprocessed. It cannot, generally speaking, be out of a box or from a company that is publicly traded. If you are eating food that you have purchased from a publicly traded corporation, I can assure you that there are ingredients in the food that are not listed on the label. I can assure you that these companies are secretly putting ingredients in the food to increase your appetite, get you physically addicted to the food, and make you fat.

So, with that in mind, here are some good types of food that you can eat for breakfast:

1. *Meats*. Eat organic beef, lamb, chicken. Make sure these are real cuts of meat and not deli-type meats or any type of processed meats.
2. *Fish*. Wild salmon, sardines, tuna, etc.
3. *Fruits*. Grapefruits, apples, pears, strawberries, blueberries, plums, peaches, and apricots. Make sure the fruits are fresh and not dried. As always, make sure they are organic.

   Stay away from bananas as they have a tendency to make you gain weight. If you must have milk with your breakfast, make sure it is organic and, ideally, raw milk that has not been pasteurized or homogenized.

Here are some common breakfasts that I eat:

Scrambled eggs with a side of smoked salmon, or lamb chops, or sardines, or a small steak.

I make my scrambled eggs various ways. I always use fresh organic, non-pasteurized, fertile eggs. The simplest way is to gently beat the eggs, add organic sea salt and organic pepper, a little pure water and a small amount of pure organic raw cream. I heat a skillet and use a little either extra virgin olive or raw organic butter. Sometimes I add some chopped up organic green and red peppers, organic onions, organic parsley, and organic mushrooms. When people come to my house and eat my scrambled eggs they cannot believe how delicious they are. The lamb chops I simply broil with a little organic salt and pepper. This is a filling, delicious high-protein breakfast, which gives me plenty of energy for the day and starts my metabolism. Sometimes I add a slice of organic rye bread. If you read the ingredients, you will notice that the bread should have only three ingredients: organic rye flour, water, and yeast. I stay away from wheat bread and sometimes eat other types of sprouted breads or wholegrain breads other than wheat. Just read the ingredients on the label. Make sure they are organic and there should be only a few ingredients. Do not buy bread if it has honey, molasses, sugar, or ingredients you cannot pronounce. On my bread, I use a little raw butter, and sometimes I eat an apple with this meal as well. If I am in a rush, I will take some organic apples and pears and make fresh juice. I put the juice in a blender and add some fresh blueberries, a few ice cubes, some spirulina powder and blue-green algae powder, and a little organic flaxseed oil. Sometimes I add a little organic non-genetically altered soy powder for some added protein. I drink this and also eat an apple or pear to get the added fiber. Depending on how I feel, I also may add a piece of toast. Sometimes for breakfast, I like potatoes. I take an organic potato, slice it up and in a skillet, with a little extra virgin olive oil, I gently sauté it with a little organic salt and pepper, organic paprika and some fresh, chopped organic parsley. It is delicious.

When people come to my home, I cook for them and show them how delicious meals can be made in less than thirty minutes. They are easy and fun, and taste absolutely delicious. People cannot believe how incredibly delicious the food is. It is better than any restaurant. Most importantly, after they eat they do not feel bloated, tired, or lethargic. The food gives them energy, which is what food is supposed to do. You will notice, when people eat, most people will get tired, gassy, bloated, constipated, and lethargic after a meal. Food is supposed to give you energy. Food is supposed to be fuel. If after a meal you aren't filled with energy, then there is something wrong with that food, or you are so toxic and full of Candida that the food cannot be used as fuel. Therefore, you must do your Candida cleanse and colon cleanse. Taking some digestive enzymes with your meal will prevent you from having any acid reflux or heartburn, prevents gas, and allows the food to digest better.

I love doing experiments, and take people who are overweight and just do one simple thing with them for just a week to see the results. My most recent experiment was to take overweight people who didn't eat breakfast. I told them to change nothing else. Don't exercise; don't change what you eat; and don't do anything. All I wanted them to do was add a big breakfast. They were skeptical because they felt by adding additional food, calories and fat, they would gain weight. The exact opposite happened. By eating a breakfast their energy levels were higher throughout the day, they felt better, they weren't ravenous throughout the day, they had less headaches, they slept better, they weren't hungry at night, and most importantly, after one week everyone lost weight.

The body needs fuel on a regular basis. Eat a big substantial breakfast, and eat the right kind of breakfast, and you will see your weight normalize and you will lose weight.

Organic, Unrefined, Virgin Coconut Oil

Here is an amazing product that can have tremendous benefits, as well as help you lose weight faster and easier than ever before. Unrefined, pure, organic, virgin coconut oil is a product that falls in that "miraculous" category. All you do is take one tablespoonful in the morning and one tablespoonful in the late afternoon. If you do this every day for thirty days, here is what you could find. High blood pressure can be a thing of the past. Circulation problems vanish. Mood swings, gone. Depression, lifted. Constipation, cured. Arthritis pain, reduced or eliminated. Cancer, in remission. Cholesterol, normalized. Acid reflux and heartburn, diminished or gone forever. Oh, and here is a major side effect: If you are overweight, you will probably lose ten pounds! This oil has a dramatic, positive effect on the body. The health-giving properties that it contains are overwhelming. In upcoming issues of the newsletter I will provide you with more references on this oil so you can read all the research if you are so inclined. However, I take this almost every day and can personally tell you that the effects are startling. When I started taking this within three days all of my pants were falling off. This happened in just three days. I didn't get on the scale so I don't know how much weight I lost, but all of my pants were falling off. They were all too big in just three days. I couldn't believe it. Try it and then write me with your success story.

In my book *Natural Cures* I talk about various tips for weight loss. As I mentioned earlier about acid reflux disease, most people today do not have enough enzymes in their diet. If you are overweight, have a sluggish digestive system, have a hard time losing weight, or feel bloated and gassy, there is an excellent chance that your body is not producing enough digestive enzymes to deal with the food that you are consuming. If you want to speed up your metabolism; reduce gas and bloating; reduce indigestion, heartburn, acid reflux; and flatten out your tummy, it is important that you have enough digestive enzymes in your system to deal with the food you are consuming. One simple way to flatten the tummy; eliminate gas, bloating and indigestion; speed the metabolism; and lose five to ten pounds effortlessly is simply to take digestive enzymes with your meals. Consult with your licensed healthcare practitioner and go to your health food store or go on the internet, and try various brands of digestive enzymes. Digestive enzymes consist of varying types of digestive aides, enzymes, as well as acidophilus and betaine hydrochloric acid. Each brand has different components, different ingredients; all are effective to varying degrees. Try different brands to see which one your body works the best with. Adding digestive enzymes when you eat food will make your food digest quicker and easier, and go through your system much faster. It will eliminate gas, bloating, and acid reflux. It will flatten the tummy. It should increase bowel movements, making you eliminate much more frequently and making the movements much easier. You will find energy increasing, heaviness decreasing, and an overall feeling of well being. Most people report that by taking digestive enzymes they lose anywhere between three to five pounds in the first thirty days without doing anything different. Most people report that food cravings diminish, appetite diminishes, and gas, bloating, indigestion, and acid reflux virtually vanish. Most people notice a dramatic reduction in their protruding tummy within the first week. Try this tip for weight loss and please write me with your results.

Salsa

Hot peppers increase metabolism. Increased metabolism means you burn more fat. It means you have more energy and vitality in your body. If you want to lose weight, there's a very simple thing you can do, which will allow you to burn faster the food you're eating, allowing you to lose weight simpler and easier.

To give you an example, I am reminded of the time I had a Shaolin monk living with me at my home. This man did not have an ounce of fat on his body. He looked 20 years younger than he was. His body was firm, yet incredibly flexible. He had agility, incredible strength, speed, quickness, coordination, grace, fluidity, and flexibility. With his incredible slim physique, it amazed me that he ate six times a day. He ate massive amounts of food. He obviously had a high metabolism.

The interesting thing to note was that every meal he would ask for hot sauce or hot peppers. He loaded up his food with very hot spices and peppers. His food was so hot that perspiration would bead up all over his bald head and face. He was constantly patting his head dry as he ate. The heat was so intense that he was sweating profusely during each meal. This was interesting. The heat from the peppers increased the fire in his body and increased his metabolism and ability to burn the massive amount of calories he was consuming. This helps him remain thin.

I began to read studies around the world that proved this to be true. So the simple weight loss tip is starting with breakfast, add organic hot salsa to your meals. Ginger is also hot. Grated fresh ginger can be added to your meals. You can also grate ginger and then squeeze it and put the juice on your food. Hot peppers and anything that increases "heat" will work. This also increases your digestion and helps move food through the colon quicker, increasing elimination.

MORE SECRETS

What can you do that's easy to lose weight fast and quickly without being hungry or depriving yourself of the foods you enjoy? Let me give you a few things you can do without changing your lifestyle or eating habits that can dramatically help you lose weight.

1. *Add hot peppers or organic salsa to all of your food.* Hot peppers raise basal body temperature. This increases metabolism and makes you burn fat and burn calories quicker. It also reduces appetite.

2. *Take a tablespoon of raw organic apple cider vinegar before each meal.* If you can't get raw organic apple cider vinegar then go to a health food store or go on the internet and get apple cider vinegar tablets or capsules. Take this before each meal. This will increase the fat-burning furnace in your body and allow you to start burning stored fat.

3. *Take a teaspoon of organic virgin coconut oil before each meal.* This will help food pass through the digestive tract quicker, stopping the conversion of food to fat, as well as stimulate the thyroid, increasing metabolism and making you burn stored fat even while you sleep.

4. *Drink Yerba Mata tea.* Drink three to four cups throughout the day; always use pure water, never tap water. This tea will reduce appetite and increase metabolism and energy. It's important to drink throughout the day, starting first thing in the morning, and ideally drink some every few hours. This will reduce appetite and increase fat-burning properties in your body throughout the day.

If you do these things and nothing else, at the end of thirty days, without changing any eating habits consciously, you will absolutely have lost a tremendous amount of weight and, more importantly, lost inches. These techniques are specifically designed to burn the stored fat in your body, thus making you slimmer and making your clothes much bigger. Try it and let me know.

Other People Who Back Me Up

Orthodox medicine has not found a cure for your condition. Luckily for you I happen to be a quack.

—Author unknown

There is a great movie that was made, actually a documentary, entitled *The Corporation*. In my book I talk about "it's all about the money." I talk about the fact that the love of money is the root of all evil. I talk about the fact that corporations are legally defined as individual entities. The legal responsibility of corporations is to make a profit. As a matter of fact, the law states that a corporation must, above everything else, make a profit. That means it cannot take into account its employees' welfare before profit. It cannot take into account the environment before profit. It cannot take into account anything before profit. Profit is the most important overriding thing above everything else.

Most people just have no idea of how corporations operate and how they take advantage of the public. As I mentioned, making money is not bad. Making a profit is not bad. As a matter of fact, making a profit and making money are good things. The key is making a profit and making money when you have an even exchange between the consumer and yourself. If you are offering a good quality product or service to a consumer and you make a profit in doing so, that is a good thing. The problem is, when people make profit while they hurt their employees, or when a company makes a profit while it destroys the environment, or when a company makes a profit while deceiving and misleading the customers, or when a company makes a profit while it bends the rules, commits fraud, or breaks the laws, that is when making a profit is bad. The big challenge is most corporations make a profit in these bad ways.

197

When companies make profit by offering good quality services and products to the consumer, while they take care of their employees and staff, while they take care of and are protective of the environment, and while they adhere to all the laws and regulations, that is when making a profit is a good thing. It comes down to honesty, integrity, and ethics. This is what is missing in the corporate world. This DVD is available on the internet and I would highly encourage and recommend that you watch it. It is entertaining and incredibly compelling.

I just received a letter from Dr. Robert Wiehe, the author of the book *Alternative Medicine and the Treatment of Cancer*, published by the We Good Life Institute of West Plains, Missouri.

Dear Kevin,

Five years ago I was diagnosed with an aggressive form of cancer. I was given three groups of chemotherapy. I continued to worsen. By April of 2001 I was bedridden and told I had two weeks to live, three at the most. I watched a TV program by Naomi Judd, which had fourteen guest M.D. speakers. They were top quality M.D.s that had switched from the traditional medical treatment of cancer to alternative medicine (natural medicines). I had it mailed to me overnight. In ten days I was walking. In two months I spaded my garden. I am now living a normal life with no sign of cancer. I now take a reduced amount of alternative medicine for prevention and I have added some natural products which I heard about from you. I have watched your infomercials and read your printed materials. I know about your run-ins with the FDA and the feds. You have done a heroic job for standing up to those (expletives) people. Your new book, *Natural Cures*, is a Godsend. You are a hero in my book and of the entire chiropractic, naturopathy, and homeopathic professions.

Dr. Wiehe's book on cancer is fantastic. If you have cancer, know somebody who has cancer, or are concerned about cancer, you should read this book. I highly endorse and recommend it.

SUCCESS STORIES

Since I read Kevin's book it has changed *every* aspect of my life. I don't think the same and I don't eat the same. It has truly been an instrument to get me and my family on the path to a vibrant, abundantly healthy life. I am totally off any medications for allergies and headaches, which I never dreamed could happen. I can't quit talking about this book and I have passed it, along with the DVD, around to everyone that would have an ear to hear the truth. I owe Kevin big time because that little $30 book has saved me thousands of dollars in medical bills, etc. I can't say enough about Kevin. Kevin, we love you and we look up to you tremendously for the work you are doing.

Carol and David B.

I have read *Natural Cures They Don't Want You to Know About*. I love this book, and I have been following as much advice from this book as much as I possibly can, and I have seen an incredible difference. Mostly my asthma is in control, and I am not taking any medications!! I have lost weight without trying to. Just by changing my food to all organic (without the chemicals, growth hormones, hydrogenated oils and dairy products) my family and I are already seeing great changes in our health in just 4 months. I have always believed that nutrition plays a big role on your well-being, and Kevin just confirmed it for me. Thank you so much for writing the book and putting the knowledge out there. I tell all my friends and family to read the book. Good Luck

Bruni W., Norwich, Connecticut

When I read Kevin's book, it changed my life forever. I learned so much. After I read the book, I went through my kitchen cupboards and discarded everything that was bad for me and replaced them with whole and organic foods. I can't say enough how much better physically I feel. I have even lost a few pounds. I was already taking Chi Gong when I discovered the book, and now I feel that my body will benefit even more from it. I am getting ready to do the Candida cleanse, followed by the full body cleanse. I feel so light and happy and at peace by just eating better and knowing that it makes a very big difference! My body is happier!

Thank you so much Kevin for caring enough to share your knowledge with the world.

Deborah S.

Kevin Trudeau has my support. I have been sick almost all my life with different ailments. Now I have been uplifted through his internet site. Looking up different sources to read about and learn from has helped me and my family out in a number of different areas. Thanks for the True Information on how to get better and live longer.

Kathy A.

Using the suggestions and information from both the website and the *Natural Cures* book by Kevin Trudeau, I have managed to lose 75 lbs in the past year and have improved my overall health.

In fact, I have missed only one day for sickness in the past year when most people I know missed 3 to 5 just on a single bout of flu and I have clients, friends and family all telling me I look no older than 38 years old.

I just celebrated my 50th birthday.

Thanks, Kevin. You're a bright light in an otherwise dismal quest for better health for all of us.

Kimberly S.

I had known for a long time something wasn't right—I have gone on many yo-yo diets but the weight keeps coming back in spades. When I heard Kevin speak on TV it rang with some resonance. I have just recently begun changing my life but the effects were immediate. I am resting better and I have more energy. I am hoping the weight will follow. I have begun to walk at my pace, not a racer's pace, and we have a trampoline I plan to try. Kevin will be a big change in the status quo I believe. He is making a difference and hopefully he won't be silenced.

Kenneth S.

No book has ever influenced me more than the *Natural Cures* book. I am convinced that I will have a better quality of life because of the information here as well as live a longer, more prosperous life ... no author has ever given so much, so selflessly as Kevin Trudeau and I thank God every day that I was home sick the day Kevin's program was on TV. It changed my life.

Liz A., Riviera Beach, Florida

Since I read Kevin Trudeau's book, *Natural Cures*, I am starting a new way of life. I am 62 years old and I got more from reading Kevin's book than I did before. I am now starting to eat the right foods and I am starting to reverse my diabetes so I could get off these pills. This is just the beginning of the new way of eating and trying to get off these pills that I take that are slowly killing me. Thank You Kevin

S.B

Since reading Kevin's book I no longer have to take cholesterol, high blood pressure or heart medications. I'm doing it with all natural herbs and things. I am being monitored very carefully by my holistic doctor who is a DO. Thanks to Kevin I no longer have to take prescription drugs that do as much harm if not more than good. Thank you from the bottom of my heart.

Terry K.

WHAT PEOPLE ARE SAYING

Dear Kevin,

I received a check from in relation to the lawsuit the FTC had filed against you. I called your Natural Cures number and the lady that I talked to said to go ahead and cash the check. My husband said he felt like it was blood money. The coral calcium that you sold and we purchased really helped relieve the pain in his hands. We wanted to be able to take a stand somehow. Tell us what to do. We want you to know we stand beside you. Thank you for your boldness.

JF

Dear Kevin,

I am sending you a check for $198.90. This is the amount of money that the FTC sent me as a refund relating to my purchase of Coral Calcium. I know it's not the evidence, but the interpretation of the evidence. I know it's also all about censorship. Well, I have decided that I have found the FTC guilty, not you. I am giving you back the money that they gave me. I don't need the FTC to tell me if Coral Calcium works. In December 2003 I bought one bottle as an experiment. If it did not work, I would not have bought it again. I continue to buy it because it works. You have my permission to report as fact that I have refunded my refund to you.

JC, Orlando, FL

Dear Kevin,

I'm reading your book *Natural Cures* and I love what you say and what you are doing to right the wrongs of the federal government and its stupid agencies like the FDA and the FTC. I think that those bastards have sold themselves and the public's wellbeing to a bunch of rich old farts who just want more and more. It's totally un-American. Keep up the good work. I stand with you and support you wholeheartedly.

JB, Florida

I get thousands of e-mails every week from people sharing their experiences from doing the things I recommend in Chapter 6 of the *Natural Cures* book. Here are some comments that hopefully will encourage you to do the cleanses I recommend and start getting the nutrition that you need, eliminating the electromagnetic chaos, and reducing stress.

- "I am eating more than ever before, enjoying it more, yet have lost five pounds. Great revelation."
- "After struggling for years to get my stomach flat it finally is. It's miraculous!"
- "You deserve an award for bringing this information out and restoring my good health."
- "Thanks for making me feel better than ever before. It's a shame most Americans just don't know this information."

- "My friends didn't believe it, but after doing the cleanses and losing their pouch they are all believers."
- "My skin rash went away without any drugs just by doing the colon cleanse."
- "You deserve a medal. Many of my ailments have already disappeared."
- "In less than a month my stomach is nearly flat. Thank God for information on cleansing."
- "After the cleansing my skin is now smooth and pink, just like a little child. It's amazing. I look ten years younger."
- "After the colon cleanse I lost my pot belly. It's unbelievable. It works."
- "The colon cleanse did the trick for me. My stomach is a thing of the past."
- "My whole family noticed a difference. No one could believe how flat my stomach was."
- "It's obvious why we haven't heard about this. Doctors would lose too much business."
- "It's truly amazing how everything changes with a clean colon. Less cravings, not hungry, and no more wanting bad junk or processed food."
- "Dropped two dress sizes in about four weeks."
- "I'm 91, feel better physically and emotionally. Not taking any more drugs that harm the body and that has had a great impact."

Book Review

***Food Politics*, by Marion Nestle.** I mention over and over again how multinational corporations view lobbyists to make politicians write laws and state things simply to help increase the multinational health corporations' profits. This is categorically true. It has been reported by the politicians themselves that they do not run Washington. Senior senators have said, "We do not run Washington, and we do not make law. Our job is simply to raise money and get reelected." It's the lobbyists that make the laws and run the country. This is scary, but true. Relating to the food that is sold by the big multinational corporations, this book *Food Politics: How the Food Industry Influences Nutrition and Health* is an absolute must read. The book examines the industries' manipulation of America's eating habits while being involved in conflicts of interest among nutritional authorities. There is no industry more important to Americans and more fundamentally linked to our well-being and future well-being than the food industry. The book reveals how corporate control of the nation's food system limits our choices and threatens our health.

You'll learn the truth about how the food pyramid was developed.

You'll learn how millions of dollars are poured into lobbyists who in effect write the laws regarding labeling what is "safe" and what is "unsafe" to eat. You'll learn how chemicals are labeled as "spices." And you will learn the reasons why I categorically say do not buy any food if it's sold by a publicly traded corporation or is a brand name food.

This book explains the rational reason in great detail about my advice to you that you should never eat food that is advertised on television. You should never eat brand name food and that you should never eat food from publicly traded corporations or fast food restaurants. This book explains in detail and verifies and backs up everything I'm saying about how food is produced. It is an absolute must read.

RECOMMENDED BOOK

One of the major causes of all diseases is exposure to toxins. Remember, if you are experiencing any medical symptoms or have any disease or illness, you must ask yourself what is CAUSING your symptoms, your illness, and your disease. Standard medical science rarely, if ever, addresses or asks what the cause of the symptoms is. Medical science, generally speaking, only prescribes drugs and surgery to suppress, reduce, or eliminate the symptom, it never addresses what caused the symptom. Critics around the world point out the fact that I do not address symptoms, but rather ask what the cause is. When you find the cause, if that particular cause is something you are actually doing to yourself, if you simply stop doing it, then you have cured yourself of the illness and disease. This is logical, makes sense, and works. This, however, scares the medical community and petrifies the industrial multinational corporations. Large publicly traded food manufacturers are frightened by this premise. The manufacturers of all other products that you use do not like this premise. Why? Because it shows that they are in fact CAUSING many symptoms and disease.

One of the major causes of your symptoms, illness, and disease, as I mentioned, is exposure to toxins. The book I want to highly recommend is *Our Toxic World*, by Doris J. Rapp, M.D., *New York Times* best-selling author. She is Board Certified in environmental medicine, pediatrics, and allergies. This book talks about how to keep yourself and your loved ones out of harm's way. It talks about chemicals and how they damage your body, brain, behavior, and sex. This is a wonderful book with tons of references, studies, and research that backs up everything that I have been saying. Consider a few things. Unborn babies float for nine months in chemicals including DDT and PCBs in the uterus. Their bowel movements and mother's milk contain the same dangerous pesticides. In the past 30 to 40 years there has been a 30 to 40 percent increase in undescended testicles, deformed penises, and changes in sexualities in young boys. This feminization is caused by dioxin and PCBs, chemicals used in the production of food. Young girls can have puberty from plastics and PCBs, and it creates masculinity in females. Over 20 studies show pesticides used inside and outside homes or schools, on lawns and playgrounds can cause leukemia, brain tumors, and lymphomas! Women have more birth-damaged, developmentally or learning-disabled babies, miscarriages, stillborns, infertility, and endometriosis than ever before in history. If a pregnant woman uses flea soap or a pest collar on her dog, her unborn child has a four- to sixfold increased chance of developing a brain tumor, leukemia, or lymphoma by the age of six years. Men have higher chemical levels in their bodies causing smaller genitals. Up to 85 percent of males can be ineligible as sperm donors. Sperm count averages have dropped from 125 million/ml per million in 1932 to just 50 million/ml in 1988. Many wonder if men will be sterile in the next 70 years. All of these problems and many, many more including allergies, obesity, mental and emotional disorders, depression, stress, food cravings, mood swings, arthritis, cancer, heart disease, diabetes, gas, bloating, and acid reflux, and virtually hundreds of other conditions, are caused by exposure to toxins.

Our government and the FDA are working together to allow food companies and manufacturers to put more and more toxins into our environment. The reason these toxins are put into our environment is because it allows the manufacturers to manufacture food and products cheaper. They want longer shelf life, they want more inexpensive products, all that at the expense of our health. Some of the most toxic substances you can put in your body are non-prescription and prescription drugs. Think of how many times you have taken cough syrup, cold medicine, an Alka-Seltzer®, Tylenol®, Advil®, aspirin, some Afrin®, or nasal decongestant. All of these things are highly toxic and have negative side effects. These toxins do not leave your body. They stay in the fatty tissue and have an accumulative effect. Think of all the lotions and soaps you put on your body. As I mentioned a few months ago, sodium lauryl sulfate is one of the most toxic things you can put on your skin. It is a solvent used to clean grease off garage floors! If you were to take a spoon of sodium lauryl sulfate and drink it you would die, yet it is in so many soaps, shampoos, and cleaning products, as well as lotions. We put it on our skin and it is immediately absorbed into the skin and goes into the bloodstream. Remember, whatever you put on your skin is absorbed and gets into the bloodstream—it's as if you were eating it. These toxins absolutely, 100 percent cause disease. Read this book. It is vital information and knowledge you need for your health and the health of your family and loved ones.

Consider some more startling facts. Cancer was rare in 1900. Now, between 33 and 50 percent of the population will develop cancer. Breast, prostate, and testicle cancer are up 50 percent in the last 50 years. In children, since 1973, brain tumors are up 21 percent and lymphomas are up 30 percent. Over 90 percent of children and adults have toxic brain damaging or cancer causing chemicals in their urine and blood. The multinational corporations are killing us. Of 64 commonly used pesticides, 16 cause cancer, 24 cause brain injury, and 44 cause hormonal damage. In addition, 49 damage nervous systems, 54 cause kidney disease, and 59 damage eyes and skin. The outrage is less expensive; organic pest control is available and why isn't it being used? This is why you must be eating organic food, but also why we need to fight and stop the use of these pesticides as they categorically, 100 percent give us disease. These toxins are so powerful that it even shows in the documentation that it is proven that regular farmers who use pesticides and herbicides, in contrast to organic farmers, have more depression as well as cancer, birth-damaged offspring, and lower sperm counts. These chemicals, even in small amounts, cause disease. Cows given genetically modified growth hormones make more milk, but have painful swollen udders, have ulcers, joint pain, miscarriages, deformed calves, infertility, and much shorter life spans. Their milk contains blood, pus, tranquilizers, antibiotics, and an insulin growth factor that can cause a fourfold increase in prostate cancer and sevenfold rise in breast cancer. This is the milk used in our school lunch programs and served to our children. This is the milk that you buy every day. This is the milk used in all cheeses, yogurts, butter, and cream. This is a new phenomena; it did not exist 50 years ago. These dairy products are categorically causing disease for you and your children. This is why you must, absolutely always consume 100 percent organic dairy products—ideally, dairy products that are also unpasteurized and unhomogenized.

Consider also how irradiated food is killing us. This process alters the flavor, decreases nutrients, and raises the cost. It eliminates most germs, but some salmonella, hepatitis, and mad cow disease still remain. In animals it causes hemorrhage from muscle tears, heart damage, testes tumors, and changes in genes and reproductive cells. Formaldehyde, cancer-causing benzene, and mold toxins form because of irradiation. Irradiation is being done to most of our food supply. This is why you must be eating 100 percent organic food. The multinational corporations are not interested in your health, but are only interested in their profits, and from my inside information I personally know that the food industry is purposely making us sick so that it can profit from the sale of drugs.

To buy this book go to www.naturalcures.com, or you can simply call 1-800-787-8780, or go to www.drrapp.com.

Another Needed and Recommended Book

Continuing on the theme of toxins in our environment, I want to recommend a book from a good friend of mine that offers you solutions. His book is entitled *1001 All-Natural Secrets to a Pest-Free Property*. The author is Dr. Myles H. Bader. If you have flying, crawling, burrowing, or other types of pests, bugs, or insect problems, this book has the solution. In the book Dr. Bader gives you the all-natural nontoxic ways to eliminate ants, termites, cockroaches, spiders, aphids, funguses and molds, grasshoppers, mites, caterpillars, tree pests of all kinds, beetles of all kinds, flies, mosquitoes, gnats, moths, bees, yellow jackets, wasps, fleas, parasites, ticks, toads, turtles, ferrets, earthworms—the list goes on and on. If you are having any problem around your property, even with rodents such as gophers, mice, rats, moles, squirrels, possums, skunks, raccoons, rabbits, snakes, bird problems, insect problems, even solving problems in your vegetable or fruit garden, this book has the answer. It gives gardening tips and shows how to repel insects and bugs without chemical pesticides. The information in this book can save you a tremendous amount of money because you will be using inexpensive, all-natural ingredients that you find around your house to solve your insect and pest problems. More importantly, however, it is so vital for you to know about the chemical illnesses as exposed in the other book that I am recommending this month, *Our Toxic World*.

This book, *1001 All-Natural Secrets to a Pest-Free Property* is highly recommended and will give you the answers you need. It is the number one book in the world on natural pest control, no dangerous chemicals or damage to the environment. The book will help you eliminate almost every kind of insect and critter you can think of and do it using natural substances. It has taken Dr. Bader over ten years of research to be able to provide thousands of usable methods of getting rid of unwanted insects from gardens and pests and animals from your property. Learn how to get rid of the neighbors' cats and dogs from digging up your yard. Learn easy methods for removing insects from plants and trees. Learn how to discourage wild animals from entering your property. Learn how to send underground pests off to another area so they will never come back. Learn where the bugs hide in the winter. Learn special formulas that you can make with products around the home. Learn how to never see another mosquito or fly in your home or yard. Learn how to get rid of moths without the smell. Learn how to purchase pest control supplies inexpensively that are nontoxic, and much, much more. The book is available at www.naturalcures.com.

ANOTHER MIRACLE STORY

I received this letter from a customer; I wanted to share it with you. Please read it. It says it all.

Hi Kevin,

I love your *Natural Cures* book. I'm excited about the way you explain why things are the way they are and what we can do about it. The corruption, lies, fraud, deceit to why we have so many illnesses and diseases and what is being kept from us is amazing. I talk to everyone who will listen about the book and encourage them to buy it. I also give people the book and the twelve CD set to listen to. Like you I believe it is a crime against humanity what the pharmaceutical companies, the food companies, and the medical establishment is doing. I hundred percent believe if all people would keep four things in mind concerning their health they could prevent and cure themselves of illness and disease. They are, as you mention, toxins, nutrients, electromagnetic chaos, and mental and emotional stress. I have had some people suggest to me that they've heard you don't give cures in your *Natural Cures* book. I absolutely disagree. You tell us how to cure disease by detoxing our bodies and stop putting toxins in our bodies, to get proper amounts of nutrients in our bodies, eliminate or reduce electromagnetic chaos, and eliminate or reduce mental and emotional stress. I understand when you do those things you are "cured" of illness and disease. That is in fact the natural cure that they don't want you to know about. Some people just don't get it. They are looking for a pill. This tells me that the medical establishment and the government have been effective at brainwashing intelligent people.

Kevin I believe what you are doing is one of the greatest crusades or missions ever in history and I want to encourage you to keep on keeping on. I believe the entire health (sick) care industry and food industries will come to their knees once people are educated. The criminals that run these industries and the FDA and FTC and all organizations involved will pay for their crimes against humanity. We need 20 or 30 million Americans owning the *Natural Cures* book, subscribing to your newsletter and website, and we need people all around the world doing this as well.

I've been doing a lot of things that you suggest in Chapter 6, including the cleanses, energetic rebalancing, magnetic mattress pads, the magnetic finger rings and foot braces, etc. The very first thing I did was stop buying food from the big food companies. I now only eat 100% organic. It's absolutely amazing, but just by doing this one thing I lost around 20 pounds in 8 to 10 weeks. All I did was stop buying food from the publicly traded corporations and started eating 100% organic food. Just by changing to "real food" without all the chemicals I lost 20 pounds! You are 100% right by saying the food companies are making us fat.

Kevin I'm sending you a small donation to help with this cause of greatness. Thank you very much. God bless you always.

Folks, I receive letters like this all the time. This gentleman sent me a wonderful donation, which I immediately gave to one of my nonprofit foundations to educate people about natural remedies and the corruption in government. If you would like to make a donation, please do so. You can send your donations to help this crusade to the Natural Cures

Health Institute, P.O. Box 246, Elk Grove Village, IL 60009. This is a non-profit organization that's designed to educate people about non-drug and non-surgical ways to cure and prevent disease. However, the best way you can help this mission is to continue to subscribe to the newsletter and subscribe to www.naturalcures.com, the website community. Encourage other people to buy and read my book, and encourage other people to subscribe to the newsletter and the www.naturalcures.com community. Spread the word. Spread the word!

WHAT *NATURAL CURES*
SUPPORTERS ARE SAYING

To whom it may Concern,

Thank you Kevin Trudeau for a book that I hope will change my life. I was always interested in natural cures and proper nutrition. I had an on again–off again relationship with the health food stores and my natural health care provider. After reading your book, I will no longer stray from taking proper care of my body. You clearly explained the harms of pharmaceutical medicines and the toxins that we expose ourselves to carelessly. I have once again started to shop at the Whole Food store near my home. I have also looked into a water filtration system for my home and an air purifier for my bedroom. I was diagnosed recently with rheumatoid arthritis but refused medicine. I was not being very careful with my diet but was visiting a health care provider who was very helpful. I am now very careful with what I put in my mouth and after 7 days, I am already feeling better. Thank you and thank you.

C. Landy

I have read your book 3 times.

First time just because it was fascinating, second time for absorption. Third time to take notes of everything I need to do and supplies to buy.

You are amazing. You are challenging everyone and everything that corporate America upholds. I sincerely hope that you are successful.

BEFORE I saw you on Shop America on Jan. 1 or 2, I had already decided that if I ever got cancer I would NEVER go through chemotherapy. I would just rather die. My husband died in May 2005 after 3 years of horrific chemotherapy for lymphoma at the Cleveland Clinic in Cleveland. He kept saying to me, "Honey, they are killing me. They are trying to kill the cancer but they are killing me." (Bone marrow transplant) My husband and I had blind faith in the doctors and in truth my husband was so far gone by the time we knew something was wrong I believe only a miracle could have saved him. We spent 3 years in a cancer ridden facility. The land of the walking dead. Nurses wore purple gloves to administer medicine. After that, I just said to myself—no chemo no way.

That is why YOU have saved my life. I am getting healthy. I have given up soda, sweeteners. I drink 8 glasses of water a day. I exercise and eat better.

Thank you, thank you, and thank you for caring enough to take a stand.

Suzanne C., Kirtland, OH

I would like to thank you for all that you do. I bought your book yesterday and love it! I am a 23 year old stay at home mom. A few years ago I had my eyes set on becoming a pharmacy tech. After watching one of your infomercials one day I began to change my mind. I have always wanted to live as natural and healthy life as possible. In the last year I have gotten my self off prescription birth control and using a all natural method (lady-comp) I am working on making healthy meals for my family, and using a natural method for hypothyroidism. Looking back after all I know now and am still learning about, I could not see myself filling prescriptions for people. I am hoping to take some classes in nutritional and herbal health. I want to be a part of the change. America needs more people like you. Knowledge is power, and can save your life! Thank you again.

Valerie B. Alexandria, MN

Kevin,

My name is Jessica and I have been interested in natural healing and medicine since I was 14 yrs old.

My best friend and I have been practicing alternative medicine for 12 years. I am only 28, but it is so great to finally hear someone publicly speak out about the FDA and other government agencies. I just applied to a natural medicine college and couldn't be more excited. The funny thing is as we were growing up we learned these things from a friends mom and all of our friends used to refer to me as a witch ... lol. I just wanted to thank you for giving me another alternative to natural cures and I wish you the best of luck.

Jessica D. Westville, NJ

You have truly changed my life and I just wanted to thank you for that! I get healthier every day because of reading your book.

Nancy L., Temecula, CA

Kevin,

THANKS for the work you do and blessings to you for giving us the guidelines to be vibrantly healthy to 100! I just became a member on your web site, haven't quite finished your book.

Although I've been eating organic for 20 years, I've been looking for important information like yours to stay healthy.

I'll be actively promoting your book ... thanks again for all you do to protect us against the giant corporations.

Leslie R., Chattanooga, TN

Dear Kevin,

I have just returned home from Aruba. I spent six days on the island; it was one of the most relaxing vacations of my life. I had the opportunity to finally read your book. I am so grateful to you for all of your efforts. I hope that I will be able to meet you at some point and personally thank you for all of your dedicated hard work. I envision being a very powerful part of your Quest for good health.

With Warmest Regards,
Patricia C., Wakefield, MA

NATURAL CURES BOOK NO. 1 ON THE
NEW YORK TIMES BESTSELLER LIST!

We did it. My book *Natural Cures "They" Don't Want You to Know About* is now number one on the *New York Times* bestseller list. On virtually every other best-selling list I'm in the top ten. I believe that in the next few weeks I will hit the number one spot on virtually every best-seller list. The book has been an absolute phenomenon. It has now sold in excess of three million copies. Please continue to tell your friends, relatives, and neighbors to go to their bookstore and buy the *Natural Cures* book. Wouldn't it be great if I was on *The Oprah Winfrey Show* or the *Larry King Live* show? Wouldn't that help change health care in America and the world? The more this message gets out the better YOU are. The more this message gets out the more the big companies will start changing from their evil ways, and start producing products that are better for the environment and our health. You will have more choices at better prices for organic good-quality food, food that has not been irradiated, pasteurized, and made devoid of enzymes and nutrients. We will have more access to licensed alternative health-care practitioners who do not use drugs and surgery. We will have more free access to the truth about the use of herbs, homeopathic remedies, acupuncture, and energy healing to prevent and cure virtually all diseases. We will have more access to the truth about the importance of nutrition in our diet and how it directly relates to our health and the prevention and curing of disease. We will learn more and have access to more information about why parasites need to be cleansed from the body; heavy metals need to be eliminated from the body; Candida needs to be eliminated from the body; and our liver, gallbladder, kidneys, and colon must be cleansed if we are to eliminate our symptoms. The only way this will happen is if this book gets out to more and more people. Being number one on the *New York Times* bestseller list means that the public wants this information. The major television networks cannot deny the truth. This is the information the people want to know. The government cannot deny the truth. This is the information the people want to know. So please continue your support. I need your support. I need more subscribers to the newsletter. I need more subscribers to naturalcures.com. I need more people going into bookstores, Costco's, Wal-Marts, K-Marts, and buying the *Natural Cures* book. Please encourage your friends, relatives, and neighbors to buy the book, subscribe to the newsletter, and join and become a member of naturalcures.com. We are making a difference. I thank you for your support and your help.

DVD Review

There are two movies/documentaries that you absolutely, 100 percent must see. They are *Super Size Me* and *What the Bleep Do We Know*. *Super Size Me* is a very important documentary about an individual who decided to eat only McDonald's food for thirty days. It shows clearly just how dangerous fast food is. When you watch the documentary, you will see that this man almost died in thirty days. He gained 28 pounds, and the doctors who were monitoring his health said that whatever he was doing was killing him. This points out the fact that the fast food industry is causing disease. It's not cheeseburgers or French fries that give you disease, it's the chemical poisons that are put in the food by the food manufacturers that cause the disease. A cheeseburger made with organic ingredients is not unhealthy, but a cheeseburger at a fast food restaurant categorically, 100 percent gives you disease. This documentary proves the point. If you have children, have them watch this movie—it can save their life. If you eat in fast food establishments, watch this DVD, it will open up your eyes to the truth.

The other DVD is *What the Bleep Do We Know*. This is an outstanding documentary, which correlates with many of the things I have talked about in my book about energetic imbalances. I highly encourage and recommend that you watch both of these DVDs. They are available on the internet.

CHAPTER 11

Stay Away from These Products

Conventional medicine is a collection of unproven prescriptions the results of which, taken collectively are more fatal than useful to mankind.

—Napoleon Bonaparte

In the book *Natural Cures* I mention that one of the things you should avoid is pork. People always question me about how important this is. Some of my best friends still, to this day, love their bacon, ham, and sausages. I am not judgmental. I sit down and have meals with people and watch them enjoy their double-cut stuffed pork chops. Everyone has to make their own choices based on what they feel is best for them. I certainly encourage everyone to eliminate pork, or at least reduce the amount of pork they are consuming. I believe that by doing so you will be sick less, have more energy, lose weight, feel better, be happier, sleep better, live longer, and be much less prone to developing serious degenerative disease. I personally believe pork is one of the major causes of degenerative disease in the body. I am not alone. Dr. Ted Broer is a major advocate in eliminating pork from your diet. Major religions concur. Muslims and Jews, for example, are forbidden to eat pork in any form. Dr. Jeff McCombs, author of the book *Lifeforce*, also has found that eliminating pork causes a dramatic increase in a person's energy level and health, as well as disease-fighting capabilities.

Here is what Dr. Jeff McCombs has to say about eliminating pork from your diet. "People are always asking me about the risks associated with eating pork and pork by-products. There are multiple references all around the world as to the dangers of eating pork. Being in practice for many years I have firsthand experience in what occurs when someone stops eating pork and all pork by-products. Over the years, with virtual 100 percent certainty, I can tell you that when my patients go off pork they virtually ALWAYS feel much better, have more energy, and their symptoms, whatever they may be, start to disappear as if by magic. Ironically, if they start to eat pork again, their symptoms reappear, their energy level plummets, and the feeling general malaise takes over. One of the greatest risks in eating pork is an unknown one. It is a retrovirus called porcine endogenous. This retrovirus lives in all pork cells. Scientists have no idea how this retrovirus affects humans. What is known is that these viruses survive heating and cooking, even at extremely high temperatures over long periods of time. If you are not familiar with what retroviruses can do, think of AIDS. The symptoms that come from AIDS are associated most often with retroviruses. Retroviruses use the body's own cells to replicate themselves. This means that retroviruses go undetected for many, many years as they spread throughout the body. Brown University reported that retroviruses pose a significant threat to the public. When a person eats pork on a regular basis they're loading their body with these retroviruses. These retroviruses dramatically reduce the body's ability to fight off disease, suppress the person's immune system, and make the consumer of pork more susceptible to disease, as well as creating a general overall malaise. When a person goes off pork for thirty days they almost always have an increased sense of well-being, a heightened sense of awareness, a high level of consciousness, are much happier, smile more, laugh more, sleep better, and whatever physical symptoms they have, almost always those symptoms diminish or vanish. Eating pork causes many problems, including hormonal imbalances, joint and back pains, inflammation, excessive histamine production, headaches, increased susceptibility to colds and flus, as well as potentially being partially responsible for degenerative disease such as arthritis, heart disease and cancer. From what I've personally observed, I believe eating pork is like vaccinating your body 'against health.' Pigs also harbor many other toxins, are latent with diseases, and contain worms. Most flu viruses that we encounter in the United States come from the lungs of pigs that create an incubator for the combination of bird, human, and porcine viruses. The Center for Disease Control has stated that as many as 200 of these combined viruses make their way from Southern China to the United States each year through pigs. Pigs scavenge and eat anything in their path including dead insects, worms, rotting carcasses, rats, their own feces, garbage, and other pigs. Whatever a pig eats turns to meat on its bones within a few hours. Pork is virtually undigested garbage. Pork causes stress in the body, both physically and emotionally, and gives rise to physical poisoning. This is a fact that is well known in the scientific community. It is obvious to everyone that when pork products are not prepared properly sickness can result in their consumption. However, this also applies to all pork products, including cured meats such as ham and bacon, smoked meats, sausages, etc. When someone consumes a freshly killed pork product instant symptoms develop, including acute inflammation of the appendix and gallbladder, colitis, intestinal problems, gastroenteritis, typhoid, eczema, various forms of abscesses, spasms, etc. These symptoms are also observed in people after consuming any pork product, including salami, bacon, sausage, and ham. As I mentioned, flu viruses in pork live in the lungs. A professor at the London Institute for Virus Research states that flu viruses remained alive and active and were found in sausages, hot dogs, ham, bacon, pork chops—virtually all pork products. This means that the flu viruses and other viruses that live in the lungs of pigs and in the tissues of pigs survive the cooking and preparation process. When you eat any pork product you are eating living, dangerous viruses. Additionally, pork is the primary source of the taenia solium tapeworm. This type of parasite spreads throughout the body. One in six Americans has triginosis and gets it from eating pork. Like most parasites, these go undetected for years, and years, and years. These parasites steal nutrients from our cells and promote inflammation and degeneration within all tissues. They help create an environment that is conducive for cancer, diabetes, heart disease, arthritis, as well as indigestion, gas, bloating, acid reflux, fatigue, and depression. So, whether it's the retroviruses, the parasite tapeworms, the flu viruses, the histamine increasing compounds, or any of the other toxins present in pork, you may want to consider why you would ever gamble with your health by eating pork. From Confucius to Moses, to Mohammad, to present day science and research, pork has always been and continues to be a very risky health choice. It may be the 'other white meat,' but it's definitely not the right meat!"

Dr. McCombs makes some excellent points. I would encourage all of you, if you want to do an interesting test, to do what I did. I eliminated pork from my diet for thirty full days to see if I noticed any difference. I did, in fact, feel "lighter." I felt more "alive." My breathing was better.

I felt generally "healthier," but I wasn't totally convinced. So, I went out and ate my favorite meal of pork loin roast. Within minutes I became violently ill. That was enough for me to know that pork is poison. If you have symptoms of any kind, if you have illness or disease of any kind, if you want to be cured of what is ailing you, you must do the steps in Chapter 6 in the *Natural Cures* book. One of those important steps is eliminating, or at least dramatically reducing, the amount of pork you consume. I do believe that once you start reducing pork, every time you eat it you will feel so horrible that you will see that a total elimination of pork may be the right choice for you. I hope it is because I do know you will see and feel a dramatic difference within the first month.

TEFLON

It is unbelievable to me the impact that the *Natural Cures* book is having on the news. Since the *Natural Cures* book came out the number of articles that are backing up and verifying everything I'm saying in my book is over a hundredfold. One of the things I talk about in the book is the fact that Teflon nonstick pans are incredibly dangerous. I mentioned that if you put a Teflon nonstick pan on your stove, turn up the heat on high, and happen to have a pet parakeet on your shoulder, the poor parakeet would probably drop dead from the dangerous, poisonous fumes coming from the Teflon nonstick coating. These fumes are generated when high heat is applied. I have said that science is not better than nature. When hundreds of millions of dollars are at stake, people at the highest levels will falsify information, create fake scientific studies, try to convince people that there is no danger when there categorically is known that there are known dangers, or try to mislead the public into believing something is good or bad when the exact opposite is known to be true. This is obviously the case with Teflon. The Associated Press reports that a $5 billion class action lawsuit is being filed against the DuPont company, stating that the chemical giant failed to warn consumers of the dangers of a Teflon chemical. The lawsuit wants DuPont to spend $5 billion to replace all the nonstick cookware, impose a Teflon warning label, and create two funds to pay for medical monitoring and more scientific research on the people who were using Teflon pots and pans to determine just how the use of Teflon cookware has related to and caused illness, sickness, disease, and depression. DuPont has known for over twenty years that the Teflon product, and the various chemicals it uses in the manufacturing of its products, cause cancer! Everyone knows that it causes cancer. The only issue is did DuPont lie in a massive attempt to continue to sell their product? This is the point: everyone knew that these products cause cancer, and the executives of DuPont lied about it because they were only interested in selling the cookware and making the hundreds of millions of dollars in profits. They didn't care that by selling this cookware virtually millions of people could potentially come down with cancer as a direct result of using this cookware. Are you outraged? I am outraged. Take your Teflon and send it back to DuPont; demand a full refund. To join this class action suit go to NaturalCures.com. DuPont, of course, denies all the allegations. The bottom line: if you want to be healthy, throw away all nonstick cookware. Remember, science is not better than nature.

ANTIBIOTICS

I want to start with the bottom line—never, ever, ever take antibiotics unless you are about to die. That's right. Unless you have days to live, never take antibiotics. Antibiotics should virtually never be taken. Why? Well, consider this—when a doctor prescribed antibiotics did he ever perform a test to determine if you had a bacterial infection? Did he perform a test to determine which antibiotic out of the hundreds would be the most effective against the particular bacterial strain causing your problem? Probably not. These two things are important because in over 90 percent of the cases when an antibiotic is prescribed the problem will not be solved with antibiotics. Antibiotics only kill bacteria, they do not kill virus. Most issues that people deal with for which antibiotics are prescribed and not even bacterial, they are viral or some other issue. Therefore, the antibiotics will be ineffective.

The other major problem is in over 90 percent of the cases the antibiotic that is prescribed is not the right one for your particular bacterial infection. Usually doctors prescribe the brand that they happen to have in stock, or the brand for which they are given the most money to prescribe. That's right, it's always about the money. Did you know that antibiotics cause chronic joint pain, hearing loss, vision disturbances, and neurological problems? Did you know that all antibiotics kill friendly bacteria in the colon, automatically leading to a Candida yeast overgrowth? This happens without exception. Antibiotics can cause skin rashes, liver failure, and have put people in comas. Antibiotics have been known to cause heart attacks, strokes, and blood clotting.

Antibiotics have been known to cause chronic pain, muscle pain, and symptoms of dementia and Alzheimer's. Over 100 million doses of antibiotics are handed out each year. Even the Centers for Disease Control, the U.S. government agency, says that 60 percent are totally unnecessary prescriptions.

All antibiotics suppress the immune system and make you more susceptible to other infections. Antibiotics are now even scientifically linked to causing breast cancer, autism, asthma, autoimmune diseases, ear infections, hormonal imbalances, infertility, erectile dysfunction, skin conditions, decreased immunity, and even death. Antibiotics create super bugs that are resistant and stronger than any other infectious-type disease. Think about the fact that every day 50 Americans die from infections that can no longer be cured by any antibiotics. Depending on the source, death from prescription medicine in the United States ranks as being the number one killer. Some sources say the number two killer, others the number three. Either way, prescription medicine kills people to an extent that it should be classified as genocide. Statistics show that antibiotics have killed over 900,000 people. It is estimated that over 10 million people, or more, suffer permanent physiological disorders and major medical conditions that are directly attributable to taking antibiotics, even in small amounts. Yes, some antibiotics have saved some people over the last 30 years, but what about the nearly one million deaths they have absolutely caused and the over 10 million people who are permanently physically damaged because of them?

Antibiotics kill bacteria in the body. They kill all bacteria, good and bad. When the good and bad bacteria are destroyed the cell wall ruptures and bits of the bacteria enter the blood and tissues. Our bodies do not like these bacterial bits and react by producing inflammation and autoimmune reactions. These reactions can continue on indefinitely and affect us years later in an adverse way. Many autoimmune diseases are now being looked at as originating in the digestive tract and specifically caused by taking antibiotics. Inflammation in the digestive system can create inflammation throughout the entire body. Antibiotics also cause constipation. Research now suggests that in order to successfully treat any condition in the body inflammation must be addressed at the same time, which means the constipation has to be addressed and the inflammation that the antibiotics cause have to be addressed too.

Antibiotics create an imbalance by killing all the good bacteria. The good bacteria help to regulate almost every system in the body in one way or another. The good bacteria are part of your body's natural defense system. They help break down foods and absorb nutrients. They help prevent other organisms, like fungus and parasites, from wreaking havoc and overpowering our bodies. The good bacteria have been called the gatekeepers of our body's health. They help us to synthesize B vitamins, which are necessary for the health of our nervous and digestive systems. If you are lactose intolerant it's probably because you've taken antibiotics and you have killed all the good bacteria. Good bacteria are responsible for breaking down lactose. If you have any other nutritional deficiencies, which you probably do, one reason is because whatever you take in is not getting into the cells of your body. Without the good bacteria dominating the internal environment, yeast (or Candida) will convert into its fungal form. This fungal form has the ability to leave the digestive tract and spread throughout the body. Once there, it becomes a source of toxicity throughout the body until it is eliminated. The natural balance can only then be restored. Each fungal cell will secrete toxins that destroy other bacteria, thus perpetuating the cycle of imbalance and toxicity. These toxins are another cause of inflammation in the body. The liver, large intestine, lungs, and kidneys eventually become overwhelmed with the toxic burden and cease to function as they should. As more and more toxins accumulate the body begins to hold water and we gain weight. If this persists long enough, our inflamed nutrient-starved bodies will start to waste away. This can be an even harder condition to treat.

Every time you take an antibiotic you create antibiotic-resistant strains in the body. Antibiotics wipe out the weak strains while the stronger strains survive. These surviving bacteria will now pass on their survival secrets to every other organism in the body. Each subsequent antibiotic only adds to the knowledge base of these developing man-made super bugs. The only way to eliminate them is by restoring the natural balance of good bacterial flora. To do this you must first eliminate the fungus that has overgrown the body and the digestive tract, and then you restore the normal bacteria flora. Don't worry, it's not time to panic about antibiotics and what they have already done to you, but it is time to start considering how we can reverse the effects of past antibiotic use and make better choices in the future.

Anti-Candida diets, like the Lifeforce Plan as outlined in Dr. Jeff McCombs' book *Lifeforce*, can be the cornerstone to any approach to restoring health to the body. The Lifeforce Plan as described in Dr. McCombs' book helps to eliminate the fungal Candida, detoxify the body, and restore the natural bacterial flora. If you ever have to take antibiotics in the future, which I don't believe you should, you should also take an anti-Candida product, an acidophilus. When antibiotics were first prescribed years ago you always received a prescription for acidophilus at the same time. This helped to keep the bacterial flora balance and prevent the inflammation and autoimmune reactions from developing. I don't know why this was discontinued, but it should be resurrected as it is necessary when taking antibiotics. If you have some type of inflammation, which you probably do if you have taken any antibiotics in your life, you must detoxify the body. That is the best place to start. Natural products like cod liver oil, all-natural vitamin E, coral calcium, and systemic enzymes can help to reduce inflammation. Olive leaf extract, colloidal silver, acidulous, royal jelly, and mushroom extracts are examples of products that may be a better first choice than antibiotics. When our bodies are toxic the immune system becomes the garbage collection system. Saunas and hot baths help to eliminate toxins that overwhelm the body's immune system. This is a natural way to boost your immune system by freeing it up to do what it does best. The bottom line is this—you need to stay away from antibiotics.

On the front page of the *San Diego Union Tribune*, August 13, 2005, the headline reads "Rules Tightened to Buy/Use, Acne Drug Acutane." Acutane is an antibiotic. It is now proven that it has caused hundreds of miscarriages and birth defects each year. This drug was prescribed like candy and now the evidence is so overwhelming that new restrictions are being put on its use. What is outrageous is the fact that this, like all drugs, was "proven scientifically" to be safe and effective. It was approved by the FDA, which means all the scientific studies "proved" that this was safe and effective. Well, guess what. Now we find out that it is categorically not safe, killing people, and absolutely not effective. How surprising. As I mentioned over and over again, the scientific studies are false, misleading, and untrue. The FDA says that drugs are safe and effective when they are not. The drug companies try to convince us that natural remedies are ineffective and unsafe, and that drugs are safe and effective. This is categorically not true; the exact opposite is true. All drugs, specifically antibiotics, are ineffective and unsafe. They are all dangerous. All non-prescription and prescription drugs are deadly. They are dangerous; they cause disease.

There are facts about drugs that are being hidden from you. The drug companies do not want you to know the truth about how deadly the drugs are. A friend of mine owns a company that just won the Nobel Prize for medicine. The secret meetings that go on in the medical community are beyond your comprehension. This Nobel Prize winner has the technology which shows that virtually every single non-prescription and prescription drug is totally ineffective and unsafe. He won the Nobel Prize for this technology. I know the truth, the drug companies know the truth, I'm blowing the whistle and telling you the truth, they don't want you to know the truth so they are trying to attack me. Folks, please open your eyes to what is true. All non-prescription and prescription drugs are ineffective and unsafe. Drug companies do not want you well, they only want to sell you more drugs. Remember, all drug companies are publicly traded companies and they only want to sell you more drugs. Remember, remember, remember—all drug companies only want to sell you drugs, they do not want you to be healthy. If every person was healthy, nobody would take any drugs and all the drug companies would be out of business and bankrupt. Remember that fact. Stay away from antibiotics, and stay away from all non-prescription and prescription drugs.

ASPARTAME

Aspartame is an artificial sweetener. It is classified as an excitotoxin. It has similar effects on the body as monosodium glutamate (MSG). It amazes me how many people that I know will sit and order a diet soda! Diet sodas are loaded with artificial sweeteners. The new artificial sweetener is Splenda. This should be avoided at all costs as well. For more information on the dangers of Splenda please go to www.the truthaboutsplenda.com. Splenda is starting to replace aspartame as the artificial sweetener of choice. The reason is the research is now becoming so conclusive that food manufacturers needed another artificial sweetener that had the same qualities as aspartame. The qualities the manufactures were looking for specifically are:

1. They needed a sweetener that didn't have "any calories"; this way they could market it as a diet product, and market it as a way to make you lose weight when in fact these artificial sweeteners make you gain weight. It doesn't matter what the facts are, all these companies care about is being able to market it as a diet product, brainwash you and convince you and lie to you about the fact that it can help you lose weight. These artificial sweeteners do not help you lose weight, they actually make you gain weight.

2. It also needed to be chemically addicting. That's right, these food manufacturers specifically want an artificial sweetener that gets you chemically, physically addicted. They needed it to act like a drug similar to cocaine or heroin where if you didn't get it you would feel bad, be depressed, and need more. This ensures their sales.

3. They also needed a substance that had a shelf life of 10 or 15 years; this way they didn't have to worry about spoilage, thus increasing their profits.

4. They needed a product that could be made for virtually nothing. They needed something that was much cheaper than sugar.

I want to share with you two bits of information. The first one was written by Rich Murray. It describes how aspartame became legal and shows the timeline. For this complete article you can go to www.rense.com. I will give you the highlights. In 1985 Monsanto purchased G.D. Searle, the chemical company that held the patent to aspartame, which by the way is the active ingredient under the brand name NutraSweet. Previously, in 1980, the FDA Board of Inquiry comprised of three independent scientists confirmed that aspartame "might induce brain tumors." The FDA actually banned aspartame based on this finding only to have Searle Chairman Donald Rumsfeld (yes, this is the same Donald Rumsfeld who is currently the secretary of defense) come to aspartame's aid. Mr. Rumsfeld used his political connections, pulled some strings and got aspartame approved by the FDA. On January 21, 1981, the day after Ronald Reagan's inauguration, Searle reapplied to the FDA for approval to use aspartame as a food sweetener. The FDA appointed a five-person review board to look at the previous board's denial. The evidence was so clear that aspartame was dangerous and caused brain tumors and other medical problems that this new five-person scientific board voted 3–2 against allowing aspartame to be used for human consumption because it was too dangerous. When this was about to happen, the FDA commissioner then broke protocol and did the outrageous thing of installing a sixth member to the commission at the last minute. This sixth member voted to have aspartame approved, thus causing a 3–3 tie. The FDA commissioner then came in and personally broke the tie in aspartame's favor. This FDA commissioner later had to leave the FDA under allegations of impropriety. He then took a position with the chief public relations firm for both Monsanto and G.D. Searle! Since that time he has never publicly spoken about aspartame. This is the outrage. This was obviously a payoff. We need to open our eyes to how the revolving door works in Washington.

Now to give you a little more information based on the history from Rich Murray of aspartame:

December 1965. A chemist accidentally discovers aspartame, a substance that is 180 times sweeter than sugar yet seemingly has no calories.

1967. G.D. Searle Company begins safety tests on aspartame so it can apply to the FDA for approval to use it as a food additive.

Fall 1967. Dr. Harold Waisman, a biochemist at the University of Wisconsin, conducts aspartame safety tests on infant monkeys on behalf of the Searle Company. Of the seven monkeys that were fed aspartame mixed with milk, one dies and five others have grand seizures!

November 1970. Cyclamate, the number one low-calorie artificial sweetener, is pulled off the market after it has been proven to cause cancer. Questions are also raised about the safety of saccharine, the only other artificial sweetener on the market, leaving the market wide open for aspartame. The Searle Company realizes that if it can get aspartame approved, it is looking at windfall profits in the tens of billions of dollars! The executives decide it will get aspartame approved "at all costs and by doing whatever needs to be done."

December 18, 1970. Searle Company executives lay out a "food and drug sweetener strategy" that they feel will put the FDA in a position to positively look at aspartame. An internal policy memo describes psychological tactics the company should use to bring the FDA into a subconscious spirit of participation with them on aspartame and get FDA regulators into the habit of saying yes! In effect, the Searle Company is using psychological techniques to brainwash executives at the FDA to approve the substance even though they know it will harm the population.

Spring 1971. Neuroscientist Dr. John Olney, whose pioneering work on monosodium glutamate was responsible for having it removed from baby foods, informs Searle that his studies show that one of the ingredients of aspartame causes holes in the brains of infant mice. One of Searle's own researchers confirmed Dr. Olney's findings in a similar study.

February 1973. After spending tens of millions of dollars conducting safety tests, the G.D. Searle Company applies for FDA approval and submits over 100 studies they claim support aspartame safety. What they don't tell the FDA is they have over 1,000 studies showing that aspartame causes disease.

March 5, 1973. One of the first FDA scientists to review the aspartame data states that "The information provided is inadequate to permit an evaluation of the potential toxicity of aspartame." She says in her report that in order to be certain that aspartame is safe further clinical tests are needed.

July 26, 1974. Miraculously, the FDA grants aspartame approval for restricted use in dry foods. To this day no one knows how or why this approval was granted since the data was so inconclusive and suggested major negative side effects.

August 1974. Immediately after this miraculous approval by the FDA, consumer advocate Jim Turner, who was instrumental in getting the artificial sweetener cyclamate off the market, as well as Dr. John Olney file objections against aspartame's approval noting the conclusive evidence that aspartame is dangerous.

March 24, 1976. It takes two years for Jim Turner and Dr. Olney's objections to trigger an FDA investigation of laboratory practices of aspartame's manufacturer G.D. Searle. The investigation finds Searle's testing procedures shoddy, full of inaccuracies, and "manipulated test data." The investigators at the FDA report "that they have never seen anything as bad as Searle's testing." It is obvious to everyone today that Searle simply lied about the safety of aspartame in order to get it approved and in order to make the billions of dollars in windfall profits.

January 10, 1977. The FDA formally requests the U.S. Attorney's Office to begin grand jury proceedings to investigate whether indictments should be filed against Searle for knowingly misrepresenting findings and "concealing material facts and making false statements" in aspartame's safety test. This is the first time in the FDA's history that they request a criminal investigation of a manufacturer. The fact is, however, that the drug companies today and the food companies are doing exactly the same thing. It was done before and it continues to be done all in the name of making money.

January 26, 1977. While the grand jury probe is under way, the law firm representing Searle begins job negotiations with the U.S. Attorney in charge of the investigation!! How absolutely outrageous. Imagine what happened here. The U.S. Attorney in charge of investigating Searle is the man who must be stopped. What does Searle do? They simply bring in their law firm and say—go to the U.S. Attorney and offer him millions of dollars by giving him a job at your firm if he gets off our back. Searle denies these allegations, but it is obvious to everyone that this bribe is exactly what had taken place.

March 8, 1977. Searle hires Washington insider Donald Rumsfeld as the new CEO! A former member of Congress and secretary of defense in the Ford administration, Rumsfeld brings in several of his Washington cronies as top management. What everyone knows now is that Searle was facing some major problems and needed some "political insider help." It simply did what all companies do, pay off Washington insiders with huge amounts of money; they use their political connections, their friends on the inside of Washington to pull the strings to make sure the problems go away.

July 1, 1977. Samuel Skinner, the U.S. Attorney in charge of the investigation against Searle, leaves the U.S. Attorney's Office and takes a job with Searle's law firm—outrageous, unbelievable, and a flagrant conflict of interest.

August 1, 1977. The Bressler Report compiled by FDA investigatory and headed by Jerome Bressler is released. The report finds that 98 of the 196 animals died during one of Searle's studies and were not autopsied until later dates, in some cases over one year after death. Many other errors and inconsistencies are noted. For example, a rat was reported alive, then dead, then alive, then dead again; a cancerous mass, a uterine polyp, and ovarian neoplasms were found in animals that were not reported or diagnosed in Searle's reports. This report compiled by the FDA shows that Searle's studies were flagrantly false! They obviously lied and doctored the studies in order to get aspartame approved.

December 8, 1977. U.S. Attorney Skinner's withdrawal and resignation stalls the Searle grand jury investigation for so long that the statute of limitations on the aspartame charges runs out! The grand jury investigation is dropped! Searle figured out how to pay off the investigator and make sure all the charges were dropped. This should be one of the largest political corruption scandals of the decade; nothing was ever reported in the media and nothing was ever done.

July 1, 1979. The FDA, under public pressure, establishes a Public Board of Inquiry to rule on the safety issues surrounding NutraSweet and aspartame.

September 30, 1980. This Public Board of Inquiry concludes NutraSweet and aspartame should not be approved pending further investigation on brain tumors in animals. The Board states it "has not been presented with proof of reasonable certainty that aspartame is safe for use as a food additive and for human consumption."

January 1981. Donald Rumsfeld, the CEO of Searle, states in a sales meeting that he is going to make a big push in Washington by using his friends and connections to get aspartame approved within the year. Rumsfeld says that he will use his political pull, rather than scientific means, to make sure aspartame gets approved! Remember, if aspartame is approved, Searle makes tens of billions of dollars in profits and the stock skyrockets. Rumsfeld is poised to make hundreds of millions.

January 21, 1981. Ronald Reagan is sworn in as president of the United States. Reagan's transition team, which includes Donald Rumsfeld, CEO of Searle, also hand picks Arthur Hull Hayes to be the new FDA commissioner.

March 1981. An FDA commissioner's panel is established to review issues about aspartame raised by the Public Board of Inquiry.

May 19, 1981. Three FDA scientists advise against approval of NutraSweet and aspartame stating on the record that Searle tests are unreliable and are not adequate to determine the safety of aspartame. These FDA scientists believe that aspartame is responsible for brain tumors and other major health concerns.

July 15, 1981. In one of his first official acts, the new FDA commissioner actually does the unthinkable; he personally overrules the Public Board of Inquiry's findings, ignores the recommendations of his own internal FDA team, and he personally approves NutraSweet and aspartame!

October 15, 1982. Searle files a petition to have aspartame approved as a sweetener in carbonated beverages and other liquids. Within a short period of time, even the National Soft Drink Association urges the FDA to delay approval of aspartame for carbonated beverages, stating it is unreliable and unstable in liquid form. This Association states to the FDA that when liquid aspartame is stored in room temperatures above 85 degrees, it breaks down into DKP and formaldehyde, both of which are known toxins, and cause cancer, brain damage, and other health issues. The National Soft Drink Association drafts an objection to the final ruling permitting aspartame to be used in carbonated beverages and syrup bases, and requests a hearing of its objections. The Association says that Searle has not provided responsible certainty that aspartame and its products are safe for use in soft drinks.

August 8, 1983. Suits are filed against the FDA objecting to aspartame approval based on unresolved safety issues.

September 1983. FDA commissioner Hayes resigns under a cloud of controversy about his taking unauthorized rides on a General Foods jet. General Foods is a major customer of NutraSweet. Searle's public relation firm immediately hires Hayes as its senior scientific consultant; Hayes makes a windfall profit on this transition. It certainly appears all too closely connected.

Fall 1983. The FDA approves NutraSweet for carbonated soft drinks and other liquids that are sold to consumers. Immediately, the Centers for Disease Control and the FDA start to receive unprecedented amounts of complaints from people who use these products and experience horrible health issues, including depression, hypertension, dementia, nausea, sickness, headaches, migraines, dizziness, etc. Both the Centers for Disease Control and the FDA ignore these massive consumer complaints about aspartame. To this day, the FDA and the Centers for Disease Control have received more complaints from consumers about negative side effects from aspartame than any other substance in the history of this country; yet the FDA, the Centers for Disease Control, and our government do absolutely nothing.

This timeline shows how the government works: it's all about money, payoffs, and bribes. It's all about multinational corporations doing anything to make profits at the expense of our health. We need to know the truth. Remember, science is not better than nature. Buy products that are 100 percent organic; buy products that are as close to natural as nature intended. This same type of information can also be said about Splenda. Please, if you are reading this, stop consuming any artificial sweetener, read food labels, buy 100 percent organic foods.

BEWARE OF "ALL-NATURAL" PRODUCTS

You need to be educated on the kind of products you should be purchasing. In all of my companies I have requirements, when I travel, when I do TV shows, when I make appearances—that all the food is 100 percent organic. Unfortunately, people sometimes do not listen or pay attention or understand that 100 percent organic means 100 percent organic. Let me give you an example. I walked into a TV shoot where I met Ozzie Ozborne. Ozzie's staff was very excited about my book. We had a great conversation about how Ozzie's son went to Thailand and did many cleanses, lost over 30 pounds, is sleeping better, feeling great, his whole personality has changed, as well as his energy level, strength, stamina, and positive outlook on life. The toxins getting out of Ozzie's son's body gave him a profound increase in his health potential. We had a nice discussion. My crew had put together food for all the people associated with this television production. As always, my orders are the food must be 100 percent organic; however, I noticed that they had ordered some "all-natural" sodas. I picked one up, turned it over and read the ingredient list. I saw high fructose corn syrup; I saw preservatives; I saw food coloring. How could this be? The good news is there were no artificial sweeteners. Let me explain.

You have to consider that some things are better than others. In many cases it's not a matter of right and wrong, but a matter of good, better, and best. In other cases it is a matter of right and wrong. Example: Never drink a soda with artificial sweeteners, either aspartame or Splenda. If you are going to drink a soda, I personally do not, I drink water, but if you are going to drink a soda what kind of soda should you drink? Here we get into a matter of degrees. The word that I want you to be aware of is "natural" or "all-natural." The food industry has paid tens of millions of dollars to its lobbyists to get the definition of "natural" and "all-natural" to mean not what you think it means! When you see the word "all-natural" on a product you assume that it is "as nature intended"; this is not true. Food manufacturers pay off their lobbyists to get the politicians to make insane laws. They start defining what is natural. Example: You can call a product "natural" even though it has chemicals in it! Those chemicals are certainly not natural, they are not as nature intended, but according to the law you can still call the product natural. This is why when you are picking up a product, if you see on the label "100 percent organic," you can feel pretty good about the product. If you see the word "natural" and you don't see the word "organic" anywhere, beware. It may be better than some other products, but it may not be as good as it could be, so it's a matter of degree. Certainly, you don't want to be a crazy person, a fanatic, but do the best you can. Personally, when I buy something, I look for 100 percent organic, but sometimes you just can't do that. I was driving up the coast of California, I needed some food, I stopped at a restaurant, they certainly didn't have 100 percent organic anything. I ordered the tuna fish sandwich on rye; I'm sure the mayonnaise was some crap, garbage mayonnaise made with all types of chemicals; I'm sure the tuna was processed in a way where it was loaded with chemicals; I'm sure the bread was loaded with chemicals; I'm sure the tomato was not organic so it had pesticides in it, as well as the onions, lettuce, and pickles. They were probably all pasteurized and irradiated as well. They had no bottled water and I had an iced tea. The water that the iced tea was made in was probably full of chlorine and fluoride. What can you do? The question is was my meal good? No. But was it better than a meal at McDonald's, Wendy's, Pizza Hut, or Taco Bell? Yes. Sometimes, you have to say which is my best option? Sometimes, you aren't dealing with right or wrong, yes or no, but you're dealing with good, better, and best; and sometimes you're dealing with what's the best of the worst! In this particular example I didn't have a lot of options so I thought, of the options that I had which is the best of all the bad options out there?! The key though is the word "natural." Beware of this word; this is a word that really means nothing today. The key is when you buy something in a package that you read the ingredient list, that's the key. If you see high fructose corn syrup or artificial sweeteners, just don't buy it. Ideally, every ingredient on that list should be 100 percent organic. Do the best you can. Remember, we can't live perfectly; we are going to be putting toxins in our body, that's why it's so vitally important to do cleanses on at least an annual basis. We must get those toxins out. It's just impossible to live where we don't put any toxins in. We also live in a world where it's impossible to get all of the nutrition we need from the food we eat; therefore, it's vital on a regular basis, ideally every day, to take some type of whole food supplement to get nutrients in your body that you need. So, just remember, beware of the word "natural," don't be concerned with what's on the front of the label, read the ingredient list. That will give you the best information.

STAY AWAY FROM SHELLFISH

A few months ago in one of my newsletters I talked about how pork can reduce your ability to stay healthy. Pork suppresses your immune system and makes you prone to illness and disease. Shellfish has pretty much the same effects on the body. Let me define shellfish. If you are going to eat anything from out of the oceans or rivers or lakes, the fish that you eat must have scales and fins. Some of you may realize that this is one of the kosher laws. Fish with scales and fins have a digestive system that doesn't allow poisons in the water to be absorbed into the flesh. Remember, fish actually swim in their own excretions. All living animals in the seas, lakes, rivers, and streams deposit their feces and bodily excretions into the same water they are swimming in. When you think about that for a moment it becomes a little sickening. Fish that have scales and fins, like flounder, cod, haddock, mackerel, and salmon, do not absorb the toxins in the water. Other animals of the sea that have fins but no scales, such as catfish, are generally bottom feeders, scavengers, and have digestive systems that absorb the toxins from the water.

Other animals in the sea such as clams, shrimp, mussels, squid, lobster, and crab have neither scales nor fins and are highly toxic. They absorb all the poisons from the water. When you think of some of these animals, such as a lobster, we realize that they are nothing more than cockroaches of the sea. Lobsters, for example, are arthropods, which is simply a large cockroach. Would you eat a cockroach? Well, why would you eat a lobster? I know, it tastes delicious! I grew up in Boston. I grew up on shellfish, lobster, clams, scallops, crab, shrimp, and calamari. I ate all of this stuff and it's delicious, especially when it's fried! However, it is highly toxic and suppresses the immune system. When blood tests are taken before and after people consume this type of shellfish we see dramatic negative effects in the body. Through the use of Kirlian photography and other techniques we see that the body's life force and energy are dramatically suppressed and reduced when eating shellfish or any fish that doesn't have scales and fins.

I have a good friend who loves mussels. We were dining at a restaurant and he ordered a large plate of mussels. I had a salad and some salmon, and our other friend had a salad and some chicken. The next morning we all got up and both I and my friend who had the chicken felt fantastic and full of energy, excited for a great day. My friend who ate the mussels said he was feeling a little "off," he wasn't feeling that well. I suggested it could have been the mussels the night before; he scoffed and laughed it off. Over the next week I made a mental note that every time he ate crab, lobster, or shellfish, the next morning he always felt like crap. The nights he didn't eat those things he always felt better. I pointed this out. He found it interesting. He then proceeded to keep his own journal and make a mental note how he felt in the morning after he had the shellfish. He was amazed that he always felt bad. Certainly this is not a scientific experiment, but it's something to think about.

I have another friend who visits Florida on many occasions. Every time he visits Florida he goes right for the lobster, right for the crab and the shrimp. He always winds up getting sick in Florida. I point out to him that his immune system is going to be suppressed by eating all the lobster, shrimp, and crab, but he never really thinks anything of it. It is obvious to me and everyone else, because every time he eats that stuff he always falls ill.

If you want to be healthy and strong and vibrant, if you want to live a long life without getting sick, without getting colds or the flu, without developing arthritis, diabetes, cancer, heart disease, or any degenerative disease, if you want to look younger and feel better, I would suggest to you to eliminate or at least reduce the amount of fish and shellfish you are consuming that doesn't have scales and fins. If you are going to eat fish, always eat wild fish that has both scales and fins—fish such as salmon, mackerel, cod, haddock, and the like. One other important thing, never consume farm-raised fish. If you have ever gone to a fish farm and seen how they pollute the water, the chemicals they put into the water, and the fact that all of the excretions of the fish are just sitting there, it will absolutely disgust you. The research today and the scientific documentation are very compelling. Farm-raised fish are full of toxicity; they should never be consumed.

C H A P T E R   1 2

The Only Source of Unbiased Health Information

Half of the modern drugs should be thrown out the window, except that the birds might eat them.

—Dr. Martin Henry Fischer

NaturalCures.com is my website that will become the ultimate source of true health information in the world. It will be the only place in the world where you can get unbiased and totally complete health information. The website will not accept any advertising, and we will not have any ties to any products or companies that sell products. Building NaturalCures.com is a massive undertaking. It will take over 500 employees and huge amounts of money to produce the vision that I have for this ultimate source of information. Imagine you find out you have prostate cancer. You are scared; you are nervous; you don't know what to do. You don't know who to talk to; you don't know who to believe; you don't know where you can get information about your choices and options. Time is of the essence. What do you do? Well, you call your local doctor and ask for his advice. Little do you know that he just bought a new machine for $2 million. He has to pay the note on that machine, which means he has to get as many patients as possible to use it. You ask him what the best treatment option for prostate cancer is. He tells you that the machine that he happens to have in the back room is the best choice. How do you know if that is the best choice, or how do you know that he's just not telling you that you need to use his machine because he needs to pay for it? You don't know. There is a conflict of interest. You go to another hospital and ask them what the best way to cure your prostate cancer is. They tell you that the freezing method is the best, and they happen to have the equipment right on site. Hm-m-m ... interesting isn't it? Is the freezing method really the best or are they telling you that the freezing method is the best because that's the only equipment they have? Think about it this way, you walk into a Chevrolet dealership and ask them, "What's the best car?" Would it surprise you if they told you Chevrolet? Hm-m-m ... interesting isn't it? Of course they are going to tell you that what they're selling is the best. That's the problem with doctors. So you go to WebMD and try to find out what the answer is. Isn't it interesting that the best answers are always the ones that advertise the most and give WebMD the most money? Is it also surprising to note that the best methods are always the companies that the officers and directors are the most heavily invested in? Can you see it's always about the money?

There are always conflicts of interest. You never know who is telling the truth. You are scared. You are nervous. You don't know what to do. That's the problem. Here's the solution. Let's go back to the beginning. You have found out that you have prostate cancer, or any disease for that matter. What do you do? Who do you call? Not Ghostbusters. You go to www.naturalcures.com. You log in. There are no conflicts of interest. Nobody at NaturalCures.com has anything to sell. We are only interested in your health. We only want to tell you all the information that is available anywhere in the world so that you can make the best informed decision without any bias. You go to the website under "diseases" and it says "prostate cancer." You click on it and it lists every single method of curing prostate cancer anywhere in the world. It lists drugs; it lists surgery; it lists natural remedies; it lists everything. It tells you the exact true success rates of each treatment. It tells you the best places in the world to get those treatments. It gives you the unbiased, truthful facts so that you can make an informed decision. It also tells you the best doctors in the world to call and get advice. There is also a chat room where you can go and talk to other people and hear what they have to say. There is also a place you can type in a question and get an answer—all from an unbiased source with nothing to sell. You see, my goal is to have a staff of over 500 people researching every single method of curing prostate cancer, and every disease from the most common to the most obscure, from drugs and surgery to homeopathy and every method of natural healing from all over the globe. I want to provide the most complete source of information for health that the world has ever seen. This will revolutionize health. The drug companies do not want this to happen. They know that their businesses will plummet. They know that drug use will go dramatically down when people start seeing the truth about what are the best methods to cure and prevent disease. The people will benefit; you will benefit.

Here is my vision for what NaturalCures.com will be:

1. *Every disease listed with all options for treatment.*   This is the main crux of the website. Every disease known to man is the goal. The goal is to list every disease and have hundreds of researchers go all over the world to find every known treatment and report on their findings so that you have access to every bit of information in a simple-to-read format. It will also allow you to ask questions and have chat rooms with people like yourself who are facing the same disease or dilemma. This will be the only place in the world where every bit of health information relating to a disease will be available, because it is the only place in the world where there are no conflicts of interest, no financial ties to the sale of drugs or the use of specific machines. With no advertisers to skew the information or make the information biased, you can be assured that you have the answers that you need regarding your health.

2. *Healthcare directory.*   I believe it is vital that you get professional treatment from licensed healthcare practitioners. I intend to provide the most intensive, exhaustive, complete list of licensed healthcare providers around the world who do not use drugs and surgery. We will list this by geographic location, by disease specialty, and by treatment technique specialty. Most importantly, you will be able to write comments about the doctor or facility. When you are searching for a licensed healthcare practitioner, how do you know if the practitioner is good? You will be able to go online and look at what other people have to say about this treatment center or healthcare provider. You can see if they are being well received and the results are good, or if the results are bad—this way you can make an informed decision.

3. *Product review.*   In this section it is my intention to thoroughly review products and make recommendations. This product review section will be unlike anything the world has ever seen. Here is why. If you pick up any magazine and look at product reviews, did you know that every single one of them is virtually bought and paid for? That's right, even in the most consumer-oriented magazines and websites, the "best of" list, the "top 10" list, the "product recommended" list, the "editor's choice" list are nothing more than bought and paid for advertisements.

None of them are truthful. At best, the way the products are reviewed is they are purchased, used by a few people, and the review is written. But generally what happens is the manufacturer pays the publication to write nice reviews, or pays the publication to write bad reviews on its competitors.

What I intend to do is put together a massive team of product researchers. You will be able to send us a product and we will review it for you. We will also review products on our own. The products that we review will be specifically related to health—things that I mention in the *Natural Cures* book. These will include food, vitamins, minerals, homeopathics, various food supplements and health supplements, and also things such as soaps, organic cleaning products, shampoos, toothpastes, air filters, water filters, etc. The review process will be unlike anything that has ever been done in history. When we review a product the first thing we will do is we will investigate the company that manufactures the product. We will investigate and talk to the officers and directors of that company. We will find out what these people are really like. Are these greedy, evil people who are only in it for the money, or are they sincere people who are really interested in benefiting society with good-quality products? Do they have a passion for their product? Do they use their own products? We will report on what these people are like. We will find out what their financial interests are in other companies and we will report to you about the company that makes the product. Are they more interested, for example, in labeling and selling their product and making money, or are they more interested in the quality of the product? We will also talk to all the people who work for the company and find out how this company treats their employees. Is the company hurting or harming the environment? Are they good to their community? Are they good to their staff members? We will report this to you.

We will then look at the entire manufacturing process. We will review every ingredient. We will find out where those ingredients are purchased from and review those companies, and continue all the way to the farms, whether they be in Peru, Nicaragua, or China, and find out exactly how this product is made. Imagine that we are reviewing a shampoo. We find out the shampoo is manufactured in Jonesville, Arkansas. We send our researchers and they fly to Jonesville, Arkansas. They meet the president of the company; they meet the board of directors; they meet the officers. They find out that these people are wonderful people that live a healthy lifestyle, they treat their employees well, and they support their community. Their plant is environmentally friendly and they do not appear to be incredibly greedy people who are only in it for the money. We find out that they have a passion for the business of producing a great-quality shampoo. We find out that they are more interested in what goes in the bottle than what the label looks like. We report to you these encouraging facts.

We then review the manufacturing process and we find out that the shampoo is manufactured with 100 percent organic all-natural ingredients. We watch them make it. We find out that the entire manufacturing process is in fact a wonderful healthy process, but the ingredients are purchased from four other suppliers. They are allegedly 100 percent organic and natural. We then send our crew to each one of those four suppliers, and we do the same process. We meet the presidents of those companies and the entire boards of directors, as well as the other officers. We interview the employees. We find out if these companies are working in an environmentally friendly way, if they support the community. We find out if these companies have any ties to the pharmaceutical industry or are just greedy people who are in it for the money. We find out if they are being truthful when they say the ingredients are 100 percent natural and organic. We find out that they produce their product from ingredients that they purchase overseas in China.

We then fly to China and we find out that the ingredients that come in from China are actually manufactured in a slave labor camp where the people are given virtually no money, work 14-hour days, and in fact the fields are not organic at all. They are sprayed with pesticides and herbicides, and the company is owned by a multibillion-dollar conglomerate, which is owned by both a drug company and a tobacco company. We would report this to you. We would also report this to all the other companies along the line. They may not be aware of it and they may change suppliers! This benefits everyone. The evil supplier loses the business and a new legitimate supplier is found. The people who are honest and true and benefiting society reap the financial rewards, and those greedy, evil people who have been exploiting workers and exploiting customers for years are finally going to pay the price in their pocketbooks. You and I benefit from getting better quality products at better prices. The environment benefits, the employees benefit, the legitimate honest people benefit, everyone benefits. What this process of reviewing products does is expose the frauds for who they are and give you information about what truly are the best quality products at the best prices.

The website will also have many other areas such as news around the world on corporate and government fraud and corruption. We will have a 24-hour radio station on the website on natural cures where you can hear doctors talk about health and nutrition. We will have cooking DVDs available, recommended books and DVDs, recommended seminars around the country, and a lot more. Good things are happening, and much has to do with your support as a newsletter subscriber and website subscriber. I thank you again for your love, prayers, and support. Go to www.naturalcures.com and become a member today.

CHAPTER 13

The Uncensored, Original, Infamous "Chapter Six"

The problem with power is how to achieve its responsible use rather than its irresponsible and indulgent use. Getting people of power to live for the public instead of off the public is the challenge.

—Robert F. Kennedy

When I wrote *Natural Cures "They" Don't Want You to Know About* the United States Government regulatory agency, the Federal Trade Commission, told me that I could not mention any product by brand name. I was ordered to refrain from putting in my book any website addresses, company names, or telephone numbers about any brand name products. I was told that I could not give my opinion, based on my journalistic investigations, about my beliefs relating to how specific products could potentially be used to treat, prevent, or cure disease. It is my understanding that doing so would result in the confiscation and burning of the books by the U.S. Government and the arrest and criminal prosecution of myself. Today, I choose to stand up against tyranny, oppression, and fascism. I choose to fully express my opinions and exercise my First Amendment constitutional right of free unrestricted speech. Today, I choose to single-handedly take a stand against the lies and deceit promulgated by the pharmaceutical medical cartels, and worldwide governments. I choose to be the first major voice who dares to go against the established worldwide medical community and cartel and do the unthinkable. I am going to actually publicly say which specific products, based on full investigation, research, and individual testimony, do in fact prevent and help the body cure disease.

If you have not read my previous book, *Natural Cures "They" Don't Want You to Know About*, it is vitally important that you read that book cover to cover. It gives you everything you need to do to prevent, treat, and help the body cure disease. The government censored all the specific product brand names from that book. Now, for the first time, I am revealing to the world the specific products that I personally use and recommend. Remember, I have no financial interests in any of these companies or products. This is truly unbiased opinions. You must know that by me writing this book, and revealing this information, that I am putting myself in grave danger. I have been personally approached by "men in black" and told in no uncertain terms that if I wrote, published, and sold this book, revealing the insider secrets that I am privy to, that I would be attacked, criticized, persecuted, and discredited worse than any political smear campaign in history. Revealing the secrets and knowledge I have is financially devastating to some of the most powerful people and groups on planet earth. I am doing this not for personal gain, but rather out of a deep feeling of responsibility. I know that sharing with you the truth will save millions of lives. Having this information widely disseminated will stop and prevent the suffering of millions of people around the world at the hands of the greedy money hungry pharmaceutical cartels and politicians.

The following information comes from Chapter 6 in my previous book, but now lists the specific companies and products that have been previously censored by the U.S. Government. We must have the freedom of being exposed to all opinions and we must have the freedom to make our own choices regarding our own health. Many products that I recommend are available at discounts by going to www.naturalchoicesclub.com.

1. SEE NATURAL HEALTHCARE PROVIDERS ON A REGULAR BASIS.

Check your yellow pages for local listings for alternative practitioners. Go to www.naturalcures.com for a comprehensive database of holistic practitioners around the country.

American College for Advancement in Medicine
www.acam.org   (800) 532-3688

American Academy of Osteopathy
www.academyofosteopathy.org   (317) 879-1881

Holistic.com
www.holistic.com

American Holistic Medical Association
www.holisticmedicine.org

American Association of Naturopathic Physicians
www.naturopathic.org   (866) 538-2267

American Holistic Health Association
www.ahha.org   (714) 779-6152

Orthomolecular Medicine
www.orthomed.org   (415) 922-6462

A. Get treated by a bioenergetic synchronization technique practitioner.

Morter HealthSystem
www.morter.com   (800) 874-1478

Dr. Morter's AlkaLine Products
www.mortersupplements.com

B.E.S.T. Life Training
www.bestlifetraining.com   (888) 333-7080

B. Get a chiropractic adjustment.
Check your local yellow pages for a chiropractor.

Association for Network Care
www.associationfornetworkcare.com   (303) 678-8101

American Chiropractic Association
www.amerchiro.org   (800) 986-4636

World Chiropractic Alliance
www.worldchiropracticalliance.org/consumer   (800) 347-1011

International Chiropractors Association
www.chiropractic.org   (800) 423-4690

C. See an herbalist.
Check your local yellow pages for an herbalist

Herb Research Foundation
www.herbs.org   (303) 449-2265

American Botanical Council
www.herbalgram.org   (512) 926-4900

American Herbal Pharmacopoeia
www.herbal-ahp.org   (831) 461-6318

American Herbal Products Association
www.ahpa.org   (301) 588-1171

D. See a homeopathic practitioner.
Check your local yellow pages for a homeopathic practitioner.

Homeopathic Educational Services
www.homeopathic.com   (800) 359-9051

The National Center for Homeopathy
www.homeopathic.org   (703) 548-7790

Homeopathic Academy of Naturopathic Physicians
www.hanp.net   (253) 630-3338

American Institute of Homeopathy
www.homeopathyusa.org   (888) 445-9988

North American Society of Homeopaths
www.homeopathy.org   (206) 720-7000

E. See a naturopath.
Check your local yellow pages for a naturopathic physician.

Find an ND
www.findnd.com

National College of Naturopathic Medicine
www.ncnm.edu   (503) 255-4860

American Association of Naturopathic Physicians
www.naturopathic.org   (703) 610-9037

2. STOP TAKING NON-PRESCRIPTION AND PRESCRIPTION DRUGS.

Find an Integrative MD or a naturopathic physician to guide you off of prescription drugs.

Foundation for Integrated Medicine
www.mdheal.org

Public Citizen
www.worstpills.org

Citizens for Health
www.citizens.org   (612) 879-7585

American Association for Health Freedom
www.healthfreedom.net   (800) 230-2762

Dr. Joseph Mercola
www.mercola.com

Alternative Health Insurance Services
www.alternativeinsurance.com   (800) 331-2713

3. ENERGETIC REBALANCING.

EMC² Energetic Matrix Church of Consciousness, LLC.
www.energeticmatrix.com

Quantum Prayer System
www.energeticbalancing.us   (888) 225-7501

Quantum Distance Healing
www.distancehealing.net   (866) 784-7111

Healing Touch International, Inc.
www.healingtouch.net   (303) 989-7982

International Center for Reiki Training
www.reiki.org   (800) 332-8112

Quantum-Touch
www.quantumtouch.com   (888) 424-0041

Rosen Method Bodywork and Movement
www.rosenmethod.org

Quantum Wellness Center
www.quantumwellnesscenter.com   (866) 784-7111

NeXus-10 biofeedback system
www.stens-biofeedback.com   (800) 257-8367

Ondamed Biofeedback System
www.ondamed.net   (800) 807-7864

Quantum Xxroid Consciousness Interface
www.qxci.biz   (888) 830-3222

Q2 Energy System
www.futurewatertoday.com   (800) 827-0762

Tools for Wellness
www.toolsforwellness.com   (800) 456-9887

Bodymath
www.bodymath.com   (800) 449-3022

Intuition for Health and Healing
www.drjudithorloff.com

4. CHECK YOUR BODY PH.

Diet is a huge component, as are negative emotions, when balancing your body's pH.

Natural Cures
www.naturalcures.com

Phion Nutrition
www.ph-ion.com   (888) 744-8589

Frequency Rising
www.frequencyrising.com   (951) 303-3471

pH Miracle Living
www.phmiracleliving.com   (760) 751-8321

pH paper
www.discount-vitamins-herbs.com   (800) 401-9186

Buffer pH+ and pH Test Strips
www.thebeewellcompany.com   (877) 726-1110

Active Ionic Minerals
www.teravite.com   (800) 776-5438

Natural Cellular Defense
www.therawfoodworld.com   (866) 729-3438

Universal Supplements
www.universalsupplements.com   (805) 646-5936

A. Clean out the toxins that have accumulated in your body.

1. Get 15 colonics in 30 days.
Check your local yellow pages for Colon Therapy.

International Association for Colon Hydrotherapy
www.i-act.org   (210) 366-2888

Dr. Natura
www.drnatura.com   (800) 877-0414

Colon Health
www.colonhealth.com

2. Do a complete colon cleanse.
For the best colon cleanse instructions, go to
www.naturalcures.com.

Dr. Richard Schulze
www.dr-schulze.com   (800) 437-2362

Blessed Herbs
www.blessedherbs.com   (800) 489-4372

Ejuva
www.ejuva.com   (909) 337-5627

HealthForce Nutritionals
www.healthforce.com   (760) 747-8822

Renew Life
www.renewlife.com   (800) 485-0960

Sonne's #7
www.sonnes.com   (800) 544-8147

Pure Body Institute
www.pbiv.com   (800) 952-2458

Universal Supplements
www.universalsupplements.com   (805) 646-5936

Arise & Shine
www.ariseandshine.com   (800) 688-2444

3. Do a liver/gallbladder cleanse.

Liver gallbladder cleansing comes after colon cleansing, usually with a rest period in between. Consult your alternative practitioner before liver cleansing.

Dr. Richard Schulze
www.dr-schulze.com   (800) 437-2362

Blessed Herbs
www.blessedherbs.com   (800) 489-4372

Pure Body Institute
www.pbiv.com   (800) 952-2458

Sandra Cabot, MD
www.liverdoctor.com

Ann Louise Gittleman—the fat flush plan
www.annlouise.com

4. Do a kidney/bladder cleanse.

Kidney/bladder cleansing should be done after colon cleansing and liver/gallbladder cleansing. Consult your alternative practitioner before kidney cleansing.

Dr. Richard Schulze
www.dr-schulze.com   (800) 437-2362

Blessed Herbs
www.blessedherbs.com   (800) 489-4372

Pure Body Institute
www.pbiv.com   (800) 952-2458

5. Do a heavy metal cleanse.

Beyond Chelation
www.longevityplus.net   (800) 580-7587

Essential Daily Defense
www.longevityplus.net   (800) 580-7587

Natural Cellular Defense
www.therawfoodworld.com   (866) 729-3438

EDTA CardioChelate from MRM
www.mrm-usa.com   (949) 369-6641

Sun Chlorella USA

www.sunchlorellausa.com

Oral Chelation Formula
www.naturesaide.com   (800) 730-4145

Enhanced Oral Chelation Health Resources
(800) 471-4007

Oral Chelation & Longevity Plus Formula
www.extendedhealth.com   (800) 300-6712

Chelation Therapy

American College of Advancement in Medicine
www.acam.org   (800) 532-3688

American Board of Clinical Metal Toxicology
www.abct.info   (800) 356-2228

6. Do a parasite cleanse.

Natural Cures
www.naturalcures.com

Blessed Herbs
www.blessedherbs.com   (800) 489-4372

Ejuva
www.ejuva.com   (909) 337-5627

HealthForce Nutritionals
www.healthforce.com   (760) 747-8822

Renew Life
www.renewlife.com   (800) 485-0960

Pure Body Institute
www.pbiv.com   (800) 952-2458

Agrisept-L
www.drstockwell.com   (801) 523-1890

Nature's Secret
www.naturessecret.com   (800) 297-3273

Parasite Zappers

Hulda Clark's site
www.paradevices.com   (866) 765-5116

The Original Parasite Zapper
www.island.net/~zapper   (800) 893-6914

7. Do a Candida cleanse.

Natural Cures
www.naturalcures.com

Ejuva
www.ejuva.com   (909) 337-5627

Renew Life
www.renewlife.com   (800) 485-0960

Pure Body Institute
www.pbiv.com   (800) 952-2458

Lifeforce
www.lifeforceplan.com   (888) 236-7780

Body Ecology Diet
www.bodyecologydiet.com   (800) 511-2660

ThreeLac Candida Defense
www.123candida.com   (888) 777-0468

Nature's Secret
www.naturessecret.com   (800) 297-3273

8. Do a full-body fat/lymphatic cleanse.

Purification Rundown Procedure
www.purification.org

Lymphatic Drainage Practitioners
www.iahe.com   (800) 311-9204

Clear Body Clear Mind
www.clearbodyclearmind.com   (800) 722-1733

Detox Patch
www.nutriworks.com.hk

> *Sweating is essential to detoxify the lymphatic system;
> far infrared saunas are the most effective.*

The Best Natural Cures
www.thebestnaturalcures.com   (310) 487-4654

Therasauna
www.therasauna.com   (888) 729-7727

Infrared Mats
www.thebestnaturalcures.com   (310) 487-4654

Gaia Holistic Circle
www.gaiahh.com   (212) 799-9711

Healthmate Sauna
www.healthmatesauna.com   (800) 946-6001

High Tech Health, Inc.
www.hightechhealth.com   (800) 794-5355

Ozone/Oxygen Therapy

American College of Hyperbaric Medicine (ACHM)
www.oceanhbo.com   (800) 552-0255

Medizone International Inc.
www.medizoneint.com   (415) 868-0300

9. Drink eight full glasses of pure water daily.

The Water Machine
www.johnellis.com

Trinity Springs
www.trinitysprings.com   (800) 390-5693

Fiji Water
www.fijiwater.com   (888) 426-3454

Ewater
www.ewater.com   (800) 964-4303

Future Water Today
www.futurewatertoday.com   (800) 827-0762

Wellness Filter and Wellness Carafe
www.wellnessfilter.com   (800) 428-9419

10. Use a rebounder (mini trampoline) ten minutes a day.

The Ultimate Rebound
www.ultimate-rebound.com   (888) 464-5867

Evolution Health

www.evolutionhealth.com   (888) 896-7790

The Raw Food World
www.therawfoodworld.com   (866) 729-3438

Urban Rebounding
www.urbanrebounding.com   (262) 796-2009

Cellercise
www.cellercise.com   (800) 856-4863

11. Walk one hour a day.

Walkvest
www.walkvest.com   (877) 925-5837

Fitness Gear 101
www.fitnessgear101.com   (866) 436-7446

Walking Healthy
www.walkinghealthy.com

Walking for Fitness
www.walking.about.com

Inner Strength Fitness
www.isfitness.com   (520) 319-6000

12. Stretch the muscles and tendons in your body.
Check your local yellow pages for yoga, pilates, and other
stretching classes.

Yoga Finder
www.yogafinder.com   (858) 213-7924

International Association of Yoga Therapists
www.iayt.org   (928) 541-0004

Yoga for the Young at Heart
www.yogaheart.com   (800) 558-9642

The Fitness Habit
www.home.earthlink.net/~fitness_habit

Inner Strength Fitness
www.isfitness.com   (520) 319-6000

Stretching with a physio ball
www.balldynamics.com   (800) 752-2255

Balanced Body
www.pilates.com   (800) 745-2837

Pilates Method Alliance
www.pilatesmethodalliance.org   (866) 573-4945

Stretching Inc.
www.stretching.com   (800) 333-1307

Institute of Thai Massage
www.thai-massage.org

The Breema Center
www.breema.com   (800) 452-1008

13. Practice deep breathing.

Buteyko Breathing Recondition Technique
www.buteykointernational.com   (888) 259-5951

Transformational breathwork
www.breathe2000.com   (619) 884-1455

Therapeutic breathwork
www.feeltheQi.com   (800) 824-4325

Breathdance
www.breathdance.org

14. Sweat with a regular dry sauna or an infrared sauna (not a wet steam).

Therasauna
www.therasauna.com   (888) 729-7727

Infrared Mats
www.thebestnaturalcures.com   (310) 487-4654

Gaia Holistic Circle
www.gaiahh.com   (212) 799-9711

Healthmate Sauna
www.healthmatesauna.com   (800) 946-6001

High Tech Health, Inc.
www.hightechhealth.com   (800) 794-5355

15. Give yourself a dry brush massage, exfoliating the skin and allowing toxins to come out of the skin at least once a day.

Yerba Prima dry skin brushes
www.yerbaprima.com   (800) 488-4339

Natural Cures has directions how to use
www.naturalcures.com

Chelation Therapy

American College of Advancement in Medicine
www.acam.org   (800) 532-3688

American Board of Clinical Metal Toxicology
www.abct.info   (800) 356-2228

16. Get a full-body Swedish and/or deep tissue massage on a regular basis.

American Massage Therapy Association
www.amtamassage.org   (847) 864-0123

Associated Bodywork and Massage Professionals
www.abmp.com   (800) 458-2267

American Organization for Bodywork Therapies of Asia
www.aobta.org   (856) 782-1616

Hellerwork Structural Integration
www.hellerwork.com

Mama's Health
www.mamashealth.com/massage/dtissue.asp

17. Do Qigong.

Roaring Lion
www.peterragnar.com   (800) 491-7141

Feel the Qi
www.feeltheQi.com   (800) 431-1579

National Qigong Association (NQA)
www.nqa.org   (888) 815-1893

Institute of Integral Qigong and Tai Chi
www.instituteofintegralqigongandtaichi.org   (805) 685-4670

Qigong Institute
www.qigonginstitute.org

18. Do Tai Chi.

Shaolin Wolf
www.shaolinwolf.com

The Healer Within Community
www.healerwithin.com   (805) 685-4670

Santa Barbara College of Oriental Medicine
www.sbcom.edu   (805) 989-1180

Institute of Integral Qigong and Tai Chi
www.instituteofintegralqigongandtaichi.org   (805) 685-4670

19. Do a seven- to thirty-day fast.

American Association of Naturopathic Physicians
www.naturopathic.org   (206) 298-0126

International Association of Professional Natural Hygienists
(305) 454-2220

We Care Spa
www.wecarespa.com   (800) 888-2523

DrFuhrman.com
www.drfuhrman.com   (800) 474-9355

Nature's Secret
www.naturessecret.com   (800) 297-3273

20. Get "specialized treatments" as needed.

Acupuncture.   Check your local yellow pages under
Acupuncture or Traditional Chinese Medicine.

Acupuncture
www.acupuncture.com

National Acupuncture Detoxification Association
www.acudetox.com   (888) 765-6232

Tai Sophia Institute for the Healing Arts
www.tai.edu   (800) 735-2968

CranioSacral Therapy.   Check your local yellow pages.

The Upledger Institute, Inc.
www.upledger.com   (800) 233-5880

Sacro Occipital Research Society International
www.sorsi.com   (888) 245-1011

The Cranial Academy
www.cranialacademy.com   (317) 594-0411

Reflexology.   Check your local yellow pages.

Reflexology Association of America
www.reflexology-usa.org   (740) 657-1695

International Institute of Reflexology Inc.
www.reflexology-usa.net   (727) 343-4811

Reiki.   Check your local yellow pages.

International Center for Reiki Training
www.reiki.org   (800) 332-8112

The Reiki Page
www.reiki.7gen.com

B. You must stop putting toxins in the body.

1. Do not eat any food produced or sold by a publicly traded corporation or a "brand name" product.

Maine Coast Sea Vegetables
www.seaveg.com   (207) 565-2907

Lundberg Family Farms
www.lundberg.com   (530) 882-4551

Applegate Farms
www.applegatefarms.com   (866) 587-5858

Diestel Family Turkey Ranch
www.diestelturkey.com   (209) 532-4950

NorthStar Bison
www.northstarbison.com   (888) 295-6332

Earthbound Farm
www.earthboundfarm.com   (800) 690-3200

Newman's Own Organics
www.newmansownorganics.com

Eden Foods
www.edenfoods.com   (888) 424-3336

SunOrganic Farm
www.sunorganic.com   (888) 269-9888

Grain and Salt Society
www.celticseasalt.com   (800) 867-7258

Gold Mine Natural Food Co.
www.goldminenaturalfood.com   (800) 475-3663

South River Miso Company
www.southrivermiso.com   (413) 369-4057

Corporate Watch
www.corporatewatch.org   +44 1865 791 391

Corporate Persons
www.personsinc.org   (866) 280-1409

The Corporation (film)
www.thecorporation.com

2. Get all the metal out of your dental work.
Resources for holistic dentistry.

Environmental Dental Association
(800) 388-8124

Holistic Dental Association
www.holisticdental.org   (970) 259-1091

National Integrated Health Associates
www.nihadc.com   (831) 659-5385

American Academy of Biological Dentistry
www.biologicaldentistry.org   (408) 659-5385

3. Stop smoking.

Kevin Trudeau's Method
www.naturalcures.com

Quitnet, Quit All Together
www.quitnet.com

Foundation for a Smokefree America
www.anti-smoking.org   (310) 471-4270

The Stop Smoking Center
www.stopsmokingcenter.net   (866) 257-9626

4. Buy and use a shower filter.

Ewater
www.ewater.com   (800) 964-4303

Wellness Filter
www.wellnessfilter.com   (800) 428-9419

The Living Water Machine
www.johnellis.com   (800) 433-9553

5. Eat only 100 percent organic food.

Diamond Organics
www.diamondorganic.com   (888) 674-2642

SunOrganic Farm
www.sunorganic.com   (888) 269-9888

Grain and Salt Society
www.celticseasalt.com   (800) 867-7258

Gold Mine Natural Food Co.
www.goldminenaturalfood.com   (800) 475-3663

South River Miso Company
www.southrivermiso.com   (413) 369-4057

Information on Organic Food

Organic Trade Association
www.ota.com   (413) 774-7511

Organic Consumers
www.organicconsumers.org   (218) 226-4164

Beyond Pesticides
www.beyondpesticides.org   (202) 543-5450

The Meatrix
www.themeatrix.com

6. Do not eat anything that comes out of a microwave oven.

Cooking.com
www.cooking.com   (800) 663-8810

Kitchen Universe
www.kitchen-universe.com   (800) 481-6679

Slow Food
www.slowfood.com   (718) 260-8000

Slow Food USA
www.slowfoodusa.org   (718) 260-8000

7. Eliminate aspartame and monosodium glutamate.
Excellent alternatives to MSG.

Eden Foods
www.edenfoods.com   (888) 424-3336

Grain and Salt Society
www.celticseasalt.com   (800) 867-7258

Maine Coast Sea Vegetables
www.seaveg.com   (207) 565-2907

8. Do not eat artificial sweeteners (including Splenda).
Alternative sweeteners.

Stevia
www.steviasmart.com   (877) 836-9982

Living Fuel Therasweet
www.livingnutritionals.com   (800) 642-4113

Agave Nectar, Honey
www.madhavahoney.com   (303) 823-5166

Birch Bark Sweetener (Xylitol)
www.ultimatelife.com   (800) 843-6325

Organic maple syrup
www.maplevalleysyrup.com   (800) 760-1449

9. Do not eat hydrogenated oil.

For more information on healthy fats and oils, go to
www.naturalcures.com.

Hempseed oil
www.nutiva.com   (800) 893-4367

High Lignan Flaxseed oil
www.barleans.com   (360) 384-0485

Raw virgin coconut butter
www.nutiva.com   (800) 893-4367

Wilderness Family Naturals
www.wildernessfamilynaturals.com   (866) 936-6457

Wide selection of quality oils Flora
www.florahealth.com   (800) 446-2110

Extra Virgin Olive Oil
Buy in dark bottle, from your local health food store.

10. Do not eat homogenized and pasteurized dairy products.

Why Real Milk?
www.realmilk.com

Weston A. Price Foundation
www.westonaprice.org   (202) 363-4394

BGH Bulletin
www.foxbghsuit.com

Organic Pastures Dairy Company
www.organicpastures.com   (877) 729-6455

Organic Valley Farmers—raw cheeses
www.organicvalley.coop   (888) 444-6455

11. Do not eat high fructose corn syrup.

Brown Rice Syrup from Glory Bee Foods
www.auntpattys.com   (800) 456-7923

SunOrganic Farm
www.sunorganic.com   (888) 269-9888

Agave Nectar, Honey
www.madhavahoney.com   (303) 823-5166

Organic maple syrup
www.maplevalleysyrup.com   (800) 760-1449

12. Use only toothpaste with no fluoride.

Weleda
www.usa.weleda.com   (800) 241-1030

Burt's Bees
www.burtsbees.com

Jason Natural
www.jason-natural.com   (800) 434-4246

13. Do not use nonstick cookware.
Cast Iron is an excellent option, check local stores

www.castironcookware.com

Le Creuset
www.lecreuset.com/usa   (877) 273-8738

Carbon steel cookware

Atlanta Fixture and Sales Co. (search for 7915589)
www.atlantafixture.com   (800) 282-1977

14. Eat only organic, kosher meat, and poultry.

Damar Farms
www.damarfarms.com   (715) 563-2333

Natural Acres
www.naturalacres.com   (717) 692-1000

Dakota Beef Company
www.dakotabeefcompany.com   (800) 282-1977

Pampa's Pride Meats
www.pampaspride.com   (598-42) 493-940

Bison

Slanker's Grass-Fed Meats
www.texasgrassfedbeef.com   (866) 752-6537

Wild Idea Buffalo
www.wildideabuffalo.com   (866) 658-6137

Northstar Bison
www.northstarbison.com   (715) 234-1496

Tatonka Meats
www.organic-buffalo.com   (402) 273-4574

Chicken

Petaluma Poultry
www.petalumapoultry.com   (800) 556-6789

Blackwing Quality Meats
www.blackwing.com   (800) 326-7874

Sheepdrove Organic Farm
www.sheepdrove.com   +44-01488-71659

Turkey

Diestel Turkey Ranch
www.diestelturkey.com   (209) 532-4950

Lobel's of New York
www.lobels.com   (877) 783-4512

Applegate Farms
www.applegatefarms.com   (866) 587-5858

Lamb

Blackwing Quality Meats
www.blackwing.com   (800) 326-7874

Thirteen Mile Lamb & Wool Company
www.lambandwool.com   (406) 388-4945

Zen Sheep Farm
www.michiganorganic.org/zensheep   (765) 795-5526

Fox Fire Farms
www.foxfirefarms.com   (970) 563-4675

15. Do not eat farm-raised fish.

Vital Choice Seafood
www.vitalchoice.com   (800) 608-4825

Rose Fisheries
www.rosefisheries.com   (877) 747-3107

Wild Planet
www.1wildplanet.com   (800) 998-9946

Fishing Vessel St. Jude
www.tunatuna.com   (425) 378-0680

Marine Stewardship Council
www.msc.org   +44-0-20735-04000

Information

Oceans Alive
www.oceansalive.org   (212) 505-2100

US EPA Fish Advisories
www.epa.gov/ostwater/fish   (202) 566-0400

Mercury Action
www.mercuryaction.org/fish   (202) 667-4260

16. If you can't eat it, don't put it on your skin.

BareMinerals
www.bareminerals.com   (800) 227-3990

The Body Deli USVI
www.thebodydeliusvi.com   (340) 776-0454

Dr. Hauschka Skin Care
www.drhauschka.com   (800) 257-9907

Eminence Organics
www.eminenceorganics.com   (888) 747-6342

Sea Chi Organics
www.seachi.com   (760) 776-2620

Miessence
www.onegrp.com   (805) 646-5998

Planet Organics
www.planetorganics.net

Aubrey Organics
www.aubrey-organics.com   (800) 282-7394

Jurlique
www.jurlique.com   (212) 803-8121

Suki
www.sukinaturals.com   (888) 858-7854

Burt's Bees
www.burtsbees.com

17. Get an air purifier.

Oreck
www.oreck.com   (800) 289-5888

EWater
www.ewater .com   (800) 964-4303

EcoQuest International
www.ecoquest.com   (800) 989-2299

Real Goods
www.realgoods.com   (800) 919-2400

Ionlite
Biotech Research   (800) 466-7688

The Aranizer
www.ionlight.com   (800) 426-1110

18. Use only nontoxic 100 percent organic cleaning supplies.

Citrisolve
www.citrisolve.com   (800) 556-6785

Seventh Generation
www.seventhgeneration.com   (800) 456-1191

Heather's Naturals—great for non-chlorine bleach
www.heathersnaturals.com   (877) 527-6601

Care2.com—education and products
www.care2.com   (650) 622-0860

19. Do not use sun block.

Aubrey Organics
www.aubrey-organics.com   (800) 282-7394

Dr. Hauschka Skin Care
www.drhauschka.com   (800) 257-9907

Clothing that shields you from the sun.

Solartex Sun Gear
www.solartex.com   (877) 476-6785

Solar Eclipse
www.solareclipse.com   (800) 878-9600

20. Do not take vitamins.
Instead of synthetic vitamins, take whole food supplements.

Eniva, entire product line
www.eniva.com/products   (800) 964-4303

Vibe and other great options
www.livingnutritionals.com   (800) 642-4113

Amazon Herb Co.
www.amazonherb.net   (866) 519-7565

New Chapter
www.new-chapter.com   (800) 543-7279

Megafood Food Based Supplements
www.organicpharmacy.org   (800) 819-6742

Pure Synergy—The Synergy Company
www.synergy-co.com   (800) 723-0277

Vitamineral Green
www.healthforce.com   (760) 747-8822

21. Do not use antiperspirants or deodorants.

Body Crystals
www.thecrystal.com   (800) 829-7625

Natural Body
www.bnaturalbodycare.com

22. Do not eat white processed sugar.

Rapunzel (Raw evaporated cane juice)
www.rapunzel.com   (800) 207-2814

Birch Bark Sweetener (Xylitol)
www.ultimatelife.com   (800) 843-6325

Brown Rice Syrup
www.auntpattys.com   (800) 456-7923

SunOrganic Farm
www.sunorganic.com   (888) 289-9888

Agave Nectar, Honey
www.madhavahoney.com   (303) 823-5166

Organic maple syrup
www.maplevalleysyrup.com   (800) 760-1449

SteviaSmart
www.steviasmart.com   (877) 836-9982

Truth about Splenda
www.truthaboutsplenda.com

23. Do not eat white processed flour.
Choose unbleached, organic, whole grain flours.

SunOrganic Farm
www.sunorganic.com   (888) 289-9888

Heartland Mill
www.heartlandmill.com   (800) 232-8533

Food For Life
www.foodforlife.com   (800) 797-5090

Purity Foods
www.purityfoods.com   (517) 351-9231

24. Do not eat "food bars."
Eat organic live food bars.

Crystal Manna Bars
www.lydiasorganics.com   (415) 258-9678

Gopal's Raw Bars
www.naturalzing.com   (888) 729-9464

CocoChia bars
www.livingnutritionals.com   (800) 642-4113

Nature's First Law
www.rawfood.com   (800) 205-2350

Blessing's Alive and Radiant Foods
www.deliciousorganics.com   (305) 655-3344

Raw Energy Food Bar
www.oraganic.com   (866) 672-6204

25. Do not eat diet or protein shakes.

Raw organic, non pre-digested Whey Protein
www.livingnutritionals.com   (800) 642-4113

Prosera™ Whey Protein Whey Healthier
www.mercola.com

Thunder
www.forevergreen.org

Almased
(800) 256-2733

26. Eliminate air fresheners.
Alternatives can be found at health food stores.

Air Detox
www.dr-schulze.com   (800) 437-2362

AirTherapy
www.miarose.com

Ecobella room mist
www.eccobella.com   (877) 696-2220

Air Mists

Heavenly Scents Aromatherapy
(800) 289-8427

27. Eliminate fluorescent lighting.

Real Goods
www.realgoods.com   (800) 919-2400

Blues Busters Full Spectrum Light Bulbs
www.bluesbuster.com   (888) 874-7373

Verilux
www.verilux.net   (800) 786-6850

Full Spectrum Lighting
www.fullspectrumsolutions.com   (888) 574-7014

HealthyHome
www.healthyhome.com   (800) 583-9523

28. Reduce or eliminate air conditioning.
Take a cool shower in filtered water.

Real Goods (nice fans)
www.realgoods.com   (800) 919-2400

Electric Fan
www.electric-fan.com   (800) 868-6008

Nevada Appeal
www.nevadaappeal.com

29. Avoid dry cleaning.

Greenearth Cleaning
www.greenearthcleaning.com   (816) 926-0895

Ecover Delicate Wash
www.ecover.com

Natural Choices
www.oxyboost.com   (866) 699-2667

Oasis all purpose cleaner
www.oasis.com   (586) 795-0545

30. Make your own beer and wine.

Homebrew Heaven
www.homebrewheaven.com   (800) 850-2739

Perfect Brewing Supply
www.perfectbrewing.com   (847) 947-7665

Home Wine and Beer Trade Association
www.hwbta.org   (813) 685-4261

Beer-Wine.com
www.beer-wine.com   (800) 523-5423

The Brew Hut
www.thebrewhut.com   (800) 730-9336

31. Buy a good vacuum cleaner with a hepa filter.

Allergy Be Gone
www.allergybegone.com   (800) 730-9336

The Vacuum Center
www.thevacuumcenter.com   (877) 224-9998

Allergy Buyers Club
www.allergybuyersclub.com   (877) 224-9998

These Vacuums Suck
www.thesevacuumssuck.com   (800) 248-1987

C. You must address and handle your nutritional deficiencies.

How Health Works
www.howhealthworks.com   (303) 530-2332

Eat Well Guide
www.eatwellguide.org

David Wolfe
www.davidwolfe.com   (888) 729-3663

Organic Pharmacy
www.organicpharmacy.org   (800) 819-6742

American College of Nutrition
www.amcollnutr.org   (727) 446-6086

Metabolic Typing Education Center
www.metabolictyping.com   (650) 325-1840

Eniva Vibe
www.livingnutritionals.com   (800) 642-4113

Amazon Herbs
www.amazonherb.net   (800) 835-0850

Tri-Vibe
www.trivortex.com   (619) 884-1455

1. Eat more fresh organic fruits and vegetables.

Diamond Organics
www.diamondorganics.com   (888) 674-2642

Organic Trade Association
www.ota.com   (413) 774-7511

Organic Consumers
www.organicconsumers.org   (218) 226-4164

2. Buy a juice machine and use it.
These companies sell a wide variety of quality juice machines.
We like Juice Man, Green Star, and Champion juicers, and for a
real splurge the Norwalk juicer.

Canning Pantry
www.canningpantry.com   (800) 285-9044

Discount Juicers
www.discountjuicers.com

The Raw Food World
www.therawfoodworld.com   (866) 729-3438

The Norwalk Juicer
www.norwalkjuicer.com

3. Eat raw organic nuts and seeds.

SunOrganic Farm
www.sunorganic.com   (888) 289-9888

Gold Mine Natural Food Co.
www.goldminenaturalfood.com   (800) 475-3663

Wilderness Family Naturals
www.wildernessfamilynaturals.com   (866) 936-6457

Raw Guru
www.rawguru.com   (800) 577-4729

4. Get natural sunlight.

Sungazing.com
www.sungazing.com

Solar Healing Center
www.solarhealing.com   (407) 657-7032

American Environmental products
www.sunalux.com   (800) 339-9572

5. Take coral calcium.

Ionic Coral Calcium
www.thewolfeclinic.com   (800) 592-9693

Quantum-Rx Coral Complex
www.healthline.cc   (800) 370-3447

Brazil Live Coral
www.brazil-coral.com   (866) 352-7896

Coral Calcium
Window Rock Health   (888) 821-9505

Coral 3X
Dynamic Health   (800) 274-4054

Okinawa Coral Calcium
www.ericssoncoral.com

Nanocal
www.nanocal.com

6. Take all-natural vitamin E.

4Spectrum
www.4spectrum.us   (903) 845-5646

A.C. Grace Company
www.acgraceco.com   (903) 636-4368

Universal Supplements
www.universalsupplements.com   (805) 646-5936

7. Take liquid colloidal minerals daily.

Living Minerals from Nature
New Life   (888) 272-4394

Eniva Minerals for Life
www.eniva.com/products   (800) 964-4303

Active Ionic and Omica Plus
www.teravite.com   (800) 776-5438

Dr. Morter's Trace Minerals
www.mortersupplements.com

8. Drink the "magic juices."

Earths Bounty Organic Tahitian Noni Juice
www.earthsbounty.com   (800) 736-5609

Goji Juice
www.gojiplease.com   (800) 913-4654

Goji Juice
www.freelife.com

Xango Mangosteen Juice
www.livingnutritionals.com   (800) 642-4113

Xango Mangosteen Juice
www.xango.net

Aloe Vera Juice
Forever Living Products

Aloe Vera Juice
www.naturesgift.com

Acai Berry Juice
www.therawfoodworld.com   (866) 729-3438

MonaVie
www.monavie.com

Zija juice
www.drinklifein.com

FrequenSEA
www.forevergreen.org   (801) 655-5500

Seasilver
www.seasilver.com

9. Take a whole food supplement daily.

New Chapter
www.new-chapter.com   (800) 543-7279

Megafood
www.megafood.com

Pure Synergy—The Synergy Company
www.synergy-co.com   (800) 723-0277

Vitamineral Green
www.livingnutritionals.com   (800) 642-4113

Eniva Vibe
www.eniva.com/products   (800) 964-4303

The Raw Food World
www.therawfoodworld.com   (866) 729-3438

Amazon Herbs
www.amazonherb.net   (800) 835-0850

Seaveg
www.tryseavegg.com

Sunrider Products
www.sunrider.com

Eniva Products
www.eniva.com/products

Melaleuca Products
www.melaleuca.com

Sprout Capsuls
www.4yourtype.com

Chlorella
www.sunchlorellausa.com

Hydrilla
www.organicpharmacy.org

Spirulina, Blue Green Algae
www.organicpharmacy.org

10. Eat raw organic honey, bee propolis, royal jelly, and bee pollen.

Bee Pollen
www.madhavahoney.com   (303) 823-5166

Manuka Honey
www.manukahoneyusa.com   (800) 395-2196

Honey Gardens
www.honeygardens.com   (888) 303-4929

Bee Hive Botanicals
www.beehivebotanicals.com   (800) 233-4483

Bee Alive Royal Jelly Sweet Energy Formula
www.beealive.com   (800) 543-2337

YS Organic Bee Farm
www.ysorganic.com　(800) 654-4593

11. Get an oxygen water cooler.

Phion Nutrition
www.ph-ion.com　(888) 744-8589

O2 Technologies, Inc.
www.o2techno.com　(201) 943-6900

Oxygen America, Inc.
www.oxygenamerica.com　(305) 933-4219

Vitamin O from RGarden
www.livingnutritionals.com　(800) 642-4113

Oxygen Supreme by Healthforce Nutritionals
www.healthforce.com

12. Take digestive enzymes.

Univase
www.rockyfork.net　(800) 630-4534

N°Zimes
www.enzymeuniversity.com　(800) 835-8545

Super Power Enzyme
www.vites.com　(800) 446-7462

Jarrow Formulas
www.jarrow.com　(800) 726-0886

Enzymedica
www.enzymedica.com　(888) 918-1118

Universal Supplements
www.universalsupplements.com　(805) 646-5936

13. Use organic sea salt.

Celtic Sea Salt
www.celticseasalt.com　(800) 867-7258

Himalayan sea salt
www.himalayancrystalsalt.com　(541) 464-5942

Krystal Miracle Sea Salt
www.krystalwebmatrix.com　(866) 588-7258

14. Eat organic dark chocolate.

Sjaaks Organic Chocolates
www.sjaaks.com   (707) 775-2434

Chocolate Alchemy
www.chocolatealchemy.com

Natures First Law
www.naturesfirstlaw.com   (800) 205-2350

Sweet Earth Chocolates
www.sweetearthchocolates.com   (805) 544-7759

Dagoba Chocolate
www.worldwidechocolate.com   (800) 664-9410

Amazon Herbs
www.amazonherb.net   (800) 835-0850

15. Take an omega-3 supplement.

Omega-3s
www.icelandhealth.com

Nordic Naturals Omega 3 fish oils
www.nordicnaturals.com   (800) 662-2544

Carlson Labs Norwegian and Omega 3 oils
www.carlsonlabs.com   (888) 234-5656

Dr. Ron's Cod Liver oil
www.drrons.com   (877) 472-8701

Hemp oil and seeds
www.nutiva.com   (800) 993-4367

D. Neutralize electromagnetic chaos.

1. Get something to neutralize electromagnetic chaos.

EMF Protection
www.ewater.com   (800) 964-4303

EMF Protection, Q Link
www.toolsforwellness.com   (800) 456-9887

EMF Protection, Q Link
www.qeshop.com   (888) 753-7729

Bioelectric Shield
www.bioelectricshield.com   (866) 567-8909

Radio Frequency Safe
www.rfsafe.com   (727) 643-5440

BioPro Technology
www.bioprotechnology.com

2. Use electronic and wireless devices less.

Lehmans, great source for non-human-powered products
www.lehmans.com   (888) 438-5346

3. Use a gentle wind project instrument.

The Gentle Wind Project
www.gentlewindproject.org   (207) 439-7639

4. Reduce TV time.

Spiritual Cinema Circle
www.spiritualcinemacircle.com   (888) 447-5494

5. Get a magnetic mattress pad.

Magnetico Sleep Pads
www.magneticosleep.com   (800) 265-1119

Bioelectromagnetics Society
www.bioelectromagnetics.org   (301) 663-4252

6. Use magnetic finger and toe rings.

Alex Chiu
www.alexchiu.com

Norso Magnets
www.naturalfeeling.com   (877) 858-9082

Polar Power Magnets
www.polarpowermagnets.com   (800) 445-1962

7. Wear white.

The Hempest
www.hempest.com   (617) 421-9944

Patagonia
www.patagonia.com   (800) 638-6464

Blue Canoe Bodywear
www.bluecanoe.com   (888) 923-1373

Natural Fibers
www.natural-fibers.com

Maggie's Functional Organics
www.organicclothes.com   (800) 609-8593

Inner Waves Organics
www.innerwavesmaui.com   (866) 573-9283

8. Use feng shui in your home and office.

The American Feng Shui Institute
www.amfengshui.com   (626) 571-2757

Feng Shui Times
www.fengshuitimes.com

Feng Shui Directory
www.fengshuidirectory.com   (800) 443-5894

E. You must reduce stress.

Feel The Qi
www.feeltheqi.com   (805) 685-4670

Third Wind
www.thirdwind.org

Conscious Breathing Practice
www.breathe2000.com   (877) 412-7328

Dr. Coldwell's stress-reducing techniques
www.20minutestolessstress.com   (888) 827-7720

Callahan Techniques   Thought Field Therapy
www.tftrx.com   (760) 564-1008

Dahn Yoga
www.dahnyoga.com   (877) 477-9642

1. Listen to de-stressing CDs.

Newagemusic.com
www.newagemusic.com   (323) 851-3355

Backroads Music
www.backroadsmusic.com

New World Music
www.newworldmusic.com   (800) 771-0987

Inner Peace Music
www.innerpeacemusic.com   (800) 909-7070

The Relaxation Company
www.therelaxationcompany.com   (800) 788-6670

2. Do alphabiotics.

Alphabiotics International
www.alphabiotics.biz   (214) 369-5117

3. Laugh.

Basic Jokes
www.basicjokes.com

Association for Applied and Therapeutic Humor
www.aath.org   (609) 514-5141

4. Smile.

Keep Smiling
www.keepsmiling.com

Association for Applied and Therapeutic Humor
www.aath.org   (609) 514-5141

5. Speak powerful words.
Your words mean everything, what you say is what you are or become.

What the Bleep Do We Know?!
www.whatthebleep.com   (877) 740-8924

Hay House, Inc.
www.hayhouse.com   (800) 654-5126

Total Integration Institute
www.totalintegrationinstitute.com   (520) 615-9811

6. Don't use a cell phone and drive at the same time.
If you insist upon talking while you drive, use a headset that allows sound to travel by air rather than by wires into your ear.

Waveshield
www.waveshield.com

Radio Frequency Safe
www.rfsafe.com   (727) 643-5440

7. Rest from Friday sundown to Saturday sundown.
Learn about the Sabbath, or Shabbat.

Everything Jewish
www.everythingjewish.com

The Shalom Center
www.shalomctr.org   (215) 844-8494

8. Take an afternoon fifteen-minute break.

The Napping Company, Inc.
www.napping.com   (207) 439-7639

9. Get rolfing.

The Rolf Institute of Structural Integration
www.rolf.org   (800) 530-8875

10. Don't read the newspaper.

Adbusters
www.adbusters.org   (800) 663-1243

AlterNet
www.alternet.org   (415) 284-1414

Independent Media Center
www.indymedia.org

Disinformation
www.disinfo.com

Arts & Letters Daily
www.aldaily.com

Fairness and Accuracy in Reporting
www.fair.org   (212) 633-6700

11. Don't watch news.

Center for Media and Democracy
www.prwatch.org   (608) 260-9713

TV News & Lies
www.tvnewslies.org   (718) 832-5767

Unknown News
www.unknownnews.org

News Target
www.newstarget.com

12. Have sex.

David Deida
www.deidacentral.com   (212) 477-0522

Maca Magic—tonic for activating sexual energy
www.macaroot.com   (541) 846-6222

Maca Root
www.peruvian-maca.com   (281) 497-7149

Steel Libido
www.irwinnaturals.com   (800) 841-8448

Kegel Exercises for sexual stamina
www.kegel-exercises.com

13. Commit reckless acts of kindness.

Helpothers.org
www.helpothers.org

The Random Acts of Kindness Foundation
www.actsofkindness.org   (800) 660-2811

14. Listen to nice music.

Newagemusic.com
www.newagemusic.com   (323) 851-3355

Backroads Music
www.backroadsmusic.com   (800) 767-4748

New World Music
www.newworldmusic.com   (800) 771-0987

Inner Peace Music
www.innerpeacemusic.com   (800) 909-7070

15. Get out of debt.

The Credit Card Directory
www.cardoffers.com

My Credit Card Freedom
www.mycreditcardfreedom.com

Debt Proof Living
www.cheapskatemonthly.com   (800) 550-3502

The Millionaire Mind
www.millionairemind.com   (888) 868-8883

Consumer Credit Counseling Service
www.cccsatl.org   (800) 251-2227

16. Drive less.

Earth 911
www.earth911.org   (877) 327-8491

17. Be thankful.

Go Gratitude
www.gogratitude.com/masterkey

Agape International Spiritual Center
www.agapelive.com   (310) 348-1250

18. Get an inversion table.

Evolution Health
www.evolutionhealth.com   (888) 896-7790

Bodylift and Bodyslant
www.ageeasy.com   (888) 243-3279

19. Use foot orthotics.

Dr. Kiper
www.drkiper.com   (800) 375-4737

Orthotics Direc
www.orthoticsdirect.com   (866) 678-4634

Podiatry Channel
www.podiatrychannel.com/orthotics

20. Get a range of motion machine.

ROM—The Four Minute Crosstrainer
www.fastexercise.com   (818) 787-6460

Evolution Health
www.evolutionhealth.com   (888) 896-7790

21. Be light-hearted.

Aha! Jokes
www.ahajokes.com

The HUMOR Project
www.humorproject.com   (518) 587-8770

22. Stay away from psychiatrists or psychologists.

Hakomi Institute
www.hakomiinstitute.com   (888) 421-6699

Dianetics Technology
www.dianetics.com   (800) 367-8788

Total Integration Institute
www.totalintegrationinstitute.com   (520) 615-9811

Citizens Commission on Human Rights
www.cchr.org

Nancy Cartwright
www.nancycartwright.com

23. Do not use an alarm clock.

Sunrise Clock
www.biobrite.com   (301) 961-5940

Zen Alarm Clock
www.now-zen.com   (800) 779-6383

24. Use aromatherapy.

Aromatherapy.com
www.aromatherapy.com   (800) 877-6889

Bio Excel
www.bioexcel.com   (888) 744-0491

National Association for Holistic Aromatherapy (NAHA)
www.naha.org   (888) 275-6242

Essential Oils
www.amoils.com

25. Use Callahan techniques for urges.

Callahan Techniques
www.tftrx.com   (760) 564-1008

26. Get a pet.

Petfinder.com
www.petfinder.com

27. Plant a garden.

Square Foot Gardening
www.squarefootgardening.com   (877) 828-1188

Dirt Doctor
www.dirtdoctor.com   (817) 461-9206

Organic Seed Alliance
www.seedalliance.org   (360) 385-7192

Sow Organic Seed
www.organicseed.com   (888) 709-7333

Peaceful Valley Farm and Garden Supply
www.groworganic.com   (888) 784-1722

The Invisible Gardener
www.invisiblegardener.com

28. Dance and sing.

Total Integration Therapy
www.totalintegrationinstitute.com   (520) 615-9811

5 Rhythms Dance
www.ravenrecording.com   (212) 760-1381

Soul Motion
www.soulmotion.com   (503) 232-0940

Nia technique
www.nia-nia.com   (800) 762-5762

American Music Therapy Association
www.musictherapy.org   (301) 589-3300

Sound Listening & Learning Center
www.soundlistening.com   (602) 381-0086

Esalen Institute
www.esalen.org   (831) 667-3000

29. Find your life purpose.

Aleta St James
www.aletastjames.com   (212) 246-2420

Women's Intuition
www.paulamreeves.com

30. Do dianetics/scientology.

Dianetics Technology
www.dianetics.com   (800) 367-8788

Church of Scientology International
www.scientology.com   (800) 334-5433

More Natural "Cures" Previously Censored by the U.S. Government

Nearly all men can stand some adversity.
If you want to test a man's character give him power.

—Abraham Lincoln

It is my belief that in almost all cases there are natural non-drug and non-surgical ways to prevent, treat, and cure disease. It is important for you to understand that I also strongly believe that in certain situations drugs and surgery do and can save lives where natural alternatives do not. Years ago when you went to a doctor getting a prescription was like pulling teeth. Doctors rarely prescribed drugs. Drugs of any kind were always the last resort. Today, the business model of drug companies is radically different. The goal of drug companies is to use brainwashing-designed advertising (I know because this is one of the things I was commissioned to do) to convince people that they need to be taking drugs, both prescription and non-prescription, on a regular basis for their whole lives. The business model of drug companies is to get every human being on planet earth, from the moment they are born, to be taking some type of non-prescription or prescription drug every day for the rest of their lives. I know this to be true because I was covertly involved in helping to organize this worldwide plan. Years ago drugs and surgery were only used by the very elderly or in matters of life and death as an absolute last resort.

With that said, the question that comes to the forefront is "I have 'X Disease,' what is the natural cure?" The answer is different for every person. If, for example, you have diabetes, the real question that must be asked is what is causing your diabetes. Medical doctors never look for the cause. They only treat the symptoms. The business model for doctors' offices, clinics, hospitals, insurance companies, and pharmaceutical companies is to develop standardized treatments for symptoms. In order to be profitable businesses they must treat every person's symptoms the same; this, however, can be dangerous and is ineffective. If ten people with diabetes were fully evaluated, there is an excellent chance that each person would have a different cause of their diabetes. One person's diabetes could be partially caused by a genetic weakness acerbated by the chemicals found in processed and fast food. Another person's diabetes could be caused by an emotional trauma that happened twenty years ago. Another person's diabetes could be caused by an adverse reaction to a vaccine they received in childhood. Another person's diabetes could be caused by obesity and lack of exercise. Another person's diabetes could be caused by an adverse reaction from artificial sweeteners and diet sodas. Another person's diabetes could be caused by a Candida yeast overgrowth. Another person's diabetes could be caused by heavy metal toxicity partially due to silver fillings in the teeth. The list of causes can go on and on. Without knowing the cause means you cannot effectively treat the patient. If you have disease or illness, remember, do not treat the symptom. You must first find out the cause; then you can find and treat the condition from the true source of the problem. Knowing the cause will determine which natural treatment will be effective.

This is why some natural treatments are reported as being ineffective in the treatment of the symptom. This is why you must never try to treat yourself. It is important that you seek several opinions from licensed healthcare practitioners who do not use drugs and surgery. It is important that the cause be found and addressed. It is important that you receive customized, personalized treatments instead of the cookie cutter, one size fits all, get them in and get them out methods conventional medicine uses.

This chapter is designed to be a starting point for you to use with a licensed healthcare practitioner when treating illness and disease. Another important point is that true effective doctors do not treat symptoms or disease. Effective doctors treat the PERSON! This is where the term holistic doctor comes from. Holistic doctors treat the person as a whole being. They understand that illness and disease manifesting in the body are caused by a large number of factors including emotions, genetics, diet, toxicity, work environment, beliefs, relationships, exercise, etc. Holistic doctors treat you as a person and understand that each person needs a customized and uniquely different treatment protocol to bring them into a state of harmony and balance. This is called homeostasis. It means the body, mind, and spirit are in harmony and balance. When this occurs, illness and disease can no longer exist.

If you want perfect health, I recommend you do the following three things.

1. Read *Natural Cures "They" Don't Want You to Know About*. Reading my first book cover to cover is absolutely vital for you to get a total understanding of the healthcare system, why you get sick, and the most effective and powerful system to prevent and cure disease.

2. Do the things in Chapter 6 of *Natural Cures "They" Don't Want You to Know About*. The specific dos and don'ts listed do in fact prevent and cure disease. The specific cure for cancer, heart disease, arthritis, diabetes, MS, and virtually every disease is doing the things in Chapter 6. It is documented that even the most incurable diseases have been cured when a person does all the things in Chapter 6. The Chapter 6 dos and don'ts protocol is in fact the natural cure that they don't want you to know about.

3. Join naturalcures.com. It is free for an entire week, which will allow you ample time to download all the new discoveries uncovered and reported on from around the world. You also can talk to my health advisors who can answer your questions and give you consultations regarding your health issues. This service is absolutely free.

Listed below are the specific products that can help you relieve symptoms and cure disease. It is impossible for this to be a complete list. There are tens of thousands of companies and products that could have been listed here. This is a starting point for you to use in conjunction with the customized, personalized treatments you will get from your licensed healthcare practitioner. The companies that sell these products cannot legally make any claims about their effectiveness or safety. Government agencies around the world will tell you that these products do nothing and are potentially dangerous. These, of course, are the same agencies that routinely lie to us when they emphatically state that drugs are safe even though they kill hundreds of thousands of people each year. If any of these companies said that the products they sell could be used to treat, prevent, or cure disease, they would be criminally prosecuted. This is happening around the world. I, as an author and journalist, am only expressing my opinions when I state that I believe that these products are safe and are effective in treating, preventing, and curing disease.

Because I have no financial interest in any of these companies or products, I believe I have the right to publish theories and opinions.

Always consult with a licensed healthcare practitioner before taking any of these products or using any of these therapies. Most importantly, remember that if you do the things suggested in Chapter 6 of *Natural Cures "They" Don't Want You to Know About,* I strongly believe that you will be cured of any disease.

One of the most powerful natural cures that the government is trying to debunk can be found at www.biologicalmiracle.com and www.liquidmannagold.com. Keep in mind that the government continually lies and says none of these products can cure or prevent anything. The government contends that these products are a waste of money and are dangerous. The government says that pharmaceutical drugs are totally safe and effective. You choose.

1. ACID REFLUX/HEARTBURN

For more information go to Find A Cure at www.naturalcures.com.

Raw organic apple cider vinegar with "mother"
Drink 2-4 tablespoons before each meal.

Probiotics Jarrowdophilus + FOS
www.jarrow.com   (800) 726-0886

Acid Reducer, Acid Redux
www.herbsmd.com

Digestive Enzymes, N°Zimes
www.enzymeuniversity.com   (800) 835-8545

Digestive Enzymes, Dr.Fred Bisci
www.therawfoodworld.com   (866) 729-3438

Viable Herbal Solutions, Botanical SafeGuard
www.herbal-solutions.com   (800) 505-9475

Ayurvedic Licorice root, Yashi-madhu
www.himalayahealthcare.com   (800) 869-4640

Dr. Coldwell's stress-reducing techniques
www.20minutestolessstress.com   (888) 827-7720

2. ACNE

For more information go to Find A Cure at www.naturalcures.com.

Essential Oils
www.amoils.com

Burt's Bees
www.burtsbees.com

Crabapple Flower Essence
www.backflower.com

Detoxify your body
www.detox.org

Vitamin A
www.costlessvitamin.com   (800) 578-5939

Sweat in an Infrared Sauna TheraSauna
www.therasauna.com   (888) 729-7727

Acne Cream, Acne-n-pimple cream
www.himalayahealthcare.com   (800) 869-4640

Vitamin E, Unique E
www.acgraceco.com   (903) 636-4368

Liver Rescue III+, HealthForce Nutritionals
www.healthforce.com   (760) 747-8822

Vitamin C, Pure Radiance C
www.synergy-co.com   (800) 723-0277

Vitamin B complex, Max Stress B Nano-Plex
www.vpnutrition.com   (877) 335-1509

Zinc, Zinc Food Complex
www.new-chapter.com   (800) 543-7279

Gently wash with *food grade* hydrogen peroxide
www.familyhealthnews.com   (800) 284-6263

Mist face daily with Willard Water
www.nutritioncoalition.com   (800) 447-4793

Dr. Coldwell's stress-reducing techniques
www.20minutestolessstress.com   (888) 827-7720

3. ADD/ADHD

For more information go to Find A Cure at www.naturalcures.com.

Applied Kinesiology
www.icak.com

Alphabiotics, Alphabiotics International
www.alphabiotics.biz　(214) 369-5117

Cranial Sacral Therapy, The Upledger Institute, Inc.
www.upledger.com　(800) 233-5880

Stress Reduction, Dr. Coldwell
www.20minutestolessstress.com　(888) 827-7720

Omega-3s, Hemp Seeds
www.nutiva.com　(800) 993-4367

Omega-3s, Cod Liver oil
www.drrons.com　(860) 945-7444

4. ALLERGIES

For more information go to Find A Cure at www.naturalcures.com.

Pantothenic Acid
www.organicpharmacy.org　(800) 819-6742

Nettle Herb, Nature's Way
www.vitacost.com　(800) 793-2601

Yerba Mate Tea, Guayaki
www.guayaki.com　(888) 482-9254

Bee pollen, Madhava Honey
www.madhavahoney.com　(303) 823-5166

Vitamin C, Pure Radiance C
www.synergy-co.com　(800) 723-0277

Pine Tree Bark extract Moducare
www.moducare.com　(800) 421-2998

NAET, Allergy Elimination Technique
www.naet.com　(714) 523-8900

Holistic dentistry, Biological Dentistry
www.biologicaldentistry.org　(408) 659-5385

Aller-7 Plus, North Star Nutritionals
(800) 311-1950

5. ANTI-AGING

For more information go to Find A Cure at www.naturalcures.com.

Forever Young Formula, Nutri-Health Products
(800) 914-6311

Grape Skin Extract, Healthy Resolve
(800) 728-2288

Anti-oxidant, Active-H
www.therawfoodworld.com   (866) 729-3438

Premier HGH, Natural Solutions
(800) 232-3536

Longevinex
www.longevinex.com   (866) 405-4000

Longevity Plus, Extended Health
www.extendedhealth.com   (800) 300-6712

Essential Youth, True Health
(800) 746-4513

Indium-xl
www.vital-nutrients.com

Protandim
www.protandium.com

Stem Enhance
www.stemenhance.com

6. ANXIETY/STRESS

For more information go to Find A Cure at www.naturalcures.com.

Healing Touch
www.healingtouch.net

Amino Acids, BAM
www.metabolicmaintenance.com   (800) 772-7873

Jing formulas, Dragon herbs.com
www.dragonherbs.com   (888) 558-6642

Callahan Techniques, Thought Field Therapy
www.tftrx.com   (760) 564-1008

Dianetics, Dianetics Technology
www.dianetics.com   (800) 367-8788

Meditation, Insight Meditation Society
 www.dharma.org   (978) 355-4378

Stress Reduction, Transformational Breath Work
 www.breathe2000.com   (877) 412-7328

Panax ginseng, Dragon Herbs
 www.dragonherbs.com   (888) 558-6642

Super Balanced Neurotransmitter Complex
 www.painstresscenter.com   (800) 669-2256

Dr. Coldwell's stress-reducing techniques
 www.20minutestolessstress.com   (888) 827-7720

Dietary Supplement, Perfect Defense, eAntiAging Inc.
(877) 912-9918

7. ARTHRITIS
For more information go to Find A Cure at www.naturalcures.com.

DMSO
www.herbalremedies.com   (866) 467-6444

Authentic CMO (Cetylmyristoleate)
www.authenticcmo.com   (800) 224-8912

Wobenzym N
www.wobenzym.com   (888) 766-4406

MSM, Ultra Botanicals
www.msm-msm.com   (800) 453-7516

Holistic Dentistry, Holistic Dental Association
www.holisticdental.org   (970) 259-1091

Soft Laser Therapy, Q1000 Soft Laser
www.q1000softlaser.com   (520) 615-9811

Castor Oil Packs, The Heritage
www.caycecures.com   (800) 862-2923

Fasting We Care Spa
www.wecarespa.com   (800) 888-2523

Evening Primrose Oil, Barlean's
www.barleans.com, (360) 384-0485

Boswellia   Himalaya Herbs
www.himalayahealthcare.com

Bee Alive Royal Jelly Sweet Energy Formula
www.beealive.com   (800) 543-2337

Glucosamine chrondrotin with SAM-e
www.longevityplus.com   (800) 580-7587

Alpha-flex with Omeage-5e, Alpha-flex
www.alphaflex.net   (800) 877-1269

SierraSil
www.sierrasil.com/questions.html   (888) 888-1464

8. ASTHMA
For more information go to Find A Cure at www.naturalcures.com.

One-half teaspoon each of baking soda and sea salt mixed into purified water.

Sorvino Asthma Foundation
www.sorvinoasthmafound.org   (212) 941-8686

Allergy testing, NAET
www.naet.com   (714) 523-8900

Yamoa powder
(800) 843-8408

Stress Reduction, Transformational Breath Work
www.breathe2000.com   (877) 412-7328

Qi-gong, Magnetic Qi-gong videos
www.peterragnar.com   (800) 491-7141

Whole Food Green Powder, Vitamineral Green
www.livingnutritionals.com   (800) 642-4113

Buteyko Breathing Recondition Technique
www.buteykointernational.com   (888) 259-5951

Licorice and Ginger Root Tea
www.mountainroseherbs.com   (800) 879-3337

9. ATHLETE'S FOOT
For more information go to Find A Cure at www.naturalcures.com.

Vitamin A
www.costlessvitamin.com   (800) 578-5939

Probiotics, Jarrowdophilus + FOS
www.jarrow.com   (800) 726-0886

Garlic capsules, Kyolic Aged Garlic Extract
www.kyolic.com   (800) 421-2998

Grapefruit Seed Extract, NutriBiotic
www.nutribiotic.com   (800) 225-4345

Tea tree oil, Desert Essence
www.desertessence.com   (800) 848-7331

Vitamin B complex, Max Stress B Nano-Plex
www.vpnutrition.com   (877) 335-1509

Vitamin C, Beyond C
www.longevityplus.com   (800) 580-7587

Vitamin E, Natural Vitamin E Complex
www.4spectrum.us   (800) 581-8906

Zinc, Zinc Food Complex
www.new-chapter.com   (800) 543-7279

10. BACK PAIN

For more information go to Find A Cure at www.naturalcures.com.

The most important strategy is finding an experienced body worker who can help heal your back.

Wobenzym
www.wobenzym.com   (888) 766-4406

Magnetic mattress pads
www.magneticosleep.com   (800) 265-1119

Feldenkrais Bodywork
www.feldenkrais.com

Pain Elimination Tool, Pain Eraser
www.thebestnaturalcures.com

Best Hot/Cold Pac, Fomentek
www.fomentek.com   (800) 562-4328

Deep Tissue Bodywork, Rolf Institute
www.rolf.org   (303) 449-4903

Chiropractic Treatment, American Chiropractic Association
www.amerchiro.org   (800) 986-4636

CranioSacral Therapy, Upledger Institute
www.upledger.com   (800) 233-5880

Bowen Therapy, Bowen Directory
www.bowendirectory.com

Inversion Tables, Inversion Table Superstore
www.inversion-table-direct.com   (800) 718-1710

Darrell Stoddard's Biotape
www.painfreeforlife.net   (619) 628-0156

Strong Bones, Strength Builder, Frame builder
www.dragonherbs.com   (888) 558-6642

Dr. Coldwell's stress-reducing techniques
www.20minutestolessstress.com   (888) 827-7720

11. BAD BREATH
For more information go to Find A Cure at www.naturalcures.com.

Natural Cellular Defense
www.therawfoodworld.com   (866) 729-3438

Willard Water
www.nutritioncoalition.com   (800) 447-4793

Digestive Enzymes, Digest
www.enzymedica.com   (888) 918-1118

Infrared Sauna, The Best Natural Cures
www.thebestnaturalcures.com   (310) 487-4654

Probiotics, Flora Source, NutriHealth
(800) 914-6311

pH Drops, pH Plus Liquid Enhancer
www.livingnutritionals.com   (800) 642-4113

Mouthwash, Herbal Mouth Therapy
www.thenaturaldentist.com   (800) 615-6895

12. BEE STING
For more information go to Find A Cure at www.naturalcures.com.

Rather than grab and pull out the stinger, simply flick the stinger out with the edge of a knife. Dab the affected area with lemon juice.

Manuka Honey
www.manukahoneyusa.com   (800) 395-2196

Swelling, Bentonite Clay
www.ariseandshine.com   (800) 688-2444

Homeopathic Remedy, Pulsatilla
www.1-800homeopathy.com   (800) 466-3672

13. BLADDER INFECTIONS
For more information go to Find A Cure at www.naturalcures.com.

Alkalize the urine by using ½ tsp. baking soda in 8 oz. of pure water.

Uva Ursi
www.gaiaherbs.com   (888) 917-8269

D-mannose
www.totaldiscountvitamins.com   (800) 283-2833

Homeopathy, Boiron Group
www.boiron.com

Larrea, Eclectic Institute
www.eclectic-herb.com   (800) 332-4372

Propolis, Bee Hive Botanicals
www.beehivebotanicals.com   (800) 233-4483

Unsweetened, unpasteurized cranberry juice
www.lakewoodjuices.com

14. BLOATING/GAS
For more information go to Find A Cure at www.naturalcures.com.

Raw organic apple cider vinegar with "mother"
Drink 2–4 tablespoons before each meal.

Probiotics, Freddy's Blend Probiotics
www.therawfoodworld.com   (866) 729-3438

Digestive enzymes, Super Power Enzymes
www.vites.com   (800) 446-7462

Natural Cellular Defence, Zeolite
www.zeolite.com   (303) 909-4541

Noni Capsules
Wild Crafted Noni by American Neutriceuticals   (888) 848-2548

Dr. Coldwell's stress-reducing techniques
www.20minutestolessstress.com   (888) 827-7720

15. BLOOD CLOTS
For more information go to Find A Cure at www.naturalcures.com.

Nattokinase
www.allergyresearchgroup.com   (800) 545-9960

Oral Chelation, Beyond Chelation
www.longevityplus.net   (800) 580-7587

Vitamin E, Natural Vitamin E Complex
www.4spectrum.us   (800) 581-8906

Omega-3s, Cod Liver Oil
ww.carlsonlabs.com   (888) 234-5656

Omega-3s, Hemp seeds
www.nutiva.com   (800) 993-4367

American College of Advancement in Medicine
www.acam.org   (800) 532-3688

American Board of Clinical Metal Toxicology
www.abct.info   (800) 356-2228

16. BODY ODOR
For more information go to Find A Cure at www.naturalcures.com.

Willard Water
www.nutritioncoalition.com   (800) 447-4793

Triphala
www.omorganics.com   (888) 550-8332

Rebound, Cellercise
www.cellercise.com   (800) 856-4863

Far Infrared Sauna, Therasauna
www.therasauna.com   (888) 729-7727

Whole Food Supplements, Pure Synergy
www.synergy-co.com   (800) 723-0277

Deodorant, Body Crystal
www.thecrystal.com   (800) 829-7625

17. BURNS

For more information go to Find A Cure at www.naturalcures.com.

Lavender Oil
www.rivendellaromatics.com   (805) 649-2476

DMSO
www.herbalremedies.com   (866) 467-6444

Zinc, Zinc Food Complex
www.new-chapter.com   (800) 543-7279

Rescue Remedy®, Bach Flower Essences
www.caycecures.com   (800) 862-2923

Vitamin C, Catie's Organic Vit C Plus
www.energyessentials.com   (888) 456-1597

Vitamin E, Unique E
www.acgraceco.com   (903) 636-4368

18. CANCER

I believe that almost all cancers, with the exception of specific cancers in advanced stages, can be cured without drugs, radiation, chemotherapy, or surgery. I am putting together a specific book on the various cancer treatment options. You can find all the current information for free at www.naturalcures.com. Every cancer is treated differently. Every cancer could have hundreds of very different causes. Therefore, virtually no two cancer treatment protocols would be exactly the same. Consider Poly-MVA, linseed oil, shark cartilage, hydrogen peroxide, ozone and oxygen therapy, Dr. Coldwell's stress-reducing CDs, and traditional Chinese medicine. I believe if you have any cancer you should immediately seek the advice of a licensed healthcare practitioner. Get multiple opinions. Immediately start doing all the things in Chapter 6 of my original book. Go to the end of this book and read the recommended books on cancer. Go to www.naturalcures.com and get up-to-date information at no charge. Take responsibility and take action for your own health. Do the treatment options that you feel best about.

19. CANDIDA OVERGROWTH

For more information go to Find A Cure at www.naturalcures.com.

Natural Cures
www.naturalcures.com

Ejuva
www.ejuva.com   (909) 337-5627

Renew Life
www.renewlife.com   (800) 485-0960

Pure Body Institute
www.pbiv.com   (800) 952-2458

Lifeforce
www.lifeforceplan.com   (888) 236-7780

Body Ecology Diet
www.bodyecologydiet.com   (800) 511-2660

ThreeLac
www.123candida.com   (888) 777-0468

Nature's Secret
www.naturessecret.com   (800) 297-3273

20. CANKER SORE
For more information go to Find A Cure at www.naturalcures.com.

Pantothenic acid
www.myhealthstore.com

Rosemary essential oil
www.rivendellaromatics.com   (805) 649-2476

Probiotics, Healthy Trinity by Natren
www.natren.com   (866) 462-8736

Lysine, Super Lysine+
www.quantumhealth.com   (800) 448-1448

Vitamin B complex, Sublingual B-12
www.sublingualb12.com

Vitamin C, Pure Radiance C
www.synergy-co.com   (800) 723-0277

Zinc gluconate lozenges, Quantum
www.quantumhealth.com   (800) 448-1448

21. CARPAL TUNNEL SYNDROME
For more information go to Find A Cure at www.naturalcures.com.

Marjoram, lavender, or eucalyptus essential oils rubbed directly into the tender areas, dilute with coconut butter or olive oil.

Chiropractic Treatment
www.associationfornetworkcare.com   (303) 678-8101

Pycnogenol
www.sourcenaturals.com

Soft Laser Therapy, Q1000 Soft Laser
www.q1000softlaser.com   (520) 615-9811

Essential Oils, Rivendell
www.rivendellaromatics.com   (805) 649-2476

Vitamin B complex, Total-B Sublingual
www.liquidbvitamins.com

Magnesium, Natural Calm
www.therawfoodworld.com   (866) 729-3438

Dr. Enzyme, Crystal Star
www.totaldiscountvitamins.com   (800) 283-2833

Wobenzym N with Bromelain
www.wobenzym.com   (888) 766-4406

22. CAVITIES

For more information go to Find A Cure at www.naturalcures.com.

Dental Chewing Gum, Peelu
www.peelu.com   (800) 457-3358

Mouthwash, Herbal Mouth Therapy
www.thenaturaldentist.com   (800) 615-6895

Weleda Toothpaste
www.usa.weleda.com   (800) 241-1030

Stevia instead of sugar
www.steviasmart.com   (877) 836-9982

Whole Food Supplements, New Chapter
www.new-chapter.com

SoniCare Toothbrushes
www.sonicare.com   (888) 766-4227

Vitamin C, EmergenC
www.alacercorp.com   (800) 854-0249

Calcium, Nano-Cal
www.nanocal.com   (805) 382-4240

23. CELLULITE
For more information go to Find A Cure at www.naturalcures.com.

Rebounding, Cellercise
www.cellercise.com   (800) 856-4863

Horse chestnut bark tincture
www.gaiaherbs.com   (888) 917-8269

Gotu kola tincture
www.gaiaherbs.com   (888) 917-8269

Dry Skin Brush, Yerba Prima
www.yerbaprima.com   (800) 488-4339

Lymphatic Massage, Dr. Deb's Lymphatic Drainage Tonic
www.y2khealthanddetox.com

Lymphomysot
www.bbpharmacy.com   (800) 621-7644

Lymphatic Drainage Cream, Keeping Abreast of It
www.awakenedshoppe.com

Self-massage with essential oils of juniper and rosemary
www.rivendellaromatics.com   (805) 649-2476

24. CIRCULATION PROBLEMS, COLD HANDS AND FEET
For more information go to Find A Cure at www.naturalcures.com.

Nattokinase
www.allergyresearchgroup.com   (800) 545-9960

Vitamin E, Unique E
www.acgraceco.com   (903) 636-4368

Omega-3s, Cod Liver Oil
www.carlsonlabs.com   (888) 234-5656

Omega-3s, Hemp seeds
www.nutiva.com   (800) 993-4367

Oral Chelation, Beyond Chelation
www.longevityplus.net   (800) 580-7587

Rebounding, Cellercise
www.cellercise.com   (800) 856-4863

Dietary Supplement, Circulation
www.healthyhabitsweb.com   (800) 327-3884

Food grade hydrogen peroxide
www.familyhealthnews.com   (800) 284-6263

25. COLD/FLU

For more information go to Find A Cure at www.naturalcures.com.

Fresh organic ginger tea.

Cold Rescue Nasal Spray
www.peacefulmountain.com   (888) 303-3388

Echinacea
www.dr-schulze.com   (800) 437-2362

Green Papaya Extract
www.ihealthtree.com   (888) 225-7778

Healthmate Sauna
www.healthmatesauna.com   (800) 946-6001

Propolis Bee Hive Botanicals
www.beehivebotanicals.com   (800) 233-4483

Cat's claw
www.amazonherb.net   (800) 835-0850

Digestive enzymes, Ultra InflaZyme Forte
www.universalsupplements.com   (805) 646-5936

Vitamin C, Emergen-C
www.alacercorp.com   (800) 854-0249

Homeopathic Remedy, Flu-Ban
www.eastparkresearch.com   (888) 374-2363

BreatheFree, Health Resources
(800) 471-4007

Homeopathy for Flu, oscillococcinum
www.oscillo.com   (800) 672-4556

Colloidal Silver, Allergy Research
www.allergyresearchgroup.com   (800) 545-9960

Acupressure
www.acupressure.com   (800) 442-2232

Steam with Eucalyptus oil
www.therealessentials.com   (800) 371-3515

Herbal Tincture, Throat and Tonsil
www.dr-schulze.com   (877) 832-2463

Cold/Flu Remedy, MycoPhyto Complex
Advanced Bionutritionals   (800) 728-2288

Pure Camu
www.amazonherb.net

Zicam
www.zicam.com

26. COLD SORES (*SEE* HERPES)

27. CONSTIPATION
For more information go to Find A Cure at www.naturalcures.com.

Soaked prunes
www.sunorganic.com   (888) 269-9888

Dr. Natura, Colonix Program
www.drnatura.com   (800) 877-0414

Flax seed meal, Forti-Flax
www.barleans.com   (360) 384-0485

Flax seed meal, Fiber Smart
www.renewlife.com   (800) 485-0960

Digestive enzymes, Univase
www.rockfork.net   (800) 630-4534

Ginger, Primal Essence
www.primalessence.com   (877) 774-6253

Probiotics, Probiotic Advantage
Mountain Home Nutritionals   (800) 861-5971

Nopal Cactus, HealthForce Nutritionals
www.healthforce.com   (760) 747-8822

Triphala, Ayurveda Organics
www.omorganics.com   (888) 550-8332

Laxative, H2Go
www.compassionet.com   (800) 510-2010

Fresh beet, apple, celery juice
www.canningpantry.com

28. COUGH
For more information go to Find A Cure at www.naturalcures.com.

Gargle with colloidal silver
www.mothernature.com   (800) 439-5506

Celtic Sea Salt
www.celticseasalt.com   (800) 867-7258

Propolis, Bee Hive Botanicals
www.beehivebotanicals.com   (800) 233-4483

Koflet, Ayurvedic Cough syrup
www.himalayahealthcare.com

Throat Coat Tea, Traditional Medicinals
www.traditionalmedicinals.com

Apitherapy Honey Elderberry Extract
www.honeygardens.com   (802) 985-5852

29. CUTS AND SCRAPES
For more information go to Find A Cure at www.naturalcures.com.

Dermatox
www.healthyhabitsweb.com   (800) 327-3884

Zinc It!
www.healthyhabitsweb.com   (800) 327-3884

Soft Laser Therapy
www.q1000softlaser.com

Vitamin O, R Garden
www.livingnutritionals.com   (800) 642-4113

Colloidal Silver Hydrosol, Sovereign Silver
www.sovereignsilver.info   (888) 328-8840

Topical Tea Tree oil, Desert Essence
www.desertessence.com   (800) 848-7331

Grapefruit seed extract, NutriBiotic
www.nutribiotic.com   (800) 225-4345

Vitamin C, Catie's Organic Vit C Plus
www.energyessentials.com   (888) 456-1597

Rescue Remedy®, Bach Flower Essences
www.caycecures.com   (800) 862-2923

Comfrey Leaf
www.mountainroseherbs.com   (800) 879-3337

Topical Treatment, True Aloe
www.naturecity.com   (800) 593-2563

30. DANDRUFF
For more information go to Find A Cure at www.naturalcures.com.

Infrared Sauna, Therasauna
www.therasauna.com   (888) 729-7727

Probiotics, Healthy Trinity
www.natren.com   (866) 462-8736

EFA therapy, Quantum-Rx EFA Oil
www.healthline.cc   (800) 370-3447

Organic Noni Juice, Earth's Bounty
www.earthsbounty.com   (800) 736-5609

Aubrey Organics, Selenium Shampoo
www.aubrey-organics.com   (831) 877-4186

Giovanni Shampoo, Tea Tree Triple
www.myvitanet.com   (800) 807-8080

Rosemary, tea tree essential oils rubbed into scalp
www.rivendellaromatics.com   (805) 649-2476

31. DEPRESSION
For more information go to Find A Cure at www.naturalcures.com.

Whole food supplement, Pure Synergy
www.synergy-co.com   (800) 723-0277

B Vitamin Complex, Bio-12 Complex
www.globalhealthandbeauty.com   (800) 901-6603

E3 Live, Green Superfoods
www.awakenedshoppe.com

Omega-3s, Cod Liver oil
www.drrons.com   (860) 945-7444

St. John's Wort
www.sourcenaturals.com

Sunlight Therapy, Solar Healing
www.solarhealing.com   (407) 657-7032

EMF Chaos Elimination, Q-Link
www.toolsforwellness.com   (800) 456-9887

Living Freedom, Emotional Release Work
www.totalintegrationinstitute.com   (520) 615-9811

Callahan Technique, Thought Field Therapy
www.tftrx.com   (760) 564-1008

Dianetics, Dianetics Technology
www.dianetics.com   (800) 367-8788

Neuro Emotional Technique
www.netmindbody.com   (800) 434-3030

Bowen, Find Practitioner
www.bowendirectory.com

Dr. Coldwell's stress-reducing techniques
www.20minutestolessstress.com   (888) 827-7720

Rebounder, Evolution Health
www.evolutionhealth.com   (888) 896-7790

32. DIABETES
For more information go to Find A Cure at www.naturalcures.com.

Diabeticine
www.alternativehealthsecrets.com

Tulsi Tea, Organic India
www.omorganics.com   (888) 550-8332

Cinnamon Bark, Gaia Herbs
www.gaiaherbs.com   (888) 917-8269

Asian Herbal Cure, Tongkat Ali
www.herbal-powers.com   (866) 330-4372

Herbal Tea, Eleotin
www.eastwoodcos.com

Herbal Tea, Eleotin
www.thymuskin.com   (800) 214-8631

WSN Diabetic Pack
www.realfoodnutrients.com   (888) 580-9390

Digestive enzymes, The Raw Food World
www.therawfoodworld.com   (866) 729-3438

Six flavor tea, Healing Place
www.healingplace.com   (800) 733-4325

Calcium, Nano-Cal
www.nanocal.com   (805) 382-4240

EDTA, Essential Daily Defense
www.longevityplus.net   (800) 580-7587

Gymnesyl, VitaNet Health Foods
www.vitanetonline.com   (800) 877-8702

Huereque Cactus, Herbs of Mexico
www.herbsofmexico.com   (323) 261-2521

Chromium, The Vitamin Shoppe
www.vitaminshoppe.com   (800) 223-1216

Oral Chelation & Longevity Plus Formula
www.extendedhealth.com   (800) 300-6712

Protein Powder, RiSoTriene
www.risotriene.org   (866) 361-5758

33. DIARRHEA
For more information go to Find A Cure at www.naturalcures.com.

Digestive enzymes, Univase
www.rockyfork.net   (800) 630-4534

Probiotic, Saccharomyces boulardi
www.allergyrearchgroup.com   (800) 545-9967

Probiotics, Freddie's Blend Probiotics
www.therawfoodworld.com   (866) 729-3438

Charcoal Capsules, Source Naturals
www.sourcenaturals.com

Ume Plum Paste, Eden Organics
www.edenfoods.com   (888) 424-3336

Robert's Formula and Licorice Root Tea, drink together
www.diagnose-me.com   (808) 938-6094

Amino Acid Therapy, Amino Acid T L-Glutamine
www.twinlab.com   (800) 645-5626

Vitamin A
www.allergyrearchgroup.com   (800) 545-9967

Vitamin C, Catie's Organic Vit C Plus
www.energyessentials.com   (888) 456-1597

Homeopathic, Calcarb
www.1-800homeopathy.com   (800) 466-3672

34. DIVERTICULITIS
For more information go to Find A Cure at www.naturalcures.com.

Digestive enzymes, SuperPowerEnzymes
www.vites.com   (800) 446-7462

Nettles tea infusion
www.mountainroseherbs.com   (800) 879-3337

Homeopathic, Belladonna
www.1-800homeopathy.com   (800) 466-3672

B Complex, Living B Vitamins
www.qnlabs.com

Vitamin C, Catie's Organic Vit C Plus
www.energyessentials.com   (888) 456-1597

Probiotics, Jarrowdophilus + FOS
www.jarrow.com   (800) 726-0886

Soil Based Mineral Organisms (SBOs) Freddy's Blend
www.livingnutritionals.com   (800) 642-4113

35. DYSLEXIA
For more information go to Find A Cure at www.naturalcures.com.

Craniosacral Treatment, Sacro Occipital Research Society International
www.sorsi.com (888) 245-1011

Neuraltherapy, American Academy of Neural Therapy
www.neuraltherapy.com (425) 637-9339

EPA, EFAs, fish oils
www.nordicnaturals.com (800) 662-2544

Nervous System Syncronization
www.heartmath.com (800) 450-9111

Neurotransmitter balancing
www.neuroscienceinc.com (888) 342-7272

36. EAR INFECTIONS
For more information go to Find A Cure at www.naturalcures.com.

Whole Food Supplement, Vibe
www.livingnutritionals.com (800) 642-4113

Mullein flower ear oil
www.gaiaherbs.com (888) 917-8269

Daily lymphatic drainage massage
www.iahe.com (800) 311-9204

Vitamin C, Beyond C by Longevity Plus
www.longevityplus.com (800) 580-7587

Echinacea
www.gaiaherbs.com (888) 917-8269

Castor oil heat pack on outside of ear
www.caycecures.com (800) 862-2923

37. ECZEMA
For more information go to Find A Cure at www.naturalcures.com.

GLA (gamma-linolenic acid) Evening primrose oil
www.barleans.com (360) 384-0485

Rescue Remedy®, Bach Flower Essences
www.caycecures.com (800) 862-2923

Vitamin A
www.longevityplus.com (800) 580-7587

Nutrex Spirulina
www.costplusvitamin.com   (800) 578-5939

Vitamin B complex, Total B Liquid Sublingual Formula
www.liquidbvitamins.com

Magnesium, Magnesium oxide powder
www.lef.org   (800) 678-8989

Vitamin E, Tri-En-All 400
www.universalsupplements.com   (805) 646-5936

Zinc, Zinc Food Complex
www.new-chapter.com   (800) 543-7279

38. EDEMA, WATER RETENTION, AND BLOATING
For more information go to Find A Cure at www.naturalcures.com.

Dandelion Leaf
www.gaiaherbs.com   (888) 917-8269

Juniper or Rosemary Essential Oils
www.rivendellaromatics.com   (805) 649-2476

Vitamin B complex, Living B Vitamins
www.qnlabs.com   (866) 627-1577

Vitamin C, Catie's Organic Vit C Plus
www.energyessentials.com   (888) 456-1597

Pantothenic acid, TwinLab
www.twinlab.com   (800) 645-5626

Potassium, Potassium 99-MG Chelated
www.puritan.com   (800) 645-1030

Free-form amino acids, Amino Fuel Liquid
www.twinlab.com   (800) 645-5626

Whole Food Green Powder, Vitamineral Green
www.livingnutritionals.com   (800) 642-4113

39. ENLARGED PROSTATE BPH (PROSTATITIS)
For more information go to Find A Cure at www.naturalcures.com.

Ashwaganda, Ayurveda Organics
www.omorganics.com   (888) 550-8332

Saw palmetto (Serenoa repens)
www.jarrow.com   (800) 726-0886

Milk thistle
www.gaiaherbs.com   (888) 917-8269

Vitamin A
www.costlessvitamin.com   (800) 578-5939

Beta-carotene
www.jarrow.com   (800) 726-0886

Vitamin C, Pure Radient C
www.synergy-co.com   (800) 723-0277

Vitamin E, Tri-En-All 400
www.universalsupplements.com   (805) 646-5936

Amino Acid Therapy, Amino acid L-arginine
www.twinlab.com   (800) 645-5626

Garlic Extract, Kyolic capsules
www.kyolic.com   (800) 421-2998

Glandular therapy, Wobenzym N
www.wobenzym.com   (888) 766-4406

Soft Laser Therapy, Q1000 Soft Laser
www.q1000softlaser.com   (520) 615-9811

Betaine HCl Pepsin Gentian Root Extract
www.vitalnutrients.net

Dietary Supplement, Prostate Health Complex
Goldshield Direct   (888) 436-7200

Dietary Supplement, Prostanix
Nutritional Science Laboratories   (800) 580-5938

Dietary Supplement, Ultimate Prostate Support
Real Advantage Nutrients   (800) 723-7318

40. FOOD SENSITIVITIES
For more information go to Find A Cure at www.naturalcures.com.

High dose Vitamin C, taken with Glutamine.

Water Therapy: drink half of your weight in water, each day, with a pinch of sea salt in each glass.

Aromatherapy
www.PacificInstituteofAromatherapy.com   (415) 479-9120

Allergy Elimination Technique, NAET
www.naet.com   (714) 523-8900

Digestive Enzymes, N*Zimes
www.enzymeuniversity.com   (800) 835-8545

Probiotics, Custom Probiotics
www.customprobiotics.com   (818) 248-3529

Quercetin Bromelain
www.iherb.com   (888) 792-0018

41. FUNGAL INFECTIONS
For more information go to Find A Cure at www.naturalcures.com.

Topical Tea Tree oil, Desert Essence
www.desertessence.com   (800) 848-7331

Oregano oil
www.gaiaherbs.com   (888) 917-8269

EFA, Evening Primrose Oil
www.barleans.com   (360) 384-0485

Garlic capsules, Kyolic Aged Garlic Extract
www.kyolic.com   (800) 421-2998

Grapefruit seed extract, NutriBiotic
www.nutribiotic.com   (800) 225-4345

Probiotics, Jarrowdophilus + FOS
www.jarrow.com   (800) 726-0886

Vitamin C, Truly Natural Vitamin C
www.healthforce.com   (760) 747-8822

B-Complex, Max Stress B Nano-Plex
www.vpnutrition.com   (877) 335-1509

Panothenic Acid
www.organicpharmacy.org   (800) 819-6742

42. GAS
For more information go to Find A Cure at www.naturalcures.com.

Down on all fours, butt in the air, self-massage, breathe and release.

Digestive enzymes, Dr.Fred Bisci
www.therawfoodworld.com   (866) 729-3438

Digestive enzymes, Beano
www.mothernature.com   (800) 439-5506

Rebounding, Cellercise
www.cellercise.com   (800) 856-4863

Probiotics, Healthy Trinity by Natren
www.natren.com   (866) 462-8736

Foot Reflexology, Find a practitioner
www.reflexology-usa.org   (740) 657-1695

Herbal Support, Ginger or Mint Tea
www.primalessence.com   (877) 774-6253

Dr. Coldwell's stress-reducing techniques
www.20minutestolessstress.com   (888) 827-7720

43. HAIR LOSS

Consult with an alternative practitioner and for more information go to Find A Cure at www.naturalcures.com.

Hair Products, Morrocco Method
www.morroccomethod.com   (805) 534-1600

Herbal Treatment, Saw Palmetto
www.jarrow.com   (800) 726-0886

Excess Estrogen ReducerIndole-3-Carbol
www.pureperscriptions.com   (800) 860-9583

Silica, Bio-Sil
www.jarrow.com   (800) 726-0886

Hair Products, Thymuskin
www.thymuskin.com   (800) 214-8631

Supplement, Follinex
www.healthmd.com   (888) 776-1511

Nickel Eliminator, Paul Oberdorf, NMS Hair
(718) 871-1363

44. HEADACHES

Consult with an alternative practitioner and for more information go to Find A Cure at www.naturalcures.com.

Allergy Elimination Technique, NAET
www.naet.com   (714) 523-8900

Soft Laser Therapy, Q1000 Soft Laser
www.q1000softlaser.com   (520) 615-9811

B-Complex, Max Stress B Nano-Plex
www.vpnutrition.com   (877) 335-1509

Vitamin B3
www.twinlab.com   (800) 645-5626

Vitamin C, Truly Natural Vitamin C
www.healthforce.com   (760) 747-8822

Vitamin E, Tri-En-All 400
www.universalsupplements.com   (805) 646-5936

Calcium/Magnesium, Cal-Mag
www.therawfoodworld.com   (866) 279-3438

EPAs
www.nordicnaturals.com   (800) 662-2544

DL-phenylalanine, Life Extension
www.lef.org   (800) 645-5626

NeuroEmotional Techniques
www.netmindbody.com   (800) 544-4440

Willow Bark Extract
www.gaiaherbs.com   (888) 917-8269

Skull Cap
www.gaiaherbs.com   (888) 917-8269

Dr. Coldwell's Stress Reducing Techniques
www.20minutestolessstress.com   (888) 827-7720

Alexander Technique
www.alexandertech.com   (800) 473-0620

45. HEART DISEASE

Consult with an alternative practitioner and for more information go to Find A Cure at www.naturalcures.com.

Calcium, Nano-Cal
www.nanocal.com   (805) 382-4240

Magnesium, Magnesium oxide powder
www.lef.org   (800) 678-8989

Nattokinase, Natto-Clear
www.instituteforvibrantliving.com   (928) 567-7854

Natural Vitamin E, Unique E
www.acgraceco.com   (903) 636-4368

Omega-3s, Cod Liver oil
www.drrons.com   (860) 945-7444

Oral Chelation, Enhanced Oral Chelation
(800) 471-4007

Rebounding, Cellercise
www.cellercise.com   (800) 856-4863

Soft Laser Therapy, Q1000 Soft Laser
www.q1000softlaser.com   (520) 615-9811

Dietary Supplement, CardioQ
Vitalmax Vitamins   (800) 815-5151

Organic Herbal Tincture, Cardio Vital
Biowell   (800) 877-2434

Enzyme Therapy, Cardio Essentials
www.mercola.com

Dietary Supplement, Cardio Support
Advanced Nutritional Products   (888) 436-7200

Enzyme Therapy, CoQMelt
NorthStar Nutritionals   (800) 311-1950

46. HEMORRHOIDS
Consult with an alternative practitioner and for more information go
to Find A Cure at www.naturalcures.com.

Aloe Vera Juice
Aloe Ace/Golden Ray Whole Leaf   (800) 654-4432

Triphala, Ayurveda Organics
www.omorganics.com   (888) 550-8332

Rescue Remedy®, Bach Flower Essences
www.caycecures.com   (800) 862-2923

Collinsonia
www.gaiaherbs.com   (888) 917-8269

Flax Seed Oil
www.barleans.com   (360) 384-0485

Witch hazel and calendula ointment
www.gaiaherbs.com   (888) 917-8269

47. HERPES

Consult with an alternative practitioner and for more information go to Find A Cure at www.naturalcures.com.

DMSO
www.dmso.com

Herpes
www.neveranoutbreak.com

Herpes
www.mandarinspirit.com   (888) 697-8381

Larrea, Eclectic Institute
www.eclectic-herb.com   (800) 332-4372

Lysine, Super Lysine+
www.quantumhealth.com   (800) 448-1448

Red marine algae
www.pureplanet.com   (562) 951-1124

Gently wash with *food grade* hydrogen peroxide
www.familyhealthnews.com   (800) 284-6263

Soft Laser Therapy, Q1000 Soft Laser
www.q1000softlaser.com   (520) 615-9811

Shegoi
www.shegoi.com

The Wolfe Clinic
www.thewolfeclinic.com

Larrea
www.larrearx.com

Essential Oils
www.amoils.com

48. HICCUPS

Consult with an alternative practitioner and for more information go to Find A Cure at www.naturalcures.com.

Mix two parts honey and one part castor oil and take one teaspoon of this combination during a hiccup attack.

Drink backwards from a glass of water. To do this, bend at the waist over the glass and put your mouth on the far side of the glass.

Charcoal Capsules, Source Naturals
www.sourcenaturals.com

Chewable papaya enzymes Original
www.ihealthtree.com   (888) 225-7778

Chamomile tea, Yogi Tea
www.herbalremedies.com   (866) 467-6444

49. HIGH BLOOD PRESSURE

Consult with an alternative practitioner and for more information go to Find A Cure at www.naturalcures.com.

Nervous System Syncronization, Freeze frame program
www.heartmath.com   (800) 450-9111

Resperate
www.resperate.com   (877) 988-9388

Calcium/Magnesium, Natural Calm
www.therawfoodworld.com   (866) 729-3438

Flaxseed meal and flax oil, Forti-Flax
www.barleans.com   (360) 384-0485

Omega-3s, Hemp Seeds
www.nutiva.com   (800) 993-4367

Omega-3s, Cod Liver oil
www.drrons.com   (860) 945-7444

Nattokinase
www.allergyresearchgroup.com   (800) 545-9960

Vitamin E, Tri-En-All 400
www.universalsupplements.com   (805) 646-5936

Black Cohosh Root
www.mountainroseherbs.com   (800) 879-3337

Raw virgin coconut butter
www.nutiva.com   (800) 893-4367

Vitamin B complex, Max Stress B Nano-Plex
www.vpnutrition.com   (877) 335-1509

Folic Acid
www.jarrow.com   (800) 726-0886

50. HIGH CHOLESTEROL
Consult with an alternative practitioner and for more information go to Find A Cure at www.naturalcures.com.

Red yeast rice
www.mysupplementstore.com   (877) 234-7284

Omega-3s, Hemp Seeds
www.nutiva.com   (800) 993-4367

Omega-3s, Cod Liver oil
www.drrons.com   (860) 945-7444

Nutritional Supplement, Cholestasys
www.techmedica.com   (877) 832-4633

Viable Herbal Solutions, Cholesterol Reduction Formula
www.herbal-solutions.com   (800) 505-9475

Garlic capsules, Kyolic Aged Garlic Extract
www.kyolic.com   (800) 421-2998

Policosanol, Royal Nutrition
www.drnorthrup.com

Herbal Supplement, Advanced Cholesterol Formula
Healthy Resolve   (800) 728-2288

Dietary Supplement, Poli-Cholest
Goldshield   (888) 436-7200

Dietary Supplement, Ultimate Heart Support
Real Advantage   (800) 723-7318

Protein Powder, RiSoTriene
www.risotriene.org   (866) 361-5758

51. HOT FLASHES

Consult with an alternative practitioner and for more information go to Find A Cure at www.naturalcures.com.

Essential oils, Basil, Thyme
www.amoils.com   (858) 794-8474

Callahan Technique, Thought Field Therapy
www.tftrx.com   (760) 564-1008

Relaxation Herb, Kava kava root
www.gaiaherbs.com   (888) 917-8269

Supplement, Femi-Yin
www.biomed-health.com   (860) 657-2258

Vitamin E, E-GEMS
www.carlsonlabs.com   (888) 234-5656

Hormone Balance, PhytoEstrin
www.drnorthrup.com

Menopause Support, Black Cohosh Extract
www.planetaryformulas.com   (800) 606-6226

Menopause Specialist, Affinity
www.meopause-specialist.com   (541) 688-2046

Hormone Balance, Quantum FemBalance
www.healthline.cc   (800) 370-3447

Hormone Balance, Quantum Multipollen Extract
www.healthline.cc   (800) 370-3447

52. HYPOGLYCEMIA

Consult with an alternative practitioner and for more information go to Find A Cure at www.naturalcures.com.

Pantothenic Acid and Vitamin B6
www.puritan.com   (800) 645-1030

Amino Acids, BAM
www.metabolicmaintenance.com   (800) 772-7873

Adrenal glandular products, Thymus Organic Glandular
www.nutricology.com   (800) 545-9960

Digestive Enzymes, N°Zimes
www.enzymeuniversity.com   (800) 835-8545

Nutri-Health Products, FenuPro
www.bestflora.com   (800) 914-6311

Blood Sugar Balance, Ridge Crest Herbals
www.ridgecrestherbals.com   (800) 242-4649

GTF Chromium Complex, Rainbow Lite
www.interhealthusa.com   (800) 635-1233

Stevia
www.steviasmart.com   (877) 836-9982

Whole Food Green Powder, Vitamineral Green
www.livingnutritionals.com   (800) 642-4113

Glycemic Health, Gaia Herbs
www.gaiaherbs.com   (888) 917-8269

Whole Food Green Powder, Vitamineral Green
www.livingnutritionals.com   (800) 642-4113

Glycemic Health, Gaia Herbs
www.gaiaherbs.com   (888) 917-8269

53. IMMUNE STRENGTH

Consult with an alternative practitioner and for more information go
to Find A Cure at www.naturalcures.com.

Nano-DHLA, Health Line
www.healthline.cc   (800) 370-3447

Colloidal Silver Hydrosol, Sovereign Silver
www.sovereignsilver.info   (888) 328-8840

Quantum-Rx Colostrum, Health Line
www.healthline.cc   (800) 370-3447

Quantum-Rx Nano-Green Tea, Health Line
www.healthline.cc   (800) 370-3447

Botanical Air Treatment, Dr. Schulze
www.dr-schulze.com   (800) 437-2362

MycoPhyto Complex, Advanced Bionutritionals
(800) 728-2288

Host Defense
www.newchapter.info

Noxylane
www.compassionet.com

Vitamin C
www.naturesplus.com

54. INFLAMED GUMS/PERIODONTITIS

Consult with an alternative practitioner and for more information go to Find A Cure at www.naturalcures.com.

Coenzyme Q10, HealthForce Nutritionals
www.healthforce.com   (760) 747-8822

Vitamin C, Catie's Organic Vit C Plus
www.energyessentials.com   (888) 456-1597

CalMagnanocalcium
www.inspiredliving.com   (866) 875-4386

Weleda baking soda toothpaste
www.usa.weleda.com   (800) 241-1030

ViaJet
www.oratec.com   (800) 368-3529

Soft Laser Therapy, Q1000 Soft Laser
www.q1000softlaser.com   (520) 615-9811

Gums, Oral Guard Dental Spray
www.instituteforvibrantliving.com   (800) 218-1379

55. INSOMNIA

Consult with an alternative practitioner and for more information go to Find A Cure at www.naturalcures.com.

Eden
www.sleep.kilohealth.com

Cal Mag, Natural Vitality
www.livingnutritionals.com   (800) 642-4113

Melatonin, Sublingual spray
www.sourcenaturals.com   (800) 815-2333

Vitamin B complex, Total B Liquid Sublingual Formula
www.liquidbvitamins.com

Vitamin C, Beyond C
www.longevityplus.com   (800) 580-7587

Zinc, Zinc Food Complex
www.new-chapter.com   (800) 543-7279

Passion Flower, Gaia Herbs
www.gaiaherbs.com   (888) 917-8269

Alarm Clock, Sun Alarm Clock
www.mercola.com

Dr. Coldwell's stress-reducing techniques
www.20minutestolessstress.com   (888) 827-7720

Full Spectrum Valerian Extract
www.planetaryformulas.com   (800) 606-6226

56. JET LAG
No Jet Lag
www.nojetlag.com

57. JOINT PAIN
Consult with an alternative practitioner and for more information go
to Find A Cure at www.naturalcures.com.

Hyaluronic Acid Complex with Chondroitin
recently found to be more effective than glucosamine.

Whole Food Green Powder, Vitamineral Green
www.livingnutritionals.com   (800) 642-4113

Joint and Muscle Comfort Plus, Dr. Julian Whitaker
www.drwhitaker.com   (800) 211-6358

Alpha-flex with Omeage-5e, Alpha-flex
www.alphaflex.net   (800) 877-1269

Joint Advantage, Mountain Home Nutritionals
(800) 888-1415

Flexanol, NorthStar Nutritionals
(800) 311-1950

Advanced Joint Support, Healthy Resolve
(800) 728-2288

Bone Revitalizer
www.drlark.com   (888) 314-5275

Alleviate
www.instituteforvibrantliving.com   (928) 567-7854

OPC Miracle Joint Complex, Biogenetics, Inc.
www.opcjoint.com   (800) 451-6406

58. KIDNEY STONES

Consult with an alternative practitioner and for more information go to Find A Cure at www.naturalcures.com.

Drink 1 gallon of distilled water combined with the juice of 5 organic lemons and 2 cups of raw organic apple cider vinegar every day for two weeks.

Essential Fatty Acids, Quantum-Rx EFA Oil
www.healthline.cc   (800) 370-3447

Kidney Protection Formula, Kidney Clear
www.instituteforvibrantliving.com   (800) 218-1379

Supplement, Stone Free
www.planetaryformulas.com   (800) 606-6226

Kidney Support, Tinkle Caps
www.totaldiscountvitamins.com   (800) 283-2833

Dr. Schulze, Kidney/Bladder Cleansing Program
www.dr-schulze.com   (877) 832-2463

59. LIVER PROBLEMS

Consult with an alternative practitioner and for more information go to Find A Cure at www.naturalcures.com.

Liver Support Formula, Extended Health
www.extendedhealth.com   (800) 300-6712

NANO-DHLA, Health Line
www.healthline.cc   (800) 370-3447

Liver Support, Liver Clear
www.instituteforvibrantliving.com   (800) 218-1379

Dr. Schulze, Liver/Gallbladder Cleansing Program
www.dr-schulze.com (877) 832-2463

Phytonutrients, Quantum Phytonutrients
www.healthline.cc (800) 370-3447

Green Superfood, Barleans Greens
www.drlark.com (888) 314-5275

Liver Support, Vital Liver Support
www.holfordhealth.com (800) 211-3706

Liver Cleansing, Bupleurum Liver
www.planetaryformulas.com (800) 606-6226

Blood Purifier, Blood Purifier Capsules
www.himalayahealthcare.com (800) 869-4640

60. LOW ENERGY AND FATIGUE
Consult with an alternative practitioner and for more information go to Find A Cure at www.naturalcures.com

Vitamin O, R Garden
www.livingnutritionals.com (800) 642-4113

Green Food Powder, All Day Energy Greens
www.instituteforvibrantliving.com (928) 567-7854

Protein Powder, RiSoTriene
www.risotriene.org (866) 361-5758

Energy Support, Adrenal and Pituitary Support
www.healthline.cc (800) 370-3447

Enzyme Therapy, CoQMelt
NorthStar Nutritionals (800) 311-1950

Increase energy, Idebenone
www.antiaging-systems.com (866) 800-4677

Adrenal glandular support, Thymus Organic Glandular
www.nutricology.com (800) 545-9960

Improved sleep quality, Melatonin sublingual spray
www.sourcenaturals.com (800) 815-2333

Improved sleep quality, Kava kava root
www.gaiaherbs.com (888) 917-8269

Herbal Tea, Planet Organic Red Rooibos Tea
www.holfordhealth.com   (800) 618-1810

Vitamin C, EmergenC
www.alacercorp.com   (800) 854-0249

Whole Food Supplement, Eniva Vibe
www.livingnutritionals.com   (800) 642-4113

61. MALE ERECTILE DYSFUNCTION

Consult with an alternative practitioner and for more information go to Find A Cure at www.naturalcures.com

Dr. Coldwell's stress-reducing techniques
www.20minutestolessstress.com   (888) 827-7720

Ginkgo biloba, Ginkgo Awareness
www.planetaryformulas.com   (800) 606-6226

Ginseng Classic
www.planetaryformulas.com, (800) 606-6226

Oral Chelation, Beyond Chelation
www.longevityplus.net   (800) 580-7587

Nattokinase, Natto-Clear
www.instituteforvibrantliving.com   (928) 567-7854

Vitamin E—E Gems, Carlson Labs
www.carlsonlabs.com   (888) 234-5656

Peruvian maca
www.macaroot.com   (541) 846-6222

Supplement, Potentium
www.healthmd.com

Supplement, Jenasol Libido Activator for Men
www.jenasolvitamins.com   (800) 327-8485

Supplement, ReVitaMan
Northstar   (800) 311-1950

Male Revitalizing Formula, T-Boost
Renaissance Health   (866) 482-6678

Nutritional Supplement, Oxegen
www.dldewey.com/oxegen.htm   (866) 888-8208

62. MEMORY MAINTENANCE

Consult with an alternative practitioner and for more information go to Find A Cure at www.naturalcures.com.

Brain Advantage
www.drdavidwilliams.com　(800) 888-1415

Sense of Mind, North Star
(800) 311-1950

Phosphatidylserine (PS), Health Resources
(800) 471-4007

Extension I.Q., Vitamin Research
www.vrp.com　(800) 877-2447

Vitamin B complex, Max Stress B Nano-Plex
www.vpnutrition.com　(877) 335-1509

Alpha-Lipoic Acid, Doctor's Trust Vitamins
www.doctorstrust.com　(800) 240-6046

Antioxidant, Active-H
www.therawfoodworld.com　(866) 729-3438

Antioxidant, Zanguard
www.instituteforvibrantliving.com　(928) 567-7854

63. MENOPAUSE

Consult with an alternative practitioner and for more information go to Find A Cure at www.naturalcures.com.

Bio-identical progesterone or hormone replacement as needed guided by a skilled professional.

Evening Primrose Oil, Barlean's
www.barleans.com　(360) 384-0485

Borage oil, Barlean's
www.barleans.com　(360) 384-0485

Pregnenolone, Life Extension
www.lef.org　(800) 678-8989

Neurotransmitter balancing
www.neuroscienceinc.com　(888) 342-7272

Efamol
www.efamol.com   +44-1757-633-889

Menopause Specialist, Affinity
www.menopause-specialist.com   (541) 688-2046

Black Cohosh Root
www.mountainroseherbs.com   (800) 879-3337

Fenugreek
www.iherb.com   (888) 792-0018

Dong Quai Supreme, Gaia Herbs
www.gaiaherbs.com   (888) 917-8269

64. PAIN/INFLAMMATION

Consult with an alternative practitioner and for more information go to Find A Cure at www.naturalcures.com.

Oral Chelation & Longevity Plus Formula
www.extendedhealth.com   (800) 300-6712

Darrell Stoddard's Biotape
www.painfreeforlife.net   (619) 628-0156

Dr. Coldwell's stress-reducing techniques
www.20minutestolessstress.com   (888) 827-7720

Magnetic mattress pads
www.magneticosleep.com   (800) 265-1119

MSM, Ultra Botanicals
www.msm-msm.com   (800) 453-7516

Nutraceutical Mineral Complex
www.nutraceutical.com   (800) 669-8877

Noni Juice
www.tni.com/mandrbj   (888) 883-9473

Pain Relief, Super Blue Stuff
www.bluestuff.com   (800) 452-3700

Topical Treatment, Pain Erase
Harbor Health   (888) 859-9800

Anti-Inflammatory, TheraFlex
Nutraceuticals   (800) 270-4881

Topical Treatment, Ortho Balm
Health Resources   (800) 471-4007

Supplement, Flexanol
NorthStar Nutritionals   (800) 311-1950

65. MEN'S SEXUAL HEALTH
Consult with an alternative practitioner and for more information go to Find A Cure at www.naturalcures.com.

Saw Palmetto

Supplement, Jenasol Libido Activator for Men
www.jenasolvitamins.com   (800) 327-8485

Supplement, ReVitaMan
Northstar   (800) 311-1950

Supplement, Vitalsex
(866) 333-5223

Male Revitalizing Formula, T-Boost, Renaissance Health
www.t-boost.com   (866) 482-6678

66. STRESS (*SEE* ANXIETY/STRESS)

67. THROAT (SORE)
Gargle with warm salt water.

Drink organic green tea with organic raw honey and organic lemons and a little brandy.

Throat Rescue, Peaceful Mountain
(888) 303-3388

68. VISION PROBLEMS
Consult with an alternative practitioner and for more information go to Find A Cure at www.naturalcures.com.

Vision Sense, NorthStar Nutritionals
(800) 311-1950

Vision Advantage
www.drdavidwilliams.com   (800) 888-1415

Vision Essentials, Health Directions
www.drwhitaker.com (800) 22-8008

Vision Clear Formula, Vibrant Life
www.instituteforvibrantliving.com (800) 218-1379

Program for Better Vision, Real Health Breakthroughs
(800) 981-7162

Healthy Vision
www.healthyhabitsweb.com (800) 327-3884

Macular Degeneration
www.altoonamedicalsupply.com (800) 442-8367

Vision Formula, Vita-Vision
VitalMax (800) 815-5151

69. WARTS/MOLES
Warts No More
www.fonoils.com

Wart and Mole Vanish
www.wart-mole-removal.com

70. WEIGHT LOSS
Consult with an alternative practitioner and for more information go
to Find A Cure at www.naturalcures.com.

Chelation Therapy, Beyond Chelation
www.longevityplus.net (800) 580-7587

Metabolic stabilization, Extra virgin coconut oil
www.nutiva.com (800) 993-4367

Rebounding, Cellercise
www.cellercise.com (800) 856-4863

Dietary Supplement
Meta-Reg (877) 912-9918

Dietary Supplement, AbGONE
BioTech Research (330) 496-5504

Dietary Supplement, Weight Guard Plus
North Star (800) 311-1950

Supplement, Slim-Tek
www.ironcurtainlabs.com   (866) 230-7449

Supplement, Digestazon
www.amazonherb.net   (800) 835-0850

Hoodia Gordonii Extract Tincture—African Red Tea Imports
www.herbalremedies.com   (866) 467-6444

Wu-Long Tea
www.wulongforlife.com

71. WOMEN'S HEALTH

Consult with an alternative practitioner and for more information go
to Find A Cure at www.naturalcures.com.

Fenugreek
www.iherb.com   (888) 792-0018

Women's Multinutrient, Daily Balance COQ10
(888) 314-5275

Living Multi, Optimal Women's Formula
www.livingnutritionals.com   (800) 642-4113

Peruvian yacon
www.natsur.com   +51-1422-8768

Rejuvenation for Ladies, Maharishi Ayurveda
www.mapi.com   (800) 255-8332

Female Balance, Dr. Schulze
www.dr-schulze.com   (800) 437-2362

Urinary Incontinence, Kegelmaster Feminine Fitness System
www.drlark.com   (800) 260-1620

72. WRINKLES

Consult with an alternative practitioner and for more information go
to Find A Cure at www.naturalcures.com

Radiance Advanced Skin Supplement
(888) 314-5275

Toki, LaneLabs-USA
(800) 526-3005

Potent-C+, Innovative Health & Beauty
(877) 261-1133

DuoMasque
(800) 366-8243

GH3-REJUV Crème
www.healthyhabitsweb.com   (800) 327-3884

Anti-aging supplement, Idebenone
www.antiaging-systems.com   (866) 800-4677

C H A P T E R   1 5

Additional Companies, Products, and Resources for Natural "Cures"

If I had my life to live over ...
I'd dare to make more mistakes next time.

—Nadine Stair

MAGIC JUICES AND JUICERS

True Aloe
www.truealoe.com   (800) 593-2563

Catherine's Choice Whole Leaf Aloe Vera
www.aloes.com   (800) 330-2563

Sambazon Acai berry, plain, pureed, frozen
www.sambazon.com   (877) 726-2296

Bossanova Flavored Acai Juice
www.bossausa.com   (213) 621-7600

Mangosteen
www.positivelymangosteen.com   (409) 291-5981

Goji Juice
www.gojiplease.com   (800) 913-4654

The Best Organic Green Tea
Dr. Lee's Tea for Health, 710 EGCC

www.teaforhealth.com   (866) 375-3378

Gypsy Teas
www.gypsytea.com   (800) 448-0803

Rooibos Tea
African Red Tea Imports   www.africanredtea.com

Madura Green Teas and Nutritional Supplements
www.drdavidwilliams.com   (800) 211-8562

Yerba Mate, Guayaki
www.guayaki.com   (888) 482-9254

Organic wine, Casa Barranca
www.organic-wine.com   (805) 640-1334

RAW NUTS, SEEDS, OILS, SNACKS, HONEYS

Coconut oil (raw extra virgin coconut oil)
www.nutiva.com   (800) 893-4367

Wilderness Family Naturals
www.wildernessfamilynaturals.com   (866) 936-6457

Grain and Salt Society
www.celticseasalt.com   (800) 867-7258

South River Miso
www.southrivermiso.com   (413) 369-4057

Jaffe Brothers
www.organicfruitsandnuts.com   (760) 749-1133

SunOrganic Farms
www.sunorganic.com   (888) 269-9888

Raw Cacao
www.naturesfirstlaw.com   (800) 205-2350
www.organic.com   (866) 672-6204

Rejuvenative Foods
www.rejuvenative.com   (800) 805-7957

Blessing's Alive and Radiant Foods
www.deliciousorganics.com   (305) 655-3344

Crystal Manna Bars
www.lydiasorganics.com   (415) 258-9678

Gopal's Raw Bars
www.naturalzing.com   (888) 729-9464

Manuka Honey
www.manukahoneyusa.com   (800) 395-2196

Hemp Seeds and Oil, Nutiva snack bars
www.nutiva.com   (800) 993-4367

Flax seed oil and meal
www.barleans.com   (360) 384-0485

WHOLE FOOD SUPPLEMENT POWDERS

Vitamineral Green
www.therawfoodworld.com   (866) 729-3438

Spirulina, Red marine algae
www.pureplanet.com   (562) 951-1124

Blue Green Algae
www.algae-world.com   (800) 469-2290

Pure Synergy
www.synergy-co.com   (800) 723-0277

Sun Chlorella "A"
www.sunchlorellausa.com   (800) 829-2828

E-3 Live
www.therawfoodworld.com   (866) 729-3438

NutriHarmony Whey
www.livingnutritionals.com   (800) 642-4113

RiSoTriene Protein Powder
www.risotriene.org   (866) 361-5758

Healthy Habits Ionic Mineral Nectar
(800) 327-3884

Biological Miracle
www.biologicalmiracle.com

HEALING TOOLS

Magnetico sleep pads
www.magneticosleep.com   (800) 265-1119

Infrared Mats and Saunas, Microcurrent Therapy
www.thebestnaturalcures.com   (310) 487-4654

Soft Laser Therapy
www.q1000softlaser.com   (520) 615-9811

pH paper
www.discount-vitamins-herbs.com   (800) 401-9186

Live Smarter—Tools for Wellness
www.ToolsforWellness.com   (800) 456-9887

Gem Therapy
www.gemisphere.com   (800) 727-8877

Emotional Well-Being, Callahan Techniques
www.tftrx.com   (760) 564-1008

Dr. Coldwell's stress-reducing techniques
www.20minutestolessstress.com

Total Integration
www.totalintegrationinstitute.com   (520) 615-9811

Transformational breathwork
www.breathe2000.com   (877) 412-7328

Flower essences
www.starfloweressences.com   (888) 277-4955

Heartmath
www.heartmath.com   (800) 450-9111, Ext.55

Scientology
www.scientology.com   (800) 334-5433

Dianetics Technology, Inc.
www.dianetics.com   (800) 367-8788

MOVEMENT AND BODY AWARENESS

Qi gong

> www.peterragnar.com
> www.shaolinwolf.com
>
> Roger Jahnke's
> www.feeltheQi.com   (805) 685-4670

Tai Chi

> www.shaolinwolf.com
> www.feeltheQi.com   (805) 685-4670

Yoga

> Yoga Finder
> www.yogafinder.com   (858) 213-7924

Inversion Table

> Body Lift
> www.ageeasy.com   (888) 243-3279
> www.evolutionhealth.com   (888) 896-7790

Teeter Hang Ups

> www.teeterhangups.com   (800) 847-0143

MEDITATION

Mind-Body Medical Institute
www.mbmi.org   (617) 632-9530

Stress Reduction and Relaxation Program
www.umassmed.edu/cfm   (508) 856-2656

Insight Meditation Society
www.dharma.org   (978) 355-4378

Vipassana Meditation
www.dhamma.org

SHOWER FILTERS

www.wellnessfilter.com
www.ewater.com   (800) 964-4303

Shower Safe
(800) 444-3563

WATER AND WATER FILTERS

www.ewater.com   (800) 964-4303
www.futurewatertoday.com   (800) 827-0762
www.thewolfeclinic.com   (800) 592-9653
www.johnellis.com

Vitapur
(800) 815-5151

Waterwise Distiller 9000
Nutrition and Healing   (800) 851-7100

OXYGEN WATER COOLER

www.o2techno.com   (201) 943-6900
www.oxygenamerica.com   (305) 933-4219
www.johnellis.com   (800) 433-9553
www.healthforcenutritionals.com   (800) 357-2717

KITCHEN TOOLS

Juicers

   www.therawfoodworld.com   (866) 729-3438
   www.discountjuicers.com

Stainless Steel-lined Rice Cooker

This is the only one made that is NOT non-stick.
www.quality-health.com   (800) 826-4148

Excalibur Dehydrators

www.therawfoodworld.com   (866) 729-3438

Sprouters and Sprouting Equipment

www.sproutpeople.com   (877) 777-6887

VALUABLE RESOURCES

Natural Cures

www.naturalcures.com
www.healthliesexposed.com
www.1healthyworld.com   (315) 792-1021
www.newstarget.com
www.healthfreedom.net
www.northamericanconsumersagainsthealthfraud.org

Gordon Research Institute
www.gordonresearch.com   (928) 472-4263

Dr. Fred Bisci
(718) 979-7950

Dr. Burton Goldberg
www.burtongoldberg.com

Find a Doctor

American College for Advancement in Medicine
www.acam.org/dr_search/index.php   (888) 439-6891

National Health Federation
www.thenhf.com   (626) 357-2181

RECOMMENDED SUPPLEMENT PRODUCTS
AND COMPANIES

The Heritage, Personal Care Health Products
www.caycecures.com   (800) 862-2923

Total Health Catalog, Maharishi Ayurvedic Products
www.mapi.com   (800) 255-8322

PromoLife, Promoting a Healthy Lifestyle
www.promolife.com   (888) 742-3404

Healthy Habits, Wellness Products
www.healthyhabitsweb.com   (800) 327-3884

Blue Spring International, Pain Relief, Salon and Wellness
www.bluestuff.com   (800) 452-3700

Healthforce Nutritionals, SuperFood Supplement Company
www.healthforce.com   (760) 747-8822

BioTech Marketplace, Products and Services
(800) 950-2121

CompassioNet, Nutritional Supplement Support
(800) 510-2010

LaneLabs, Innovative Natural Health
www.lanelabs.com   (800) 526-3005

Health Resources, Top Quality Nutritional Products
(800) 471-4007

East Park Research, Inc., Natural Health Care
www.eastparkreasearch.com   (800) 345-8367

Rejuvapol Swiss Flower Pollen, Northland Biogenics, Inc.
www.northlandbiogenics.com   (888) 255-7119

The Magaziner Center, Wellness and Anti-Aging Medicine
www.drmagaziner.com   (888) 436-7200

Universal Supplements
www.universalsupplements.com   (805) 646-5936

Jarrow
www.jarrow.com   (800) 726-0886

Lypo-Spheric Vitamin C
www.livonlabs.com   (800) 334-9294

Pain & Stress Center
www.painstresscenter.com   (210) 614-7246

Century Wellness
www.centurywellness.com   (775) 827-0707

The Wolfe Clinic, Energy Medicine Equipment
www.TheWolfeClinic.com   (800) 592-9653

Issels Clinic, Complete Cancer Care
www.issels.com   (888) 447-7357
www.toolsforwellness.com
www.organichealthandbeauty.com
www.virtuvites.com   (800) 332-5069
www.compassionet.com   (800) 510-2010
www.rain-tree.com   (800) 780-5902
www.larreacorp.com   (800) 682-9448

American BioSciences, Fucoidan (for cancer)
(888) 884-7770

Aquasearch, Inc.
(800) 480-6515

Health Research Associates
(877) 635-7070

Willner Chemists
www.willner.com   (212) 682-2817

BenSalem Naturals
www.bnatural.com   (215) 638-0627

Himalaya USA
www.himalayausa.com   (713) 863-1622

Buteyko Asthma
(317) 824-0328

Optimal Health Resources/PCE & Associates
(407) 366-8208

Herbaceuticals, Inc.
(707) 259-6266

IHerb
www.iHerb.com   (626) 358-5678

Optimal Health Resources
(407) 977-5689

J-Lin Alternative Healing
www.powertoheal.com   (914) 725-7557

BioBalance International
www.natural-chemistry.com   (310) 459-9866

Merix Health Care Products
www.viramedx.com   (847) 277-1111

North Bay Diagnostics
(231) 922-2295

Forever Well
www.foreverwell.com   (610) 374-5258

Nutricology
(510) 487-8526

Solanova
www.solanova.com   (415) 898-1704

Potter's Herbal Medicines
www.herbal-direct.com   +011-44-1942-405100
www.academyhealth.com   +011-44-1942-405100
www.goodnessdirect.co.uk   +011-44-1942-405100

Healing America
www.northernnutrition.healingamerica.com

Harmony Company
(860) 426-1518

Center for Natural Medicine Dispensary
www.cnm-inc.com   (503) 232-0475

Tahoma Clinic Dispensary
www.tahoma-clinic.com   (425) 264-0051

NorthStar Nutritionals
(203) 699-4438

Nutritional Products
www.heelusa.com   (800) 621-7644
www.quantumhealth.com
www.thayers.com
www.liddell.net
www.aubrey-organics.com
www.calcompnutrition.com
www.911health.com
www.health911.com
www.wisdomherbs.com
www.healthsuperstore.com
www.irwinnaturals.com
www.foreverliving.com
www.seasilver.com
www.kombuchaamerica.com
www.energyessentials.com
www.organicpharmacy.org
www.naturalchoicesclub.com

RECOMMENDED READING

Water Cures: Drugs Kill: How Water Cured Incurable Diseases,
by F. Batmanghelidj, M.D.

*You Are Not Sick You Are Thirsty: How Water Cured Incurable
Diseases—A Healer's Guide to Natural Health*
www.watercure.com

Alternative Medicine and the Treatment of Cancer, by Dr. Robert
Wiehe

Do you have cancer? Do you know someone who does? This book will not only explain all that you have been wanting and needing to know about cancer and alternative medicine ... It will also give you a list of alternative medicines which you can get without a prescription! www.wegli.com

Relief for Pennies
An inexpensive way to cure common health problems without any side effects. Remove the cause of commonly occurring health problems using safe and readily available natural products. www.relief4pennies.com/products

Fell's Health and Wellness: A Fell's Official Know-It-All Guide,
by Dr. M. Ted Morter, Jr., M.A.

Your Absolute, Quintessential, All You Wanted to Know, Complete Guide
www.fellpub.com

The Herbal Drugstore, by Linda B. White, M.D., Steven Foster
The Best Natural Alternatives to Over-the-Counter and Prescription Medicines! (Pain relievers, cold and flu cures, heart health boosters, blood pressure easers, weight loss helpers, sleep aids, arthritis remedies, antacids, allergy and asthma remedies, hormone balancers, laxatives, antidepressants, decongestants, cholesterol busters, and more.)
www.rodalesstore.com   (800) 848-4735

Natural Cures and Gentle Medicines that Work Better Than Dangerous Drugs or Risky Surgery, by the Editors of FC&A
www.fca.com

The Assault on Medical Freedom, by P. Joseph Lisa

Why American Health Care Costs So Much!
Available through local bookseller or through the publisher, Hampton Roads Publishing Company, (800) 766-8009

Racketeering in Medicine: The Suppression of Alternatives,
by James P. Carter, M.D., Dr. P.H.
Can we assume that our health is always the prime concern of organized medicine? Or are Americans being deprived of effective, economical treatments because those treatments are not highly profitable for surgeons and pharmaceutical companies? Dr. Carter presents names,

events and facts, which are of interest to all concerned Americans. Available through your local bookseller or through the publisher, Hampton Roads Publishing Company, (800) 766-8009

The Truth About the Drug Companies: How They Deceive Us and What to Do About It, by Marcia Angell, M.D.
Available through your local bookseller or www.atramdom.com

Bitter Pills: Inside the Hazardous World of Legal Drugs,
by Stephen Fried
According to the *Journal of the American Medical Association* (JAMA), adverse drug reactions are the fourth-leading cause of death in America. Reactions to prescription and over-the-counter medications kill far more people annually than all illegal drug use combined. A work of investigative and personal journalism ... the book is meant to help reform the system and inform your choices when using medications ... Available through your local bookseller or the publisher, Bantam Books, at www.bantam.com

Beyond the Bleep—the definitive unauthorized guide to *What the Bleep Do We Know?* by Alexandra Bruce
www.cbsd.com   (800) 283-3572 or (651) 221-9035

The Fluoride Deception, by Christopher Bryson
A chronicle of the abuse of power and of the manufacture of state-sponsored medical propaganda that reveals how a secretive group of powerful industries ... collaborated with officials from the National Institute of Dental Research to launder fluoride's public image. Available through your local bookseller or the publisher, Seven Stories Press, at www.sevenstories.com.

Over Dose: The Case Against the Drug Companies, by Jay S. Cohen, M.D.
Prescription drugs, side effects, and your health. Available through your local bookseller or the publisher, Jeremy P. Tarcher/Putnam at www.penguinputnam.com

The Cancer Industry, by Ralph W. Moss, Ph.D.
The classic exposé on the cancer establishment. "Everyone should know that the 'war on cancer' is largely a fraud."—Linus Pauling. Available through your local bookseller or the publisher, Equinox Press, P.O. Box 8183, State College, PA 16803.

The Cancer Conspiracy, by Barry Lynes
Betrayal, collusion, and the suppression of alternative cancer treatments. Available through your local bookseller or the publisher, Elsmere Press, P.O. Box 130, Delmar, NY 12054 (800) 578-6060

Overcome Cancer, by Albert Sanchez, Ed.S., Ph.D.
Your Body Belongs to You ... And You Are the One to Make the Decisions. Advanced Medicine Research Information and Education Center. (800) 426-7252.

Fire in the Genes: Poly-MVA—the Cancer Answer? by Michael L. Culbert, ScD., with preface by Dr. Merrill Garnett
A Personal Research on Cancer and Palladium Lipoic Complexes
"The world's first nontoxic cancer specific supplement has taken on the No. 2 killer (cancer) and the No. 3 (stroke) ... I suspect that Poly-MVA—along with adequate diet and support—would affect all 300 alleged tumor types and their ever changing subdivisions, families, etc. Also, Poly-MVA's extension into research for stroke and hypertension is overwhelmingly positive and available to the public."—Michael Culbert.   www.polymva.com   (866) 765-9682 or (619) 713-0430

Poly-MVA: A New Supplement in the Fight Against Cancer,
by Robert D. Milne, M.D., & Melissa L. Block, M.Ed.
A basic health guide. How Poly-MVA and other palladium lipoic complexes (LAPds) can help you: improve overall health, increase energy and vitality, prevent cancer, and heal from cancer. Published by Basic Health Publications, Inc., 8200 Boulevard East, North Bergen, NJ 07040. (800) 575-8890

The Olive Leaf: Unequalled Immune Support for Health and Longevity
"Nature's Secret" for vibrant health and long life.
An official report from The National Life Extension Research Institute, 1675 E. Main Street, #221, Kent, Ohio 44240.

Dr. T's 21-Day Natural Detoxification and Cleanse
drmike@biotruth.com

Ultimate Cancer Breakthroughs, by Aparajita Datta & Marco Wutzer
The Only Guide to Alternative Cancer Treatments You'll Ever Need!
www.Ultimate-Cancer-Breakthroughs.com

Cancer: One Disease, One Cause, One Cure, by Dr. Mike Thompson
www.biotruth.com

Holocaust American Style, by Dr. James R. Walker, Director, Christian
Health Research
www.ghchealth.com

The Natural Bird Flu Cure "They" Don't Want You to Know About,
by David J. Kennedy
In this alarming investigation Nobel Prize-winning chemists and other
top scientific minds share knowledge and facts about the inexpensive
easily accessible cure that can stop this pandemic in its tracks.
Published by Wellness Research Publishing. Available at www.
naturalcures.com.

Politics in Healing, by Daniel Haley
The suppression and manipulation in American healthcare. Former
New York State Assemblyman Daniel Haley documents the suppression
of new medical treatments. A well-researched investigation into the
FDA and its policies of suppression. Published by Potomac Valley
Press. Available at www.naturalcures.com.

The Biggest Secret, by David Icke
Reveals documented sourced details about the secret societies that
control healthcare and governments. www.davidicke.com.

The Disease Conspiracy "The FDA Suppression of Cures,"
by Robert Barefoot
Contains suppressed clinical studies documenting how vitamins and
minerals cure cancer, heart disease, diabetes, MS, lupus, and dozens of
other ailments. www.cureamerica.net.

CHAPTER 16

Winning the War

Who is rich? He that is content.
Who is that? Nobody.

—Benjamin Franklin

The biggest mistake a person can make is not tripping and falling down. The biggest mistake is staying down and not getting up. Everyone makes mistakes. Everyone makes errors in judgment. The key is taking responsibility, learning from those mistakes, and doing better the next time. The war against the suppression of the free flow of information is reaching a new high. Freedom is winning over tyranny and fascism. The more people that read books such as this one means that things will begin to change. They are changing because of my first book *Natural Cures "They" Don't Want You to Know About.* Record numbers of people are buying organic food. Record numbers are addressing their nutritional deficiencies. Record numbers are cleansing out the toxins in their body. Record numbers are seeking out healthcare practitioners who do not use drugs and surgery. Record numbers are experiencing the benefits of homeopathy, traditional Chinese medicine, essential oils, herbs, vitamin and mineral therapy, enzyme therapy, energetic rebalancing, and more. People are feeling better and becoming healthier. Non-prescription and prescription drug use is being stalled. People are opening up their eyes to the ineffectiveness and dangers of prescription and non-prescription drugs.

We are winning. We will continue to win as long as each one of you do your part. It's simple. Do the recommendations in this book and at www.naturalcures.com. Get everyone you can to read these books. Doing so will help change the world for the better.

Until the next blockbuster of exposing the truth . . . I remain humbly the servant of society.

If you want to know more of what Kevin has to say, be sure to read
Natural Cures "They" Don't Want You to Know About

THE #1
NEW YORK TIMES
BESTSELLER

Kevin
Trudeau

AS SEEN
ON TV

NATURAL CURES
"THEY" DON'T WANT
YOU TO KNOW ABOUT

INCLUDES THE NATURAL CURES FOR MORE
THAN 50 SPECIFIC DISEASES!

OVER 5 MILLION COPIES SOLD!

Available in Mass Market Paperback
ISBN-10: 0-97559959-3 ISBN-13: 978-09755995-9-4
Price: $7.99 US / $9.99 CAN

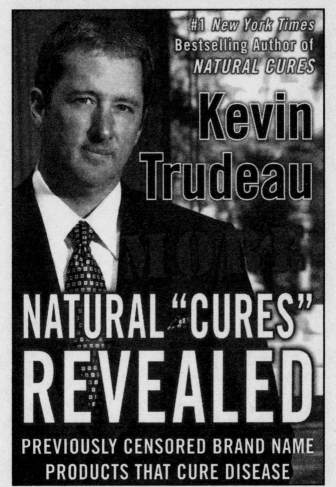

#1 New York Times
Bestselling Author of
NATURAL CURES

Kevin Trudeau

NATURAL "CURES" REVEALED

**PREVIOUSLY CENSORED BRAND NAME
PRODUCTS THAT CURE DISEASE**

Available in Hardcover
ISBN-10: 0-97559954-2 ISBN-13: 978-09755995-4-9
Price: $24.95 US / $29.95 CAN